# THE BLACK GAME

Also by Ellic Howe

URANIA'S CHILDREN: THE STRANGE WORLD OF THE ASTROLOGERS
THE MAGICIANS OF THE GOLDEN DAWN

# THE BLACK GAME

British Subversive Operations against the Germans
during the Second World War

## Ellic Howe

Michael Joseph

LONDON

First published in Great Britain
by Michael Joseph Ltd
44 Bedford Square, London WC1
1982

ISBN 0 7181 1718 2

Printed in Great Britain by
Butler & Tanner Ltd, Frome and London

For Janet Morgan

# Contents

# CONTENTS

# List of Illustrations

# Acknowledgments

I am particularly indebted to two wartime contemporaries who read copies of the typescript and offered the kind of help and encouragement for which an author can never be sufficiently grateful. They are Mr Clifton Child, OBE, who was from 1969-76 the Assistant Secretary of the Cabinet Office in charge of the Historical Section, with responsibility *inter alia* for the production of the official histories of the Second World War and Mr A. R. Walmsley, CMG, who generously allowed me the use of his unpublished typescript, 'EH/PID/PWE German and Austrian Intelligence: Recollections of A. R. Walmsley', written in January 1946. Any gross errors or misstatements which they failed to identify are my own.

I must also express my gratitude to Mr Harold Robin, CBE, until his retirement Chief Engineer of the Diplomatic Wireless Service, who was in charge of the technical side of our secret broadcasting activities (1939-45). Without his help I would have known little or nothing about their development and, in particular, the installation of the giant Aspidistra transmitter. My friend Mr Frank Lynder ('the Sergeant'), one of the few remaining survivors of the late Sefton Delmer's wartime 'black propaganda' team, was most helpful.

Professor Michael Balfour, CBE, yet another member of the wartime Political Warfare Executive organisation, also provided authoritative information. Lord Ritchie-Calder, CBE, once PWE's Director of Plans, kindly discussed my project with me at an early stage. But for the fact that until his death in January 1982 he was mostly resident in the USA I would have liked to trespass upon his patience more than was possible during our brief conversations when he was in London.

Anthony Gishford, T. G. Harman and Thomas Barman, none of them still alive, discussed their memories of the Department with me. Mrs Shirley Beck, widow of the late Dr Leslie Beck, an important member of PWE's French Section, sent me a number of helpful letters, and Madame Vivian de Poerck-Watts (as a young girl Dr Beck's secretary) summoned up her memories of a now very remote past when we met in Paris.

Among friends who had no connection with the Department I must particularly mention the help given to me by Terence Charman of the Department of Printed Books at the Imperial War Museum and Miss Barbara Mockert at the London Library. Mr R. G. Auckland (Co-Founder of the Psywar Society) and Herr Dr Albrecht Götz von Olenhusen of Freiburg im Breisgau both helped to provide illustrative material relating to our tampering with the issue of the

*Völkischer Beobachter* which we planted on Rudolf Hess soon after the latter arrived in the British Isles in May 1941. Professor Dr Manfred Messerschmidt, Director of the *Militärgeschichtliches Forschungsamt* at Freiburg i. Br. kindly read the manuscript and suggested some corrections.

I must also express my gratitude to Father Robert Graham, SJ, in Rome a co-editor of *Actes et documents du Saint Siège relatifs à la seconde guerre mondiale*, for generous help and permission to describe him here as 'my man at the Vatican'. I am grateful, too, to Mr Herbert A. Friedman for lending me copies of the American philatelic publications in which he so carefully described and analysed some of our more exotic productions.

Finally, I am indebted to the Leverhulme Trust for a grant which enabled me to pay for a very large number of photocopies at the Public Record Office, also to the Foreign and Commonwealth Office for allowing me to refresh my memory from certain official papers which have not yet reached the PRO.

Transcripts/Translations of Crown-copyright records in the Public Record Office appear by permission of the Controller of HM Stationery Office.

Ellic Howe
London 1982

The author and publishers would like to thank the following for permission to reproduce extracts from the publications mentioned:

Methuen Military, *Baker Street Irregular* by Bickham Sweet-Escott; Mac-Gibbon and Kee, *My Silent War* by Kim Philby; Jonathan Cape, *Nemesis: The Story of Otto Strasser* by Douglas Reed; Secker and Warburg, *Black Boomerang* by Sefton Delmer; Hamish Hamilton, *Diplomatic Correspondent* by Thomas Barman; and *Very Special Admiral: The Life of Admiral J. H. Godfrey, CB*, by Patrick Beesly.

# Introduction

This book is mainly concerned with certain British propaganda activities during the Second World War which were classified as 'black'. The BBC's broadcasts to Germany and enemy-occupied Europe, also leaflets bearing the imprint of HM Government and dropped by the RAF, were all 'white'. Black operations, however, never indicated their British origin. Various clandestine broadcasting stations, all of them outside the control of the BBC, sought, sometimes with surprising success, to give the impression that they were actually operating inside Germany or elsewhere in Europe. Great pains were taken to disguise the fact that a strangely variegated range of black printed matter had not, in spite of its convincing appearance and, where necessary, bogus imprints, been produced in Germany, France, Belgium, etc. Indeed, it was all manufactured in London. Little of it was disseminated by the RAF since other and far more covert methods were performed.

There were various shades of nigritude, ranging from dense black to grey according to the target and objectives, but subversion – the disruption of the enemy's will and power to fight on – was the common factor in all the output intended for German ears or eyes. Furthermore, nothing perpetrated by the black specialists could possibly be acknowledged by HM Government as being of British origin. Indeed, the black operators could do a great many things that would have been absolutely impossible for respectable white propagandists.

From August 1941 onwards propaganda work in both the black and white areas was controlled by a secret department designated as the Political Warfare Executive (PWE). It was the direct successor of two previous secret organisations, namely Department Electra House (EH) and Special Operations 1 (SO1). Both SO1 and PWE operated under the cover of the Political Intelligence Department of the Foreign Office (PID), which was a small and *non-secret* section of the Foreign Office and one that is duly recorded in the FO Lists (or 'Red Books') of the Foreign Office of the day. When the PID was closed in 1943 the PWE continued to use its name and initials. Those who, like myself, were employed in PWE thought of ourselves as working in PID. Indeed, many of my contemporaries, and particularly those who arrived after March 1943, were probably unaware of the previous existence or functions of 'the real PID'. Furthermore, my own impression is that the term PWE was unknown to outsiders until after the war.

PWE was a temporary wartime department with many ramifications. Nothing like it had ever existed in the past because during the First World War there was no radio propaganda (black or white) and printed 'black' was only produced on a very small and amateurish scale. In the absence of a host of precedents PWE evolved, often painfully, by a process of trial and error.

In my early chapters I have briefly described Department EH's pre-war origins, also certain later developments which have no connection with the black side. The latter's emergence and later expansion cannot be understood, however, without some knowledge of the organisational background from which the whole black business came into existence. Thus I have sketched in PWE's pre-history, although I am far more interested, for example, in the Department's rather loose connection with Section D (SOE's immediate precursor which dabbled with black activities) than with its really important white propaganda functions. Hence the reader must look elsewhere for information about PWE's work and responsibilities outside the specifically black area.

I must emphasise, too, that in relation to the Department as a whole its black side consisted of a number of small and separate groups which not only operated under conditions of very tight security but completely outside and away from PWE's very large white divisions. Indeed, the average member of PWE was totally unaware that the Department was engaged in highly secret black propaganda activities.

The Germans signed an instrument of unconditional surrender to the Western Allies and Russia on 7 May 1945 and almost immediately PWE, as I and many others had known it, ceased to exist and we all went our separate ways. It is significant, however, that whereas former members of SOE founded the Special Forces Club there was never any similar PWE 'Old Boys Association'. I soon lost touch with all but a handful of former colleagues and largely forgot about my wartime experiences in the Department where, incidentally, I specialised in the production of printed fakes and forgeries, largely for the benefit of the Germans. There was an unexpected reminder of those now distant days in *The Times* on 16 May 1973 when the late Richard Crossman proposed, in an article headed 'The wartime tactics which led to Watergate', that 'Subversive operations and black propaganda were the only aspects of war at which we [British] achieved real pre-eminence.'

For three years until he left to join the American psychological warfare warriors at Algiers in May 1943 the future cabinet minister and author of the famous *Crossman Diaries* had been PWE's stormy petrel and one of the Department's most intriguing characters. Extracts from his article and from the subsequent correspondence in *The Times* will serve to introduce the reader, if only obliquely, to the strange world of black propaganda. Crossman's purpose was to make a distinction between the wartime Political Warfare Executive's covert activities and some of the Watergate affair's tangled aspects. The relevant passages follow:

I have just come across a remark by Neil Sheehan, of *The New York Times*, which seems to me to get near to the heart of the [Watergate] matter. He made it when the Pentagon Papers first came into his newspaper office and he had to read them through. 'My first impression', he observed, 'was that the government of the United States was not what I thought it was; it was as if there was an inner United States government . . . it had its own codes which are quite different from public codes.'

Commenting upon Mr Sheehan's observations, Mr Crossman continued:

This inner government is, of course, a necessary apparatus of total war; and the best paid and the most attractive of its departments are those which deal with covert operations in which we British have always excelled. Indeed, apart from the RAF success in pioneering the firestorm which cooked 50,000 Hamburgers and 150,000 Dresdeners while officially claiming we were bombing military targets, subversive operations and black propaganda were the only aspects of war at which we achieved real pre-eminence. We trained a small army of gifted amateurs for all the dirtiest tricks from lying, bugging, forging and embezzlement to sheer murder – all, of course, in the name of preserving the democratic way of life.

The Americans adored subversion, but they were too heavy-handed and never learned from us to *play it as a game* [author's italics] and give it up when the war was over. Whereas here the secret departments withered away harmlessly, in America they multiplied and found plenty of opportunity in Korea and Vietnam, not to mention the Dominican Republic and Guatemala. It was only a matter of time before the wartime experts were being employed by business firms and by political parties against their rivals. As for the inner central government in Washington, how could it fail to employ those techniques against anyone who obstructed it when the

United States was engaged in a cold war against the Communists who regularly used every kind of dirty trick?

I am sure that Crossman wrote the truth when he suggested that our black activities represented a game which we played, often with laughter, especially against the Germans. It must be remembered, too, that until the tide began to turn in our favour in 1943 there was precious little connected with the war about which we could actually laugh. However, the 'jokes' were strictly private and unknown to any outside a very small circle.

Then, on 4 June 1973 *The Times* printed a letter from Mr George Martelli, who had been head of PWE'S Italian section, in which he forthrightly declared that the whole black business had been a scandalous waste of time and money. According to Mr Martelli:

So far, in fact, from achieving pre-eminence in the conduct of the war, I would say that the whole of the Woburn Abbey set-up, with its clandestine broadcasting stations, comfortable country houses cosily presided over by the wives of the chief executives enjoying priority in the employment of any domestic help available, its printing presses and vastly inflated intelligence sections (I once calculated that one hundred times as much intelligence material was being churned out daily as anyone expected to make use of it could possibly digest), its bevies of personal assistants and private secretaries, its luxurious transport and pretty chauffeuses, was a gigantic waste of human effort and public money which could have been much better employed in other ways more conducive to winning the war. This is intended as no reflection on the enthusiastic band of civil servants, journalists, dons, artists, advertising men, administrators and expatriates, who crammed the ducal mansion from attics to basement and overflowed into the ducal stables; but I suspect that they were sustained in their zeal more by blind faith in their mission and by the superiority of the democratic cause than by any proof that they were contributing to victory. Some inkling of this eventually leaked out – the Foreign Office was always sceptical about our efforts – but by then, like other government departments, the PWE had become a vast vested interest which was politically impossible to liquidate.

There is a place in war for a foreign information service, as was shown by the BBC, which by eschewing propaganda and sticking strictly to the truth, however unpleasant, acquired an enormous influence on the course of the war. There is also room for a professional secret service, trained in and with long experience of dirty work.

But there is none for the sort of amateurs with whom I also worked for

4

a while. Nor did Goebbels, who knew a thing or two about it, bother with black propaganda.

In retrospect Mr Martelli got it all wrong, because he somehow confused the Woburn Abbey set-up, which was wholly concerned with white propaganda, i.e. the production of the leaflets dropped in vast quantities by the RAF and policy guidance for the BBC's essentially truthful European Service, with the black sections. The latter consisted of small, sometimes even minute teams whose members were kept well away from the Abbey. In any case, except for a few administrators who continued to work in adjacent buildings, the Department vacated the ducal mansion in the spring of 1942 and transferred Mr Martelli's 'enthusiastic band of amateurs' to London. Finally, Dr Goebbels did bother with black propaganda but without ever watching our expertise in the art and, in particular, Sefton Delmer's.

Lord Ritchie-Calder's reply to Mr Martelli's criticism was published on 11 June 1973. Extracts from his letter follow:

As Director of Plans and Operations of the Political Warfare Executive, I was in a good position to evaluate the conduct not only of our overt propaganda services but also of our subversive operations and black propaganda. I shall not dispute Mr Martelli's estimate of the inefficiency of our black operations against Italy when he was in charge of them but when Sefton Delmer, who was in charge of German 'black' took over Italian 'black' as well, he was demonstrably effective, e.g. his subversive *Radio Livorno* had a decisive role in preventing the Italian navy from getting into German hands after the fall of Mussolini.

His description of the sybaritic days at Woburn makes me regret that I did not make more use of his hospitality when he was a 'housemaster'. I worked in the ducal china closet, slept in a 'bed-sit' in the village and ate in the cafeteria where the wartime austerity was mitigated by a rather good beer.

As a poacher turned game-keeper, keeping a practised eye open for international abuses of the kind we generated and used during the war, I am not likely to boast about nor excuse the 'black' arts of subversion and black propaganda but, perversely, I get indignant about the clumsiness of our imitators. 'Pre-eminence', for claiming which R. H. S. Crossman is taken to task, is comparative. We were more efficient on the whole than the others.

No one will ever be able to measure the effectiveness of our role – specific operations, yes. I have never believed that we could effectively divide the Germans after the announcement of unconditional surrender (which applied to Italy as well), but we did confuse and disturb them and soften them up. In terms of the occupied countries I would maintain that political warfare (overt and covert) did a praiseworthy job in restoring morale, recruiting resistance and producing a strike force.

I entirely agree with Mr Martelli about the BBC. It was our Grand Fleet-in-being. It was a concern of the Political Warfare Executive to keep it immaculate. Its veracity and credibility made it one of our most important weapons.

As far as the Germans, and to a lesser extent the Italians, were concerned, Lord Ritchie-Calder's suggestion that we did 'confuse and disturb them and soften them up' was acutely perceptive. Although the technical expression 'destabilisation' (i.e. of a country) was not then in use – it was a later American CIA invention – Delmer and Co. certainly helped to 'destabilise' German morale, and that of the U-boat crews in particular. However, I cannot sufficiently emphasise that black propaganda is not a war-winner and only begins to become effective when the enemy is losing confidence.

Letters from a few other members of PWE were also published in *The Times*. They did not agree with Mr Martelli. Sefton Delmer did not contribute to the discussion. His health was already poor and it is possible that he supposed that Lord Ritchie-Calder had said all that was necessary.

Richard Crossman's article and the subsequent correspondence in *The Times* stimulated my curiosity to the extent that I began to frequent the Public Record Office and read those PWE files (FO 898 series) which specifically concerned information about our black activities. I also had a number of conversations with old friends who had been involved in the black business. Their recollections were sometimes disappointingly tentative, not surprising, perhaps, in view of the fact that thirty years had elapsed since they had been concerned with black affairs.

The 545 messy files which are available at the PRO survived more by chance than by any scientific archival policy. On the administrative side PWE never employed more than a handful of career civil servants and was not (and could not) be run on conventional civil service lines with a central registry and anything like the efficient filing system which the great Eyre Crowe introduced in the Foreign Office itself after the First World War. As far as the regional directorates and other sections were concerned, papers were kept in personal working files and when cabinets became overloaded, unwanted papers were simply jettisoned without reference to higher authority. During a period of almost six years the

Department generated an enormous amount of *paperasserie* and, at a guess, ninety per cent of it was of no great interest much more than a month after it had been produced.

Immediately after the war PWE was liquidated as speedily as a few administrators could complete the task. When I returned to London early in August 1945 after spending ten weeks in Germany I found our offices at Bush House literally deserted. In the meantime PWE had engaged a lady archivist whose knowledge of the Department cannot have been very great. Her instructions were to destroy rather than preserve. The Foreign Office library eventually received the equivalent of the contents of thirty filing cabinets, but I would imagine that ten times their number might have existed. As could be expected, no files containing material which was regarded as sensitive eventually reached the PRO. Furthermore, no personnel records are available and, since the clandestine broadcasting stations were under the technical control of a branch of the Secret Intelligence Service, very few particularly informative papers about their activities reached the PRO. Our SIS colleagues were essentially radio technicians and *not* propagandists.

It seems that the regional directors and other heads of sections were instructed to leave their filing cabinets intact. 'Mr Howe's unit' was either so obscure or so secret that nobody remembered our existence and I did not receive any directive about the disposal of papers and, above all, hundreds of specimens of black printed matter, including two rather spectacular pornographic items. Before I left for Germany my secretary and I deposited all our files into sacks whose contents were immediately removed for pulping under secure conditions, thus there is very little documentary evidence that my unit ever existed. A search at the PRO will reveal documents which refer to black printing although my name is seldom mentioned in them. Luckily a fairly complete set of printed specimens, which had existed at Sefton Delmer's office, eventually reached the Imperial War Museum via the Foreign Office library, and a smaller one will be found at the PRO. The world of scholarship will search in vain for the pornography.

By comparison with SOE – those once secret initials have been so extensively publicised that it should hardly be necessary to explain that they refer to the wartime Special Operations Executive – the PWE literature is relatively small. Sir Robert Bruce Lockhart, who had been the Department's Director-General, published his wartime memoirs in 1947. His *Comes the Reckoning* was a notably discreet performance since the Official Secrets Act then made any reference to black activities impossible. It does, however, contain some mildly interesting material

about his experience in PWE's stratosphere and dealings with war-
ring cabinet ministers, the Foreign Office's top mandarins and various
Allied governments-in-exile. (The second volume of Lockhart's *Diaries*
was published late in 1981 when I was completing this book. I did not
find much that contributed to my 'black propaganda' story, but the
diaries will certainly interest zealous students of the overall PWE
'phenomenon'.)

Sefton Delmer's autobiographical *Black Boomerang* did not appear
until fifteen years later in 1962, hence five years before the first and main
collection of PWE files reached the Public Record Office. It contains the
first account, written by an insider, of PWE's black operations. Although
long out of print and difficult to find outside libraries, this is an important
source of information and reliable except for a few minor details. (Many
of Delmer's stories of 'black operations' will only be found in his book,
since I have preferred to work from documents which were not then
available to him. My own offering can be described as a 'supplement' to
*Black Boomerang*.) Delmer was far too modest to explain that until he
arrived in the spring of 1941 nobody had the slightest idea of what was
possible in the black department. Indeed, as far as the British were
concerned, Sefton Delmer created a new concept of psychological
warfare.

A general account of PWE's evolution and operations was published
in 1977. This was Dr Charles Cruickshank's *The Fourth Arm: Psychological Warfare, 1939-45*, which was largely based upon those files which
had found their way to the PRO. The fact that he was able to produce a
coherent account of the Department's incredibly tangled annals reflects
both his patience and his skill as a historian.

Dr Cruickshank's book was soon followed by Professor Michael Balfour's *Propaganda in War, 1939-45: Organisation, Policies and Publics*.
Unlike Dr Cruickshank, Balfour had worked in the wartime propaganda
field, first at the Ministry of Information and then from April 1942 in
PWE. Various appointments in the Department's planning and intelligence sections had given him a detailed knowledge of its personalities
and atmosphere. Whereas Dr Cruickshank limited his enquiry to PWE,
Balfour contrived an invaluable comparative study of the propaganda
output of the MoI, PWE and the BBC's European Service, and the
German Propaganda Ministry.

The leaflet war, black and white, British, American, Soviet and Ger-
man, was first discussed at any length by German writers in Ortwin
Buchbender's and Horst Schuh's *Heil Beil! Flugblatt Propaganda im
Zweiten Weltkrieg*, 1974, which contains a fair selection of colour

illustrations. At the time of publication its authors were on the staff of the *Bundeswehr*'s School for Psychological Warfare at Euskirchen, near Cologne. At Erlangen, Herr Klaus Kirchner, an enthusiastic collector of wartime printed propaganda, has begun to publish a series of volumes which cover most aspects of its production.[1] His book, *Krankheit rettet* (*Illness saves* - the title is derived from one of Delmer's most successful productions), contains evidence of contemporary German reactions to our black output which is not easily available elsewhere.

Illustrations of a small number of our black publications will also be found in Dr Heinz Gittig's *Illegale antifaschistische Tarnschriften 1933 bis 1945* (*Illegal anti-Fascist camouflaged publications, 1933-45*), published in the German Democratic Republic in 1972. This was originally a doctoral dissertation by a member of the staff of the *Deutsche Staatsbibliothek* (German State library) in East Berlin. When I met him in 1977 he was employed as a librarian by the *Institut für Marxismus-Leninismus*. His book contains a bibliography of no less than 550 booklets, all with camouflaged covers, which circulated in Germany between 1933-9. All or most of them had a Communist Party background and were smuggled into Germany from neighbouring countries. Dr Gittig listed only thirty-four wartime productions, of which a dozen originated in PWE. The others appear to have been manufactured in the Soviet Union.[2]

As far as 'Mr Howe's unit' and PWE's black forgery and faking operations are concerned, I am the only survivor with a personal knowledge of how the unit originated and operated. Hence, owing to the unfortunately premature destruction of its records, I have been obliged to include some autobiographical material in this Introduction.

Since the production of what forensic scientists would call 'suspect documents' is an unusual occupation, I should explain how I came to acquire the technical knowledge which equipped me to undertake the work which kept me busy for more than three years at PWE. I must also describe the circumstances which led to my recruitment by the Department.

I became a printer more by accident than design. I had nothing to show for my disgracefully idle time at Oxford and left at the end of 1930 without taking a degree. I spent the next three years in Paris, Berlin, Rome and Vienna - still idle, but an unearned income helped - and at least became fluent in three languages. Then, in the spring of 1934, some months before my twenty-fourth birthday, I decided to acquire the training for a useful occupation and preferably one which did not need an academic qualification. A process of elimination suggested printing, about which I knew absolutely nothing. Nor did I have any contacts in the printing industry.

For a very modest premium – £100 per annum for two years – I became a trainee pupil at Simson and Co. (later Simson Shand Ltd), a medium-sized book, periodical and general letterpress printing firm at Hertford, twenty miles north of London. There was very little photo-lithographic printing in those days and the process was mostly used for poster colour work. Fortunately my master was James Shand, who was not only an exceptionally accomplished craftsman but had the tempera-ment of an artist. James was the eldest son of the proprietor of the firm, Alexander Macleish Shand, and he had every intention of making his personal Shenval Press imprint as well known to contemporary discri-minating print buyers as were those of the handful of top-quality firms which existed in Great Britain at that time. When he died in 1967 The Shenval Press had an international reputation among connoisseurs of good printing – not in the artificial field of so-called limited editions, but for industry, commerce and important institutions.

Looking back, I now realise with what tolerant and sympathetic insight James directed my early training, because he must have sensed that I would never be a very conventional printer if, indeed, I remained in the industry at all. For instance, within a few months it was becoming evident that my multifarious interests were tending to be those of, say, a 'gentleman scholar' (what is known in Germany as a *Privatgelehrter*) rather than those of someone who intended to become a conventional book or commercial printer. What happened was that I very soon become immersed in the artistic, social, cultural and economic history of printing from its infancy in the 1450s to the present day.

My reference library grew with surprising speed, particularly after January 1935 when I first met that extraordinary man Stanley Morison who was to become my second teacher. Morison was the world's greatest authority on the history of type design and equally familiar with related departments of historiography, e.g. the development of newspaper print-ing and publishing from the seventeenth century onwards, the evolution of the scripts used in the sixteenth-century Papal chanceries, Carolingian palaeography, the Roman Catholic liturgy and the design of Victorian and later steam-driven railway locomotives.[3]

When I first encountered Morison he was the typographical adviser to the Monotype Corporation, manufacturers of composing machines (the hot-metal predecessors of photo-composition and electronic word-processors), also to the Cambridge University Press and *The Times*. During the early 1920s he initiated the Monotype Corporation's new and ambitious programme of type design and engraving and was the moving spirit behind the British typographical renaissance which flourished between the two World Wars. A decade later he was responsible for the major industrial design operation which led to the typographical restyling and re-equipment of *The Times*, and during the early 1950s he became a highly influential *éminence grise* at the old *Times* office in Printing House Square. My sense of indebtedness to both James Shand and Stanley Morison is very real because it was they who made my early and formative years in the printing industry a singularly rewarding experience.

While my 'typo-cultural' education was in progress with Morison, my practical training continued at Hertford. James Shand very sensibly kept me in the composing department for all but a month or two of my two years. I learned to set type, operate Monotype composing machinery, design and set periodical advertisements, make up pages, read proofs, impose a thirty-two-page forme on the stone, etc., in fact everything that happens in a letterpress printing office before printing begins. James never encouraged me to spend any time in the printing department because he very quickly realised that my still obscure future would probably be concerned with design and the organisation of the production of printed matter rather than with the mechanics of presswork.

When my 'apprenticeship' came to an end I remained with the Shands on an informal basis until the summer of 1938. The basis of our unwritten agreement was roughly as follows: I was not their employee, but they would pay me a commission of ten per cent on all the work I introduced with an annual (!) settlement of accounts. I was soon able to develop a satisfactory clientele but had plenty of time for my private interests. James Shand patiently looked after my customers when I was happily researching in libraries in France, Germany, Belgium and Holland. At that time I was immersed in the study of the type specimen sheets and books issued for the information of their customers by the European type foundries during the period 1580–1800.

On every possible occasion during my travels I collected and hoarded specimens of jobbing printing from the seventeenth century onwards. There were then very few collectors of ephemeral printing and I used to return to London with inexpensive hauls of eighteenth- and nineteenth-century material which would today be regarded as quite spectacular. I was also beginning to assemble a large collection of contemporary specimens of jobbing printing: hotel bills, commercial stationery of all kinds, handbills and leaflets, for example. It all demonstrated *how* a compositor in any western European country would tackle any particular task, no matter how humble, at that time. I learned too, about the extent to which national printing styles or conventions varied. In the course of analysing the typographical components of hundreds of specimens of jobbing printing I learned to identify at sight almost every printing type in current use in western Europe, i.e. I knew its trade name, who originally designed it and when, also who cast and marketed it. This was before the invention of 'Letraset' and the availability of various methods of film-setting for the provision of display types. Half a dozen hot-metal type foundries were still busy in Germany and exporting their products to the specialist advertisement typesetters in London. Hot-metal type foundries were also operating in France, Switzerland and Holland. They have practically all disappeared today or, if they have survived, are active in the new technological fields. Forty or more years ago my encyclopaedic knowledge of a number of areas relating to the contemporary printing trade had no identifiable commercial value although I was to find it extremely helpful when I joined PWE in 1941.

The only occasions when I thought about forgery in those days was when travelling by train from London to, say, Vienna via Calais, Paris and Zürich. Then, as now, one had a wire-stitched *carnet* containing tickets for the British, French, Swiss and Austrian railway systems which a succession of inspectors punched or clipped. I used to analyse the typefaces and coloured papers and speculate upon the apparent ease with which one could travel from London to Vienna and back with forged tickets. By comparison with present-day air tickets they were very simple documents from a potential forger's point of view. The tickets could mostly have been produced very simply by line blocks, but the fun was to suppose that process engraving had not yet been invented and to calculate how many different founts of quite undistinguished jobbing types would be needed and where they could be purchased. I must confess, too, that I sometimes considered the possibility of faking absurd but intriguing literary productions, such as minuscule editions of hitherto unknown pamphlets by famous authors. A short piece, ostensibly by Lenin, on 'Hegel and Dialectical Materialism', allegedly written and printed in Zürich when he was there in 1915, would have set the cat among the Marxist pigeons but I knew no one who could write it. However, having attentively studied John Carter's and Graham Pollard's classic *An Examination of certain Nineteenth-century Pamphlets* (their brilliant exposure of the T. J. Wise forgeries), published in 1934, I had at least learned what mistakes to avoid.

During the summer of 1938 I decided to give myself a sabbatical year in order to work on *The London Compositor: Documents relating to Wages, Working Conditions and Customs of the London Printing Trade, 1785–1900*, which was eventually published for the Bibliographical Society by the Oxford University Press in 1947. The project had been suggested to me by Morison.

Then, at the height of the Munich crisis I enlisted in a Territorial Army anti-aircraft unit, supposing that since a war with Germany seemed inevitable I might as well pre-empt my own hopefully modest role in it. When the Germans invaded Poland on 1 September 1939 I was an acting unpaid Lance-Corporal in 306 Company, 27th Searchlight Regiment, Royal Engineers, and leading a distinctly al fresco existence with nine genuine Cockneys (typical 'Battersea Boys') in a field near Cardington in Bedfordshire.

I can now take the reader without further delay to September 1941, when I happened to be due for a week's leave. In the meantime I had somehow managed to 'lose' the 27th Searchlight Regiment (actually in February 1940) and had become a Warrant Officer Class II, hence a Sergeant-Major, at Headquarters Anti-Aircraft Command at Stanmore, in the northern suburbs of London. I was in charge of the so-called Secret Registry, which was a distribution centre for the very large number of secret documents which arrived daily. For an eccentric who could recognise and identify almost any printing type engraved since 1500 the task of remembering the titles and often the numbers of the hundreds of files in current use was child's play. However, in spite of my sergeant-major's badges, which I wore not without a certain degree of modest pride, I was really a sort of British 'Good Soldier Schwejk' dressed up as a sergeant-major. It is true that I could have applied to be sent to an Officer Cadet Training Unit (OCTU) but was too indolent to make any move in that direction. The following year I returned to civilian life and became PWE's unique specialist in the manufacture of mainly typographical fakes and forgeries.

The Monotype Corporation's large works at Horley, where I had spent an instructive week early in 1935 as part of my training at Hertford, could be reached by bus from my aunt's home in Merstham. I happened to know that a certain John Tarr was now in charge of the type-drawing office. The Corporation was almost wholly engaged on wartime precision engineering but there were occasional urgent orders for 'special sorts' (e.g. mathematical characters) or sets of Arabic matrices, and Tarr dealt with them. When I telephoned him and said that I was in the neighbourhood he invited me to lunch with him in the factory canteen.

At noon there was an air-raid warning. This was surprising: there had been very little enemy action over England during the past few months because the *Luftwaffe* was fully engaged on the Russian front. The punch store, a small single-storeyed, heavily sandbagged and allegedly safe building was close to Tarr's office, so we went there. There was obviously no immediate danger but Tarr needed a box of punches.

A typographical punch is a small precision-engraved steel artefact which is used to 'strike' the copper-alloy matrices from which hot metal printing types are cast. Over the years the Corporation had accumulated a vast collection of punches. In the event of their destruction by enemy action it would have been a formidable task to replace them, even providing that the master patterns, which were kept elsewhere, had survived.

Inside the store there were rows of steel cabinets containing shallow drawers or trays and every one of the latter contained the punches for one size of any particular fount or design. I pulled out a drawer at random and inspected the record card which listed the dates when matrices had been made and for which customer(s). The card I held referred to a German *Fraktur* (i.e. 'Gothic') design. During the early 1930s a single set of matrices had been struck from these punches and the latter had not been used again. What fascinated me was to discover that the type design in question had been engraved for the exclusive use of the *Reichsbank* in Berlin. It immediately occurred to me that, given a specimen of the printing for which the *Reichsbank* employed this particular type, forgery would be comparatively easy providing that one could solve any associated paper and watermark problems.

I knew that the Corporation had engraved a large variety of *Fraktur* designs for the German, Austrian and Swiss markets and had exported the matrices. I was aware, too, that these designs, which were intended for use on 'Monotype' composing machines, were no more than exact copies of those produced by the German type foundries for hand-composition. Every one of the more important German type foundries had its standard lines and, when the German printing trade began to use the 'Monotype' system during the early 1900s, the Corporation simply copied them. I asked John Tarr to give me a list of all the series numbers of the *Frakturs* designed for the German market and then checked the corresponding record cards. I wanted to know what matrices had been supplied to British printing firms during the past twenty years and if the cards would reveal that any particular customer had assembled a really interesting collection of these specifically German types. The answer was that this had never happened. I also inspected the cards which recorded the export to France and the Low Countries of certain designs which were widely used in those countries but *never* in Great Britain. But no matrices for these had ever been delivered to any British printing firm.

My immediate conclusion was that HM Government's forgers, whoever they might be, must be unaware of the existence of this material at Horley. It is true that they could produce more or less acceptable forgeries of routine documents such as travel passes and *cartes d'identité* by making enlarged photographs of the originals and then retouching the line negatives to try to eliminate certain inevitable deficiencies. However, I was tolerably sure that they were unable to manufacture completely new documents which, although they looked exactly like those which already existed, should contain different and, above all, misleading texts. I reckoned that the 'misleading text' gambit might cause a lot of useful confusion. One hypothetical example will suffice: the Gauleiter at Breslau is accustomed to receiving a copy of a secret printed circular from the Nazi Party Chancery in Berlin and its format and general appearance have become familiar to him. Then another copy arrives, this time containing our 'misleading text'. The Gauleiter reads it and is surprised but then, after all, 'Those idiots in Berlin are capable of anything!' He stares at the document and makes a mental note that it looks exactly the same as the last one he received. If he goes so far as to compare the two documents, the latest one obviously came from the same printer even if the shade of paper was very slightly different, but then, after all, they could have run out of the old stock.

It was in the bus on my way back to Merstham that I thought up the following apothegm: 'If it's printed it's true and if one can find a plausible excuse for using or faking a rubber stamp impression on the printed document, then it must be doubly true!' I knew that the Germans loved using rubber stamps on every possible occasion. As for mailing or conveying the bogus document from Berlin to Breslau, I naturally supposed that our omniscient and omnipresent Secret Service would know how to arrange that.

A few days later, on Monday 22 September 1941, I read *The Times* and learned how Dr Hugh Dalton, the Minister of Economic Warfare, had spent the sabbath. He had travelled to Peterborough to address a National Council of Labour demonstration and, furthermore, had there revealed that the Prime Minister had made him, together with the Foreign Secretary and Minister of Information, responsible for British propaganda to enemy and enemy-occupied countries.[4] It then occurred to me that Dr Dalton might conceivably be interested in the plan that I was beginning to formulate.

When I returned to HQ Anti-Aircraft Command a couple of days later I wrote a paper headed 'Political Warfare and the Printed Word: A Psychological Study'. I offered a lot of technical and other information which, I hoped, might give the impression that I had a lifetime's experience of interfering with the efficient operation of various kinds of 'machinery', ranging from municipal to mechanical, by the simple process of depositing bits of paper where they were liable to block drains, overheat ball-bearings and cause the maximum amount of doubt, confusion and inconvenience. The piece read as if it had been prepared for publication by a learned society and did not contain any reference to the interesting discovery which I had just made at the Monotype Corporation's works. In fact, with prophetic foresight I provided a tolerably accurate blueprint for much that happened later in the Department, except that it was to be the gifted Sefton Delmer who supplied most of the best ideas while I was responsible for the manufacturing processes. It now remained only to manœuvre the paper into the hands of someone in a position of authority who might perhaps react by inviting me to put theory into practice.

Because I was serving in His Majesty's armed forces there was no question of mailing the piece to Dr Dalton together with a polite note asking him to forward it to an appropriate destination. Nevertheless the fact that I was employed at an army command HQ was an advantage because this eliminated all the conventional channels, i.e. regimental, brigade, divisional and corps headquarters. I consulted Major George Francis, the Camp Commandant at HQ Anti-Aircraft Command. He said that I should talk to Major-General Richard Bond, the M.G. (Administration), and a few minutes later escorted me to his office. The General read the document, not without indications of surprise and approval, and said that he would immediately send it to an unspecified branch of military intelligence. A few hours later I was instructed to report to a Brigadier X at an address in St James's Street – it was probably a branch of MI5 – at 11am the following morning. When I saw him the Brigadier had already read the paper but all he cared to tell me was that it had already been forwarded to an unspecified address.

Thereafter there was a succession of visits to London at weekly or fortnightly intervals. At one stage Major Avison, our liaison officer with MI5, told me that I was probably destined for a place called 'Baker Street' and would forthwith be promoted to the rank of Major, he supposed in the Intelligence Corps. 'Baker Street' was the headquarters of SOE, of whose existence I was ignorant. In any event, this never happened and my most important contact with the secret world now became John Rayner. I already had a slight acquaintance with him because he was skilled in the highly specialised area of newspaper typography and moved in book-collecting circles. He wrote to me from the Political Intelligence Department of the Foreign Office (Box 100, Western District Post Office) which, yet again unknown to me, was the 'cover' for the Political Warfare Executive. During the first week of November 1941 he summoned me to London and announced that he would no longer be concerned with my affairs because he was going to 'work for the Minister', but without specifying which Minister. He escorted me from his office in Lansdowne House, Fitzmaurice Place, at the southern end of Berkeley Square, across the road to Berkeley Square House, the headquarters of the Ministry of Economic Warfare, to the office of a Mr Leonard Ingrams. Ingrams sat behind a desk on which there were red leather boxes containing Cabinet papers and spoke with evident authority.

'Why aren't you already with us?' he immediately asked. I could only reply that I had no idea. Then he wanted to know if I was acquainted with someone whom he vaguely described as my 'Chief'. I thought that he was referring to Major-General Bond, but in fact he meant Lieutenant-General Sir Frederick Pile, Bt., the Commander-in-Chief of Anti-Aircraft Command, with its three Corps and twelve divisions. I replied that I was acquainted with the General to the extent that we occasionally exchanged a polite 'good morning' and that he knew my name. Ingrams said that he expected to encounter him at a 'Thirty Club' luncheon that very day and would speak to him. When I left Ingrams I lunched at my club and then went to a cinema because it never occurred to me that my absence from the Secret Registry that afternoon would be noticed.

When I arrived at the Registry the following morning I was told to report to the Camp Commandant's office without delay. Major Francis, who was evidently enjoying the situation, then told me the following story: 'You were the cause of an incredible flap here yesterday afternoon,' he said. 'The Chief [General Pile] telephoned the Major-General (General Staff) from London and said, "Howe is returning to civilian status and is to go to London immediately. He knows to whom he should report." The Major-General (GS) said it was all very irregular but the Chief said it didn't matter and that the administrative mess could be cleared up later.'

Thereupon Major Francis handed me a document which certified my transfer to the Class 'W'(T) Reserve' and told me to obtain a civilian ration book at the local Food Office. I bade farewell to a few people including the Chief Clerk, who was an elderly lieutenant.

'Is it true', he asked in a conspiratorial whisper, 'that you are going to be dropped into Germany by parachute?' I told him that his supposition was correct. 'But for heaven's sake keep your mouth shut, because it's all terribly secret!' I said.

I had no idea that Leonard Ingrams was an Under-Secretary at the Ministry of Economic Warfare and MEW's principal liaison officer with the Political Warfare Executive, nor that he had close links with SOE and the SIS. I could only surmise that my paper bomb had caused a very small explosion, not at PWE but at the Political Intelligence Department of the Foreign Office or MEW or perhaps both. My ignorance of the interlocking world of the Secret Departments was soon to diminish. My new employer was PWE.

Because the 'black game' was primarily and, indeed, most effectively played against the Germans, I have concentrated in this book upon that particular aspect of PWE's covert output. In any case the Germans were by far our most important target. Whatever we produced for other 'publics', e.g. in France, the Low Countries and Scandinavia, was addressed for the most part to the Allied resistance movements, albeit also for the German army units stationed there. While I worked for all or most of the PWE regional directorates, although relatively seldom for those concerned with Scandinavia and the Balkans, at the time I knew practically nothing about their other clandestine operations.

It is necessary to make a distinction between black broadcasting and printing because the two activities were never particularly co-ordinated. Whereas the broadcasting began in a very small way in May 1940, the fakes and forgery unit did not become really active until the early spring of 1942 when Sefton Delmer began to exploit its potential. In retrospect my little firm was mainly responsible for providing a back-up service for Delmer's black radio activities, and its work for the French, the Low Countries and other sections was far less regular or ambitious. For about eighteen months until the end of 1943 'Mr Howe's unit' led a completely independent and unsupervised existence. It came under Delmer's wing late in 1943 but it was typical of PWE that I was never informed in very precise terms about any new arrangements.

The authorities always knew, more or less, what was happening on the black broadcasting side but probably next to nothing about how I operated. Delmer and others were able to flourish specimens of my unit's output at various top-level meetings so there was at least satisfactory visual evidence of activity in the black printing department. Further-more, since there were reports that our productions were actually being delivered by SOE to anonymous readers in Europe, everybody seemed to be completely satisfied.

To return to Crossman's claim that the British achieved 'real pre-eminence' in the fields of subversion and black propaganda, the fact that certain successes could be recorded (and they were mostly Delmer's!) was solely because the authorities allowed the black division to run on a very loose rein subject to admirably tight security. In the unlikely event of indiscreet enquiries even the fact of the black operator's existence would have been cynically disavowed. Today PWE's black activities would hardly last for a month without being 'exposed' by the now unfailingly petulant left-wing weekly with which Mr Crossman himself was once associated. Times have changed.

I have suggested above that Sefton Delmer created a new concept of psychological warfare. It did not arrive with him 'ready made' but was evolved during a period of about two years after May 1941 as he grew in experience and confidence. 'Black' à la Delmer at the height of his wartime maturity was not merely a distortion or disregard of the truth, nor just sensational rumour-mongering, nor merely the most sensational dig at the enemy which could possibly be contrived. Its success (and damage to the Germans) depended upon the black operator being able to *indentify himself completely* with his (in our case, German) target. This was a most difficult and, indeed, subtle operation, relying to a significant extent upon the use of psychology. Hence the employment of Dr John T. MacCurdy, Lecturer in Psychopathology at Cambridge University, an eminent Canadian psychologist, as Delmer's professional adviser in this department.

Delmer had an unusual, indeed phenomenal capacity for 'tuning in' to, or penetrating the German mind and its mental processes, almost as if he himself resembled an ultra-sophisticated radio receiving set. This ability should not be equated with 'knowing Germany' (or 'the Ger-mans') in any conventional sense, because there were a number of people in PWE who could claim some kind of expertise in that context. Later in this book the reader will discover that Robert Walmsley, one of his PWE contemporaries who knew him well but was never a member of his team, described him as a 'genius', no doubt because that single word, *tout court*, best described his own assessment of Delmer's qualities. I believe, too, that some of Delmer's genius 'rubbed off', as it were, on some who worked closely with him on the scriptwriting and broadcasting sides, and that under his leadership they could achieve 'performances' of which they would have been incapable on their own.

Looking back at Delmer's work forty years after I first met him, I have realised (although without any feelings of satisfaction) how important is the role which 'black' plays in the modern way of political life, both nationally and internationally. However, TV documentaries and the press appear to indicate that neither the KGB nor the CIA, with their inflated staffs, are likely to match what Delmer achieved with a handful of gifted colleagues.

1  Herr Kirchner is in the building trade and runs his *Verlag für Zeitgeschichtliche Dokumente und Curiosa* (Luitpoldstrasse 58, D-8520 Erlangen) as a hobby. He has been active in organising exhibitions of all forms of Second World War printed propaganda. In Great Britain the Psywar Society, founded in 1958 by Mr R. G. Auckland (60 High Street, Sandridge, Herts.) caters for the interests of collectors and students of similar material and has an international membership of about two hundred. Mr Auckland edits and publishes *The Falling Leaf* (quarterly). He and his colleagues have produced a chronological list of PWE's white leaflets, i.e. those disseminated by the RAF from 1939 onwards.

2  Considering the care with which the *Institut für Marxismus-Leninismus* has collected and preserved 'illegal anti-fascist camouflaged publications' of the pre-war period, it is extraordinary that nothing produced by Otto Strasser's *Schwarze Front* (Black Front) is listed or, in the unlikely event that nothing has survived, that neither Strasser nor the *Schwarze Front* is mentioned in the index. During the years 1933-7 nobody was more active than Strasser in organising the despatch of black anti-Nazi propaganda literature across the Austrian and Czechoslovak borders into the Reich. However, the fact that Otto Strasser is probably a non-person in the German Democratic Republic would explain this *suppressio veri*.

3  For Stanley Morison see Nicolas Barker's biography, *Stanley Morison*, 1972.

4  On Saturday 20 September, the day before he went to Peterborough, Dr Dalton must have received the document (dated 20 September) prepared for the information of the Prime Minister and about forty other members of the Establishment, which formally announced the formation of 'a secret organisation which has recently been set up under the name of the Political Warfare Executive (PWE)'. An early public reference to PWE can be found in *Hansard*, 9 October 1941: 'Broadcasting to enemy countries and occupied territories is controlled by the Political Warfare Executive which has displaced the former miscellaneous agency. The PWE is under the ministerial direction of . . .' etc.

# 1

# The Munich Crisis

In the spring of 1938 HM Government was reluctantly beginning to realise that Hitler might decide to solve the Sudetenland problem by occupying that region of Czechoslovakia by force.[1] The Germans had annexed Austria on 15 March, the situation in Central Europe remained dangerous and Great Britain was unprepared for most eventualities. In the event of war with Germany our lack of preparation on the propaganda side was unhappily conspicuous.

The Committee of Imperial Defence had recently drafted plans for a shadow Ministry of Information, but in the spring of 1938 the MoI existed only on paper. Nevertheless, the Director-General designate was Sir Stephen Tallents, the Public Relations Controller at the BBC. He had previous Civil Service experience and had been a successful director of public relations activities at the Empire Marketing Board and the Post Office. In 1938, as far as his MoI work was concerned, Tallents, with the help of a couple of assistants, was concerned only with contingency planning.

However, I am not concerned with the future MoI but only with Tallents's shortlived connection with the concept of a wartime Propaganda to the Enemy Department. It was supposed that a specialist, self-contained department outside the MoI but responsible to the Minister of Information, whoever he might be, would be required. Sir Campbell Stuart had already been invited to take charge of this notional department, but nothing except a provisional appointment and a vague plan existed in September 1938.[2]

Campbell Stuart was a Canadian. When he arrived in England in 1916 as a young staff officer in the Canadian Army he was quickly in touch with influential social and political personalities. He impressed Lord Northcliffe, the proprietor of the *Daily Mail* and *The Times* newspapers, who invited him to direct, as his deputy, the new Propaganda in Enemy Countries department for which Northcliffe was responsible to the War Cabinet. The department was known as 'Crewe House' from its location at the Marquess of Crewe's residence in Curzon Street. It began to function early in 1918 but achieved little until the failure of the last major German offensive in the spring of that year. Then, with the deterioration of morale in Germany and Austria-Hungary and the intensification of the British propaganda effort, the message that Germany could only expect defeat was ruthlessly driven home.

It was widely believed in Germany after the war that her collapse on the home front was largely due to the diabolical efficiency of British propaganda. This hypothesis became part and parcel of the 'stab in the back' legend. But Crewe House's success was largely due to the fact that the tide had begun to run in the Allies' favour. A later generation was to learn how difficult it is to contrive convincing wartime propaganda when one reverse follows another.[3]

Stuart received a knighthood in 1918 at the unusually early age of thirty-three, and Northcliffe made him managing editor of both the *Daily Mail* and *The Times*. After Northcliffe's death in August 1922 Stuart played an important role in the negotiations which led to Major John Jacob Astor's purchase of The Times Publishing Company's shares from the Northcliffe estate. A seat on the board was one of his rewards and he became prominent in Establishment circles with fingers in many respectable pies, including the Imperial Communications Advisory Board of which he was Chairman in 1938. Stuart, then, was neither a professional propagandist, publicist nor foreign affairs specialist and, as Professor Balfour has remarked, 'Planning for 1939 tended to begin where 1918 had ended.'

Stuart's involvement in propaganda activities began in the spring of 1938 when the Prime Minister (Neville Chamberlain) asked Sir Warren Fisher, Head of the Treasury and Civil Service, to approach him.[4] At this stage he was merely asked to consider and report informally on the steps necessary for the creation of a new Propaganda to the Enemy Department. Stuart's preparatory work was conducted behind the scenes and Tallents acted as his representative. At the time of the Munich crisis his role was hardly more than peripheral because his proposed department did not even have a skeleton existence. By 30 August 1938, when the Cabinet discussed secret intelligence reports to the effect that the German armed forces were already partially mobilised, nothing had really been settled on the propaganda front.

During the first fortnight in September the situation continued to deteriorate and soon became critical. Chamberlain's first meeting with Hitler took place at Berchtesgaden on 15 September. His second encounter with the *Führer* was at Bad Godesberg a week later. In the event of war our ability to acquaint the German people with the British point of view would hardly have been impressive, although at this stage the RAF was making hectic preparations in case it was required to drop propaganda leaflets over Germany.

While the Prime Minister was still in Germany on Friday 23 September there was a meeting attended by Sir Hugh Knatchbull-Huggeson, who had latterly been Ambassador in Peking, and Wing-Commander A. L. Fiddament, representing the Air Ministry's Directorate of Planning. They had been informed by HM Stationery Office, which was responsible for all government printing, that ten thousand copies of an octavo leaflet for dropping over Germany by the RAF would weigh 40 lb. Only at this very late stage was elementary logistical information of this kind being collected and analysed.

The next day there was a larger meeting at which Tallents was present. He was accompanied by Robert Byron, a young man whom he had recruited to help him with his MoI work, and Mr D. S. Todd from the Stationery Office was also present. Fiddament reported that 'twelve Whitley bombers flying separately and at night could on one trip drop ten million leaflets' and added that two trips might be possible. He said that these aircraft were 'likely to be available in the first days of the war', also that they would be able to fly a little beyond Berlin.

It was accordingly resolved that an experimental leaflet should be produced up to proof stage. Mr Todd had brought with him some specimens of printing composed in a German *Fraktur* type. These met with criticism, probably because Tallents sensed that the types in question were somehow old-fashioned or otherwise unsatisfactory. Byron was asked to investigate two related problems: the identification of more suitable or legible types and the printing firms where they might be available. It is likely that the specimens had been prepared by Harrison and Sons Ltd, who had printed many of the Crewe House leaflets and still stocked the *Fraktur* matrices used in 1918. The reasoning which led Tallents to suppose that it was strictly necessary to use a German type design to convey a specifically British message was false. A legible Roman design would have served the purpose equally well.

While Knatchbull-Huggeson & Co. were fiddling with typographical minutiae Sir Campbell Stuart was also busy. According to a memorandum written by Tallents some weeks later, 'Authority to approach Sir Campbell Stuart was given and acted upon during the week ending 24 September. He devoted himself to the problem during the crisis, making his private house available for the purpose.' Robert Byron's paper on 'Preparation of Leaflets, 23–30 September 1938' was submitted to Tallents on 5 October and indicated that he had not yet solved the problem of access to more satisfactory *Fraktur* types. He observed that the trial leaflet which had been produced a couple of weeks earlier looked shoddy and old-fashioned, in fact unconvincing in terms of straightforward propaganda requirements. In this context he wrote:

> It is essential in the early stages that all printed propaganda should have a *normal* appearance in the eyes of those to whom it is addressed. The slightest abnormality gives an impression of inefficiency and even absurdity: the document ceases to be serious.
>
> There was no assurance that the leaflet which was in preparation would have the desired look of normality.
>
> The ideal solution of this difficulty would be to enlist the help of an expert on German [typographical] layout. But in case that should be impossible it is suggested that a collection should be made of comparable documents actually issued in Germany, so as to have models available for the typesetters to follow. It might also be worthwhile getting a commercial firm which has business in Germany to approach a German advertising agency (if there are such things there) with a request for designs for leaflets advertising its wares.

Byron's lack of familiarity with the whole typographical design area was leading him up the wrong path. It was never necessary for specifically white leaflets, meaning those which were intended to inform rather than deceive, to be printed with *Fraktur* types and to look as if they had been printed in Germany. He was confusing black requirements with those for white propaganda. In fact we continued to use *Fraktur* for white leaflets until 1941.

It is improbable that Byron had also been briefed to investigate the black printing area but it obviously interested him. He had undoubtedly read Campbell Stuart's *Secrets of Crewe House* and noticed the following on page 104: 'Perhaps, as a gratuitous hint to the curious, it may be added that the outside covers with titles of works by revered German authors did not always correspond with the contents of the books,' because he wrote:

> If the precedent of the last war is followed, there will be a stage when it is desired to circulate documents which look as if they are of official or at least domestic origin.
>
> To give these a proper aspect needs a careful study of Nazi methods of presentation and use of symbols. Designs of swastikas, wreathed, tilted and straight, of the eagle-cum-swastika, and of Hitler's personal standard, should be ready for blockmaking, and themes for which each type of

design is suitable should be known beforehand. It might also be useful to have actual photographs of Hitler and other leaders suitable for block-making. The badges of different organisations such as the *Hitlerjugend* [Youth Movement], in whose name it might be desirable to issue appeals, should also be available. Current leaflets and other publications from German official sources should also be scrutinised for printers' imprints so that these could be copied exactly.

Byron was never able to implement his black ideas, which were on the right lines. Soon after the completion of his memorandum he went to the USA on behalf of Tallents, and when he returned to London at the end of 1938 he learned to his dismay that his patron was about to be dismissed from his MoI job. Tallents gave him an introduction to Campbell Stuart but the latter was unwilling to consider him for future employment.[5]

The Air Ministry was not only prepared to disseminate printed matter; it was also willing to provide the actual propaganda texts. Thus on 25 September it submitted a draft for a leaflet which, it was suggested, could be dropped over Germany after the German air force had bombed England. Its purpose would be to warn the German population that we would take counter-action against the Ruhr region after giving twenty-four hours' notice of our intention to do so. The fact that any preliminary notice would give the Germans time to mobilise additional anti-aircraft defences was ignored. With memories of what had been done in Iraq in the 1920s the Air Ministry noted that,

> ... there is a specific type of propaganda which is of more particular interest to the Air Staff; namely the dropping of warning notices to the civil population to evacuate an area selected for attack, on similar lines to that which has been done for many years in the underdeveloped territories of the Empire.

Memories of India's north-west frontier died hard. Later the RAF was to be less solicitous for the safety of German civilians.

By the evening of Thursday 27 September those with inside know-ledge were becoming aware that an armed conflict might be unavoidable and the Cabinet decided to mobilise the fleet. On the propaganda front six different leaflet texts had been drafted at the Foreign Office and were in due course submitted to Sir Alexander Cadogan, its Permanent Under-Secretary. Cadogan made his choice, the translation was put in hand, and Tallents instructed HMSO to be prepared to print ten million leaflets at an agreed cost of 6d. per thousand at very short notice.

Apart from the RAF's slow Whitley bombers there was another method, given a favourable wind, of sending leaflets at least in the direction of Germany, namely in containers attached to balloons. This procedure had been used extensively during the First World War. The leaflets were released by a pre-set clockwork mechanism. Tallents learned on 29 September that while the Air Ministry had no suitable balloons in stock it had that very day purchased two hundred alarm clocks. There was, after all, a convenient source of supply just across the road from Adastral House at Messrs Ingersoll's premises in Kingsway.

The printing presses did not turn, the Whitley bombers did not set forth laden with ten million pieces of printed matter. The Munich Agreement was signed late on 29 September and the next day the Prime Minister returned to London, soon to declare with misplaced confidence: 'This is the second time in our history that there has come back from Germany peace with honour; I believe it is peace in our time.'

There were the inevitable *post mortem*s. The crisis period had demonstrated that our preparations for propaganda to Germany had been so rudimentary as to be almost worthless. On 4 October Tallents wrote to Sir Donald Banks, Permanent Secretary at the Air Ministry:

> Last week's dress rehearsal for the Ministry of Information taught us various lessons, but the sharpest and most urgent of them was the need for properly co-ordinated arrangements for the conveyance of information into enemy countries. The attention of the Committee of Imperial Defence should clearly be drawn to this subject, and I imagine that this might best be done by a paper put up by me to its Ministry of Information Sub-Committee.

Tallents's paper was circulated in November and discussed when the sub-committee met on 14 December. This document reveals that very little thought had so far been given to broadcasting as a propaganda weapon. It also indicates that Tallents, and possibly also Campbell Stuart, was still thinking almost exclusively in terms of printed leaflets.

> Of all the preparatory work for the Ministry, that on Propaganda in enemy countries was most in arrears. ... Last September it might have been very important to get a very important message into Germany at short notice. There were only a limited number of ways in which this could be done. Broadcasting was no doubt a valuable method in peacetime, but it appeared more likely that, in the event of war, German wireless receivers would be

confiscated and that the ordinary citizen of the country would be cut off from the messages broadcast from foreign stations. This means that the only means of getting a message distributed on a wide scale in an enemy country in the early stages of a war would be by dropping leaflets from the air, but such a method involves a great deal of preliminary preparation. Last September there had been no advance preparation of any kind.

At the same meeting Reginald Leeper (Foreign Office News Department) optimistically observed that

> if a crisis arose it would be comparatively easy for the FO, who would be abreast of the position in Germany, to prepare leaflets and other propaganda within a few hours, and they were prepared to undertake this task. It was true that in September last they had been unable to do so, but since then their organisation had been expanded. He personally had handed over his responsibilities for press work and was now engaged in publicity work.

Mr Leeper, who held the rank of Counsellor, was at that time unaware of the extent to which he would be involved in propaganda work, and to the Germans in particular, during the next four years. The News Department's function was to provide a press liaison service. The inference is that the recent leaflet-planning operation had taxed the department's limited resources. Leeper vaguely described one meaning of 'publicity work':

> Proposals were being submitted to the Cabinet which, if adopted, would result in the intensification by various means of British publicity work in Germany ... Contacts were being established through businessmen who were continually visiting that country. It was proposed to get into touch with heads of firms to enlist their support.

According to Leeper more arcane propaganda techniques were now also being considered. In addition various other methods were also being considered. '... various other methods were being tried by the SIS [Secret Intelligence Service] which for obvious reasons he could not enlarge upon.' He was referring to the obscure operations of Section D, which are discussed in the following chapter.

Tallents was soon to disappear from the pre-war propaganda scene. He was no longer *persona grata* at either the Treasury or the Foreign Office and was succeeded as Director-General designate of the MoI by Sir Ernest Fass, the Public Trustee, whom ill-health obliged to retire in June 1939. By then Sir Campbell Stuart's organisation was beginning to take shape and he never had any close connection with Fass.

1   The material for this chapter is largely based on the documents in FO 898/1.

2   For Campbell Stuart, see his *Secrets of Crewe House*, 1920, and his autobiographical *Opportunity Knocks Once*, 1952.

3   See J. D. Squires, *British Propaganda at Home and in the U.S. from 1914 to 1917*, Cambridge, Mass., 1935.

4   This information relating to the pre-war history of Department EH is based upon a memorandum written for me in 1973 by the late Anthony Gishford, who had been Stuart's personal assistant at this time.

5   Robert Byron (1905–41) was educated at Eton and Oxford. At Eton he used to go to the cinema dressed as an old woman, presumably to escape detection by the school authorities. During the 1920s he travelled extensively in the Near East and established a reputation as a Byzantinist. His best-known book was *The Road to Oxiana*, 1937, a study of Islamic architecture. He was commemorated by Christopher Sykes, with whom he travelled in Persia and Afghanistan in 1935, in *Four Studies in Loyalty*, 1946.

It is probable that Campbell Stuart found Byron altogether too overwhelming because, as his sister (Mrs Rohan Butler) remarked in a memorandum written for me in *c.* 1975: 'Robert's outspokenness did not make employing him easy or even desirable. . . . During the following months [i.e. after February 1939] Robert did not cease to importune various ministries for a job in some capacity dealing with propaganda. Nothing came of his efforts trying to enlist when the war started. . . . It was not until October 1939 that he became a sub-editor in the European News Department of the BBC.' Byron eventually found a niche in SOE and lost his life at sea on the way to Greece in February 1941.

# 2

# Section D

Section D, of whose existence Leeper had merely hinted at the meeting held on 14 December 1938, was a small offshoot of the Secret Intelligence Service. Indeed, it was SOE's direct precursor and at the time of the Munich crisis, when the Foreign Office was fumbling with plans for printing a leaflet for the RAF to disseminate over Germany, it was already dabbling with black printed propaganda for infiltration into Germany by underground channels.

Section D was run by Major Laurence Grand, a Corps of Royal Engineers officer, whom Admiral Hugh Sinclair, who was 'C',[1] i.e. chief of the SIS, had engaged for very special and secret work. Tallents learned a little about Grand's activities on 30 September 1938, and some more on 5 October, because 'C' had decided that it would now be advisable to let Tallents know something about parallel efforts in the covert propaganda field. His intermediary was Captain Robert Henniker Heaton, R.N., who made contact with A. P. Ryan, Tallents's liaison officer for MoI planning work. He had been a member of the *Manchester Guardian*'s editorial staff before joining Tallents at the Empire Marketing Board and was senior to Robert Byron.

Ryan wrote a report for Tallents on 30 September 1938:[2]

S[ecret] S[ervice], etc.

Through Captain Henniker Heaton (Passport Control, Broadway Buildings, Whitehall 7446) I saw:

Col. W. Hinchley-Cooke (No. 3 Entrance, 7th Floor, Thames House, War Office MI5). He translated the FO approved text and said he would be willing to do any other translation work.

Major Grand, address as Henniker Heaton.
Major Thornton, ditto
Mr Wren, ditto

The first of these two are soldiers who took me to see some of their foreign contacts.

Major Grand expressed strong views on how this type of [black] propaganda should be conducted and had had printed in German a leaflet. He

29

did not tell me how it was to be distributed but it was for immediate release. The printers were Williams Lea and Co. Ltd, Clifton House, Worship Street, EC2. As I have not seen the leaflet, I cannot judge whether these printers are better supplied with German types than are Harrison's. But if we are to go ahead, it would be worthwhile asking the S[tationery] O[ffice] about them.

In 1938 Williams Lea was one of the few London printing firms which specialised in printing in foreign languages and employed one or two monotype keyboard operators of German or Polish origin. They had a small range of *Fraktur* matrices but were not 'better supplied with German types' than Harrison and Sons Ltd.

Ryan learned more about Grand's activities on 5 October and immediately drafted a report for Tallents:

Major Grand rang me this afternoon and said he wanted to let me know about developments on his side. I had a long session with him this afternoon, at which I began by making it clear that I had no standing in this matter and could not say what would happen immediately or in the long run on the Ministry of Information side.

I am still not certain to whom Major Grand is responsible. He told me that he was not directly under either the War Office or the Foreign Office, but that the right way to get at him with a letter was c/o MI1 at the War Office. The points he made were:

1 On Monday afternoon, 26 September, he was sent for by his Chief [i.e. 'C'] and told to form immediately a section dealing with the dissemination through all channels *outside this country* of material into enemy and neutral countries. The limitation means that anything sent from here by the BBC, by Air Force machines or ships of war, would not concern him. This section is now in the process of active formation, though I gathered it had only taken on one man, J[ohn] Walter, of the *Times* family.[3] His name was mentioned to me by Henniker Heaton last week in connection with the proposed index of neutral papers which I reported to you. ... Grand was proposing to describe him as a member of the Ministry of Information. When I explained that this was impossible, he asked whether he might be attached for camouflage purposes to the BBC and I told him that this was equally impossible, and he is thinking again.

2 Grand had been asked last week to distribute as widely and thickly as possible over Germany the German texts of one of the Prime Minister's statements and of Roosevelt's appeal. Nothing has come of this.

3  As you already know, Grand has had some leaflets printed in German and has apparently got a few of them into Germany.

Ryan added that Grand was proposing to be active in four ways:

(a) *Broadcasting*: by broadcasting outside this country, e.g. Luxembourg etc. He wanted to be put unofficially in touch with the BBC, but he emphasised that he did not wish to trespass on anyone else's preserves. I advised him not to move until this position has been cleared up.

(b) *The Press*: by indexing papers with the names of correspondents etc. in all neutral and friendly countries adjacent to enemy territory, and taking steps to introduce desirable editorial matter into them.

(c) *Leaflets distributed by any and every means* – balloons, communists, commercial travellers, seamen. He emphasised that it would be necessary to have all sorts of leaflets, since one that a social democrat would willingly risk his neck to disseminate would be anathema to a communist and vice versa.

(d) *Whispering campaigns* which were most effective in the last war.

Grand said he was most anxious to do nothing that would in any way cut across the Ministry of Information. He realised that the preparation and printing of material was a MoI responsibility, and here merely wished to be the channel of distribution. He would not himself initiate any leaflets or whispering campaigns. He said he hoped you would bring his side in whenever there are any discussions and hoped that all danger of overlapping with his outfit and with the Services might be avoided.

It was tactful of Grand to express a desire not to impinge upon the Ministry of Information's territory. However, the MoI still only existed on paper, and Section D itself was an incredibly amateurish affair.

It is unlikely that a detailed account of Section D's origins and early days will ever be written. There are references to Grand in a handful of books, but their respective authors, e.g. Bickham Sweet-Escott, Joan Bright Astley, Julian Amery and Kim Philby[4] were not recruited until late in 1939 or even early in 1940, whereas Grand himself had been running the section since the spring of 1938. Kim Philby found his way to the SIS via Section D and SOE. When he joined Grand's outfit in July 1940, in fact only a few weeks before Grand himself was sacked and what was left of the section became SOE, he was instructed to report to none other than Guy Burgess 'at an address in Caxton Street in the same block as the St Ermin's Hotel'.[5]

Bickham Sweet-Escott thought that Section D had been created 'shortly after Munich', but it was then that Grand began to expand its hitherto minute personnel. He wrote, too, that it had been formed 'with the object of doing those things which assisted the execution of HM Government's policy, but which HM Government preferred not to acknowledge as the actions of its agents'. Before he joined the section in March 1940 the man who recruited him said: 'For security reasons I can't tell you what sort of a job it would be. All I can say is that if you join us, you mustn't be afraid of forgery, and you mustn't be afraid of murder.' His initiatory experiences reminded him of somewhat similar episodes in John Buchan's novels.

Bickham Sweet-Escott recalled that Grand was,

... tall and thin, with a heavy black moustache. He never wore uniform, always had a long cigarette holder in his mouth, and was never without a red carnation in his buttonhole. What was remarkable about him was the fertility of his imagination, the imperturbability of his character under the most trying circumstances, and he also had an uncommonly pretty wit. I have never I think met anyone who had such a fine flow of ideas about what we should do, nor anyone for whom it was easier to work.

Kim Philby wrote:

Grand never had the resources to carry out his ideas, though they were given freely to his successors. His London staff could fit easily into a large drawing-room. We regularly did so on Sundays at his headquarters in the country, where plans, plans, plans were inexhaustible topics of discussion. In the field he had little more than bits and scraps. His efforts to get a larger slice of the secret cake were frowned on by the older and more firmly based intelligence-gathering side of the service.... Thus Grand's demands on the Treasury and on the armed services were often blocked within the service. At best they were given lukewarm support.

I had two long conversations with the late Major-General Grand in 1973. His memory was often hazy – for instance, he could tell me very little about his printing operations – and his remarks were often somewhat disjointed as he flitted from one reminiscence to another. Thus I have distilled my notes into a more or less narrative form.

At the beginning of 1938 Grand was approaching the end of four happy years at the War Office where he was concerned with vehicle design. He already had a loose connection with the SIS for whom he had previously supplied information about Syria. He expected to be posted to Egypt in the autumn of 1938 but in March was summoned to see 'C'.

The latter was convinced that war with Germany was inevitable and was making certain preparations.

'I want you to do sabotage,' said 'C'.

'Is anything barred?' Grand asked.

'Not a thing!' 'C' replied.

This was the first time that Grand had encountered 'C' and he thought that he looked like a Mexican gangster. 'He wore a hat with a very wide brim and a blue suit with brown shoes,' he recalled. In those days brown shoes with a blue suit were a sartorial solecism.

Grand said that Section D was more or less formally established on 1 April 1938 and added, 'The date itself was very appropriate!' During the next few months he recruited two or three congenial colleagues who would presumably not be afraid of either forgery or murder.

'What you are going to do won't be very popular on our side,' 'C' remarked, adding that he would encounter opposition from certain ultra-conservative individuals in the higher echelons of the War Office. In fact 'C' named five people. He said, too, that he was worried about the existence of a number of identifiable potential quislings. They were highly placed politicians and civil servants.

Grand said that it was not long before 'C' sent him to Czechoslovakia on a solitary reconnaissance expedition. The objective was to find ways and means of denying the Germans the use of the huge Skoda armaments plant by the simple process of blowing it up. The simplest method was to discuss the matter with the Skoda directors and this was done. But the 'big bang' never happened.

The financial arrangements could be informal. Grand was in the Chief's office one day when 'C' asked him if he needed any money.

'What do I need money for?' Grand asked.

'Well, you might want to do some entertaining,' said 'C', who then fished around in a drawer, pulled out £100 in notes and handed them to him.

Grand recalled a particular black operation. A certain Mr Walter Hauck, whom he had enlisted, went to New York and took with him a large number of addresses of senior Nazi party officials. In due course they received friendly letters posted in the USA, saying that the writer was grieved to learn that there was a severe shortage of food in Germany and that he would send a parcel. The packages were sent by sea mail and included subversive printed propaganda in addition to chocolate, tins of meat and so on. At the same time the Gestapo received a tip-off letter. The plan was that the Gestapo should harass the recipients of these gifts and according to Grand this actually happened.

Grand remembered very little about his black propaganda activities but implied that a steady flow reached Germany before the outbreak of hostilities.

'A lot of it arrived at North German ports by sea transport,' he said. 'Consignments were carried by the eel boats which sailed from small ports in Essex. We received quite useful help from the seamen's trade union.' Postal operations were conducted from the Swiss side of the border at Constance.

The same route was used by SOE for similar purposes in 1943, but across the border inside Germany. Gramophone records with misleading labels were manufactured for infiltration into Germany.

It seems that rather wider recruiting for Section D did not begin until after the Germans occupied Czechoslovakia in the spring of 1939. At this stage Grand enlisted several dozen adventurous young men who might otherwise have joined conventional Territorial Army units because the TA was expanding fast at this time. He mentioned that during the summer of 1939 they secretly surveyed practically every port in northern Europe, perhaps on the principle of when in doubt, blow up a crane.

I suspect that Grand's part-time apprentice saboteurs were all 'warrior children of the upper classes'. The anonymous reviewer who used this phrase also observed that 'the Establishment went to war in the secret services'.[6] During the early part of the war this probably applied to the SIS, certain branches of military intelligence, Section D and its successor SOE. The intellectuals, and the mathematicians in particular, tended to go to the Government Code and Cypher School at Bletchley, but the secret propaganda departments (Department EH and its successors SO1 and PWE) were never the Establishment's happy hunting ground.

By the spring of 1940 when the Germans invaded France, Section D consisted of about three hundred officers. This was Grand's estimate. Grand said that he knew that his own days were numbered when Dr Hugh Dalton, the Minister for Economic Warfare, was placed in charge of sabotage and subversion in July 1940.

Dalton sent for me and asked me to get Leon Blum, a fellow socialist politician, out of France. I saw him a couple of days later and told him that I would need a submarine or a Lysander aircraft, also that he would have to ask the War Cabinet for approval. Dalton said that he could not do this. I don't suppose that the Conservatives were all that interested in Blum. I said that I couldn't hazard lives and that the operation could not be mounted because it wasn't a 'top war priority' affair. So Dalton sacked me and I was damned glad to return to ordinary soldiering.

## SECTION D

Kim Philby, who was around and observant, recalled that Section D was purged during the summer of 1940, and that many familiar faces disappeared. What was left of Section D became Special Operations 2 (SO2) and in due course SOE.

1 In those days the name of the Chief of the SIS was never mentioned, even in private conversation, and he was simply called 'C'. Indeed, his identity was unknown outside a small circle.

2 This and other contemporary documents quoted in this chapter are in FO 898/1 (PRO).

3 *The Times* newspaper was founded by the first John Walter in 1785. In 1939 a senior member of the Walter clan was a director of *The Times* Publishing Company Ltd although the family had lost control many years previously.

4 See Bickham Sweet-Escott, *Baker Street Irregular*, 1965; Joan Bright Astley, *The Inner Circle*, 1971; Julian Amery, *Approach March*, 1973 and Kim Philby, *My Secret War*, 1968.

5 Philby: '... I found myself in the forecourt of St Ermin's Hotel, near St James's Park station, talking to Miss Marjorie Maxse. She was an intensely likeable elderly lady. ... I had no idea then, as I have no idea now, what her precise position in government was. But she spoke with authority, and was evidently in a position at least to recommend me for "interesting" employment.' – Kim Philby, *My Secret War*, 1968. Miss Maxse had latterly been Chief Organisation Officer at the Conservative Party Central Office, a fact which would have amused Philby.

6 Review of Julian Amery's *Approach March* in *The Times Literary Supplement*, 16 November 1973.

# 3

# The Mobilisation of Department EH

At the height of the Munich crisis on 27 September 1938, when war with Germany seemed inevitable, the Cabinet took two important decisions: to mobilise the Fleet and to invite Sir Campbell Stuart to organise a secret Department of Propaganda to Enemy Countries, outside the general framework of the Ministry of Information but under the ultimate jurisdiction of the Minister.[1] While the Fleet was presumably in a position to fire a few broadsides, the Propaganda Department simply did not exist. In any case, after Munich the propaganda project was put on ice until 23 December 1938 when Stuart was appointed chairman of a sub-committee of the Committee of Imperial Defence to report on 'possible methods of conducting propaganda to the enemy'. He met Sir Ernest Fass, Tallents's successor as Director General designate of the MoI, probably for the first time, on 16 January 1939.

According to the surviving (and not very informative) minutes of that meeting, Captain R. J. Herbert Shaw was to be the 'Head of Section'. Next, 'For liaison with the four Intelligence Services [i.e. SIS and naval, military and air] an officer of the Royal Marines. A confidential typist would be required and Mr Gishford, who is on Lord Camrose's staff, might also be used.'

Shaw was an old acquaintance of Stuart's, a former member of *The Times* staff and reputed to be an authority on Irish affairs. There is no reason to believe that he had any particular knowledge of Germany. The Royal Marines officer, who had clearly already been earmarked, was Lieutenant-Colonel Reginald Alexander Dallas Brooks (always known as Dallas Brooks), later to be promoted to Brigadier and then Major-General. Later in his career he was Governor-General of Victoria, in his native Australia. He spent most of the war years with the Department. Mr Anthony Gishford, a young friend of Sir Campbell's and his future personal assistant, was soon to leave the Camrose group of newspapers (*Daily Telegraph*, *Sunday Times*, etc.) and work for the Hon. Leo Russell, the advertisement director of Illustrated Newspapers Ltd.

Twenty years earlier journalists with a detailed knowledge of European politics and personalities – Wickham Steed of *The Times* was one of them – had made a notable contribution to the work of Crewe House and Stuart was looking for their successors. By the end of January 1939 he had also enlisted Cecil Sprigge, one of the *Manchester Guardian*'s veteran correspondents and an Italian rather than a German specialist, and Valentine Williams, the author of a famous best-selling spy story (*The Man with the Club Foot*, 1920), whom he had first encountered many years earlier at the *Daily Mail*.

A. R. (Robert) Walmsley was one of the very few who was recruited without being a member of the 'old boy' network with which Stuart was in touch. He was then twenty-seven years of age and unknown to anyone in Stuart's milieu. After Oxford he had gone to Vienna to work for Julius Meinl, an Austrian captain of industry, who had required him to treat German as his working language. He returned to London at the time of the Munich crisis and wrote to Reginald Leeper asking to be put in touch with anyone concerned with propaganda to Germany in the event of war. An unsigned note in the file states that, 'This man wrote a "Dear Sir" letter stating his qualifications.' In those days it was preferable to be on first-name terms with someone or other if one wanted to be admitted to the charmed circle which inhabited the secret world.

Walmsley heard nothing until 17 March 1939, two days after the Germans entered Prague. He then received a letter, not from Leeper but from Grand who, disguised as 'Major Douglas', invited him to a meeting at a cover address. After the war Walmsley recalled that,

At this and other meetings it turned out that Major Grand ... had been given charge of clandestine propaganda against Germany up to the outbreak of war. Grand asked me to send him any suggestions I had for methods of propaganda, and I sent him a large number of individual suggestions ranging from points for insertion into a speech by the Foreign Secretary to a suggestion for forging Nazi Party Literature passing between Germany and abroad. It has always been a matter of great regret to me that Grand never put the second suggestion through, though he promised to do so, since it would have started genuine 'black' propaganda two years earlier than actually happened.

Grand had accumulated a few other people working for him, of whom I met three. His main project, as far as I know, was the production of a regular 'news sheet' to be smuggled into Germany and distributed as if from an oppositional organisation. This was an extremely crude affair by later standards.

Walmsley evidently impressed Grand because a brief minute recorded that, 'He is considered to be the best German leaflet writer in the United Kingdom. He will shortly be coming to see C[ampbell] S[tuart] and would be at our disposal in war.' Walmsley knew nothing about the latter proposition before he met Stuart for the first time on 18 April 1939.

> Grand asked me to go along and have dinner with him and Campbell Stuart. Immediately we entered Campbell Stuart's house he shook me warmly by the hand and asked me, somewhat to my surprise, to join 'his organisation'. During the evening it turned out that Grand's organisation would be responsible for propaganda against Germany up to the outbreak of war and that Campbell Stuart's organisation (also secret) would be responsible after the outbreak of war. I think this was the first occasion when Grand and Campbell Stuart met to discuss their plans.

While Walmsley had a hand in drafting many of the early wartime leaflets, he was soon diverted to mainly intelligence activities, where his most interesting achievement was to identify the signs in German propaganda from which their strategic intentions or expectations could be guessed. At the end of the war he was probably the Department's longest-serving member and proceeded to a successful career at the Foreign Office.

On 3 April 1939, about three weeks after the German occupation of Czechoslovakia, Stuart's small inner circle received the following communication. It was probably signed by Leo Russell, whom Gishford had brought into the fold.

> Sir Campbell Stuart has asked me to let you know that an office at the above address [Room 207, Electra House, Victoria Embankment, the headquarters of the Imperial Communications Advisory Committee, of which Stuart was Chairman] has been opened. A Reuter's tape machine is being installed and a wireless set, maps etc. are available. This office and the services of a stenographer will be at your service at any time.

Thus Stuart's department inevitably became known as 'Electra House' or 'Department EH' for cover purposes.

Until Department EH was mobilised at the end of August 1939 it existed on an informal or 'blueprint' basis without a Treasury grant, although Stuart received a modest subsidy for expenses from 'C'. Hence on 27 July 1939 Leo Russell sent Valentine Williams a cheque for £50 'as a slight appreciation of the services which you have been rendering during the past month'. The recipient had been writing memoranda on German topics.

Department EH's connection with Woburn Abbey, the seat of the Duke of Bedford, was entirely fortuitous. It was assumed that London would be bombed immediately by the German Air Force and it was decided that most of the staff should be accommodated outside London. The preliminary arrangements in connection with Woburn, which was conveniently close to the metropolis (forty-three miles), were made by Leo Russell, who was a kinsman of the old Duke of Bedford. At that time there was no question of taking over the Abbey itself and Russell arranged for Department EH to occupy merely the vast stable wing and the Riding School. The latter was to be used for offices and the flats above the stables, once inhabited by a large staff of coachmen and grooms and their families, would provide somewhat spartan sleeping accommodation. No rent was required and it was stipulated that His Grace would not have to set eyes upon, let alone encounter, any of his unwanted guests. The fact that they would be there at all was because the Duke preferred temporary civil servants to a mob of children evacuated from the London slums. However, the ducal estate was so large that even chance meetings with the secret propagandists could be avoided without too much trouble.

The final crisis in due course manifested itself. During the evening of 19 August 1939 Stalin informed the Politburo that he intended to sign a non-aggression pact with Germany. The news that Ribbentrop, the German Foreign Minister, would be flying to Moscow was released by the Soviet Tass news agency very late on 21 August and the pact was signed on 23 August. Department EH's elaborate mobilisation instructions reached Valentine Williams on 19 August, two days before the Tass press release was published. The news of Ribbentrop's forthcoming journey to Moscow had been leaked to London by Wolfgang von Putlitz, a German diplomat stationed at the Hague, who escaped to England just before hostilities began and then went to the USA. In fact he returned to England early in 1944 and, much to his surprise, found himself at Woburn.

Germany invaded Poland at dawn on Friday 1 September. Walmsley received a telegram from Leo Russell: 'Mobilise today at 7pm.' Only a few selected initiates already knew that Department EH's secret Country Headquarters were to be located at Woburn Abbey. Walmsley and others who had their own transport were instructed to go to the Sugarloaf Hotel at Dunstable, thirty-four miles north of London on the old A5 London-Holyhead road. Walmsley found his way there in an ancient

Morris which he had recently acquired for £15 when Major Grand paid him £50 for services rendered. 'It seemed like a fortune at the time,' he wrote.

Upon arrival at Dunstable they were told to ask for Mr Gibbs-Smith, who had been appointed Administrative Officer at Country Headquarters. The latter was soon known to all as 'CHQ', or by those who remained in London as 'The Country'. The place name Woburn was never mentioned. The subsequent procedure at the Sugarloaf was roughly as follows: after checking each new arrival's identity Mr Gibbs-Smith whispered the name Woburn Abbey and provided a rough sketch map showing its location (nine miles further north), also a pass which would admit the bearer at one of the entrances to the Duke's estate.

Walmsley mentioned that some of the administrative staff had arrived a few days earlier and the partitions for twenty-four small cubicles had already been erected in the Riding School. According to the mobilisation order the advance party of propagandists was to be provided with two typewriters, one box of pins and two red and two blue pencils!

During the next few days about sixty people settled in at Woburn, including catering staff supplied by J. Lyons and Co. – later they were replaced by the A.B.C. – and two compositors from the University Press at Oxford. The latter contrived a composing room in the small hangar which had once housed the late Duchess's small aircraft. The compositors were employed to do the typesetting for the propaganda leaflets which were to be printed at HM Stationery Office's works at Harrow. Department EH already possessed what Stuart called a 'war store' of leaflets for use during the first few days of hostilities.

Various documents attached to the mobilisation order reveal the names of the team of propaganda warriors which had been picked to represent Great Britain against Dr Goebbel's Propaganda Ministry. As well as those of the pre-war recruits these included Vernon Bartlett (a well-known journalist and broadcaster who had recently been elected a Member of Parliament), Ian Colvin (a young journalist with recent experience of working in Berlin), Thomas Barman from *The Times* and Ralph Murray, an energetic young man from the BBC who was later to be HM Ambassador to Greece. Few of them survived, or rather elected to survive, for very long although both Barman and Murray achieved a certain eminence in the later (1941–5) PWE period.

There were also typists, telephonists and sundry other camp followers, and a sizeable transport section as Woburn was some miles from the nearest town and railway station. The typists were mostly recruited from the Imperial Communications Advisory Board and Thomas Cook and

Son Ltd. The eight telephone operators came from such places as the Dorchester and Grosvenor House hotels, Keith Prowse Ltd's theatre ticket agency and the Derry and Toms department store. Mr C. M. Baatz, the *chef de cuisine* supplied by Messrs Lyons, was initially in charge of four waitresses, two counter hands and two kitchen porters.

All, from the highest to the most humble, were under strict instructions not to communicate their address to any outsider nor to tell anyone what they were supposed to be doing. Letters were not to be posted locally and were to be sent to London for mailing.

The mobilisation instructions contained the following peremptory behest: 'Engage ten housemaids; obtain six Boy Scouts for immediate duty and arrange for others to succeed them in shifts.' Housemaids still existed in England at that time but were soon to become a dying race. It has not been possible to discover if the Boy Scouts, who were presumably intended to function as messengers, were ever recruited.

Sir Campbell Stuart and two or three of his close associates were accommodated at Paris House, a French half-timbered building which had been on exhibition in Paris in 1889. It had greatly impressed the then Duke of Bedford who had had it dismantled and transported to Woburn. Many other propagandists were lodged in various houses at Woburn or the surrounding district.

The Department's military wing, then a small affair headed by Colonel Dallas Brooks, remained in London at Electra House. Campbell Stuart oscillated between London and Woburn in his Rolls-Royce, accompanied by three personal assistants and a filing cabinet. There was also a small liaison section in Paris whose members included Nöel Coward. When 'C' learned of this somewhat surprising appointment he is supposed to have said, referring to Coward's appearance in naval uniform, 'I suppose he had it specially designed for him.'

According to the mobilisation orders accommodation was also to be provided at Woburn for, 'SIS, 6 men, including one "occasional", 3 senior females and 4 female typists.' They were, in fact, members of Grand's Section D propaganda team. According to Anthony Gishford, Stuart's interest in black propaganda and subversion was minimal, and Grand's black cuckoos were unwelcome in Stuart's white propaganda nest at Woburn. Thus in November 1939 they moved to a house at Hertingfordbury where they remained in apparently peaceful obscurity until the summer of 1940 when a few of them joined the white leaflet production team at Woburn.

It remains to mention what Walmsley called 'the real PID' (i.e. Political Intelligence Department of the Foreign Office), with which

PWE has often been confused. The reason for the confusion is that from the early autumn of 1941 onwards PWE used the title PID as a cover. The revived PID – it was a reincarnation of a small department which had existed during the First World War – was also located at Woburn but was non-secret. Reginald Leeper was placed in charge of it in September 1939 and also acted as Foreign Office adviser to Stuart's propagandists. From 1946 onwards he was its Superintending Under-Secretary.

The PID's main task was to produce a weekly summary, country by country, of political intelligence information from a wide variety of sources. The latter was printed on the pale blue paper characteristic of all FO printing from about 1830 onwards. Its classification was Secret rather than Most Secret because a copy used to arrive at Headquarters Anti-Aircraft Command every Sunday morning and I used to read it with great interest before sending it up to the GSO I (Intelligence) who conceivably never bothered to look at it.

Bruce Lockhart, later PWE's so-called 'FO and Whitehall' Director-General, spent a few mildly unhappy months at Woburn as a member of the PID in 1939. In due course the PID engaged the services of distinguished scholars like R. W. Seton-Watson, whose *Britain and the Dictators: A Survey of post-war British policy* (written under the pseudonym 'Scotus Viator') attracted attention when it was published by the Cambridge University Press in 1938. The PID also provided a genteel employment for various distinguished ambassadors who were without embassies, Sir Percy Loraine and Sir Reginald Hoare, for example, whom the Germans had evicted from Rome and Bucharest respectively. The PID was dissolved in March 1943 when most of its members were transferred to a new Foreign Office Research Department which was mainly staffed by Chatham House people under the direction of A. J. Toynbee at Balliol College, Oxford.[2]

1 The material for this chapter is based on the documents in FO 898/1 and 2, Mr Robert Walmsley's unpublished notes, and information supplied by the late Anthony Gishford.

2 The 'real PID' people at Woburn also included Maxwell H. H. Macartney, Professor John Hawgood, Clifton Child, G. M. Gaythorne-Hardy, Denis Brogan, E. D. Gannon and Brigadier Eric Scaife (formerly military attaché in Moscow). When the PID ceased to exist at Woburn early in 1943 Hawgood and Child both joined PWE. Furthermore, Child became an important member of Delmer's black team.

# 4

# The Department at Woburn
# 1939–42

I shall attempt no more than a brief sketch of the background from which the Department's black propaganda activities emerged in a very modest way in 1940 but with increasing vigour in 1941. In any case its black side has very little connection with its history's main stream, which has already been described in Dr Charles Cruickshank's *The Fourth Arm* and Professor Michael Balfour's *Propaganda in War, 1939–45*.

From September 1939 until the French débâcle in June 1940 Department EH was nothing more than a small organisation mainly concerned with leaflet propaganda for Germany and policy directives for the BBC's German service which in any case never welcomed them. The fall of France, which followed the German occupation of Denmark, Norway, Belgium and Holland and led to Italy's entry into the war, found it unprepared, bewildered and in a state of suspended animation. The assumption of new responsibilities, i.e. the conduct of propaganda to the enemy-occupied territories, which required an immediate expansion of staff, was complicated by a complete change of management when Sir Campbell Stuart disappeared to Canada in July 1940. Furthermore, the Department was involved in sinister ministerial battles for the control of propaganda, internecine warfare with one half of the newly created Special Operations Executive (SOE), of which it was the other half, and was disliked and mistrusted by the BBC. If Dr Goebbels had been given even an inkling of the confusion which prevailed in the British 'Propaganda Ministry' he would have experienced a delicious sense of *Schadenfreude*. However, in the course of time the problems diminished and by the middle of 1942 the Department was operating on a fairly even keel.

In 1939 Department EH was little more than a reincarnation of the First World War's Crewe House propaganda organisation. Nobody realised how difficult it would be to create an even tolerably efficient

43

successor in the light of the completely different conditions which prevailed at the time.

The Department's black propaganda side began to emerge in the autumn of 1940: at first tentatively, certainly amateurishly, and without inheriting anything identifiable or useful from Section D. When Sefton Delmer arrived on the scene early in 1941 no one anticipated that it was he who was destined to transform a black propaganda 'popgun' into a genuine weapon of psychological warfare.

If the Department's installation at Woburn resembled scenes from the Beatles' comic TV *Magical Mystery Tour* film, the early annals of its sojourn there also had qualities which were sometimes more akin to surrealism than reality. The formula for a 'mad' atmosphere was ready made. Plant an ill-assorted collection of journalists etc. in and around the purlieus of a ducal mansion and more or less isolate them from the outside world – during the first fortnight of the war they were confined to the Riding School and stables area – and there is the perfect recipe for a black comedy. Even two years later the Abbey and its denizens presented an extraordinary phenomenon when I first beheld them.

According to Robert Walmsley: 'The atmosphere of the early days was one of bustling amateurishness and, with one exception, almost complete ineffectualness. The only pre-war appointments which stood for some time were Shaw as Deputy Director and Valentine Williams as German Editor. All the other appointments were shuffled around, if indeed any were made at all.'

The problem confronting the Woburn people was that they were required to produce propaganda to the Germans in a vacuum. The shooting war had not yet begun and there was nothing very important to say to them, certainly nothing which was calculated to lessen their belief in the *Führer*.

At that time Department EH's main task was the production of leaflets for the RAF to drop over Germany. Close on twenty million were delivered in September 1939 but during the remaining months of the year the number steadily dwindled and only two million were disseminated in November and December and these could have been scattered by three Whitley bombers on one trip. In any case the RAF was not invariably enthusiastic about leaflet operations. Department EH was also supposed to provide policy guidance for the BBC's German service. Walmsley wrote:

I do not think it is an exaggeration to say that the relation of Electra House to the BBC was an organisational disaster. In the early months there was as good as no control whatever. There were two liaison officers with the BBC. Both were members of the BBC who considered it their duty to prevent EH from having any effect on BBC output. The Director and the German Editor of EH time and again vetoed rebellious suggestions from more junior members that any instruction should be given to the BBC. Only a 'recommendation' was in order. The only channel for these recommendations was via the two liaison officers. I do not think it unjust to say that these two officers acted purely as servants of the BBC. They probably considered this to be in the general as well as in the BBC's interest. [Thirty years later Walmsley thought that the BBC had probably been right.] Apart from the organisational decision which permitted them to beat off Electra House, it is of course true that a number of the suggestions put up by Electra House were fairly amateurish, but this was because the senior members of EH had not the qualifications for directing BBC output and were compelled to rely on junior members who themselves lacked experience.

However, there were consolations. Walmsley recalled:

Even in those days work was apt to go on until the early hours of the morning. This was not quite as arduous as it sounds, since the Lyons canteen was supplemented by an excellent small bar in which you could have five sherries or a reasonable bottle of French claret for half a crown. I was told that one tenth of the salary bill of the whole Department passed through this bar. Those were also the days in which gallon jars of sherry and bottles of gin enlivened the working hours of secretaries and others, somewhat to the surprise of the regular civil servants who visited us from time to time. It was not unusual, also, for people to take two or three hours off in the afternoon, encouraged in this by Valentine Williams himself. There was wonderful skating on the lakes (January 1940 was an unusually cold month) and the Duke of Bedford's park was full of interest to the zoologically inclined.

The minutes of a meeting of the Services Consultative Committee (6 March 1940) indicate that Department EH was not solely engaged in the production of relatively anodyne printed propaganda. On this occasion the following items were discussed:

With regard to the attempt to shake the credit of a German bank: Zeiler & Co., a bank at Munich of which detailed information is available in this country, has been selected and the necessary enquiries are being made.

With regard to the suggested rumours of the ill effects following a starch diet, the latter is being scientifically investigated and suggestions are shortly expected.[1]

The committee next considered 'a suggestion for an apparatus to project [propaganda] images or clouds' over the German lines, no doubt supposing that the battle-front in France would remain static for long periods as during the 1914–18 war. A few weeks later the German armoured columns were approaching the channel ports at a speed which would allow no time for 'magic lantern' operations. Finally, there was 'Hitler's astrologer', who was supposed to exist but was actually as insubstantial as a ghost. The same set of minutes reported:

> A large number of Germans are superstitious and it is believed that a good deal of interest is taken in astrology. There was a rumour that Hitler, himself, believes in astrology and had employed the services of an astrologer. We suggest obtaining from a well-known astrologer a horoscope of Hitler predicting disaster to him and his country and putting it into Germany by secret channels.

A month later there was further information about these nefarious schemes. Letters which, it was hoped, would adversely affect the credit of the *Bankhaus* Zeiler were ready for mailing, perhaps from Zürich, when the addresses of some of its clients had been obtained. This was just one part of a small-scale letter campaign which was evidently already in progress because the committee was informed that 'a letter compromising Professor Herlein, head of the IG Farbenindustrie and a leading authority on bacteriological warfare has been sent on its way', and 'the distinguished Professor will find still further awkward missives in his postbag'.

I find it difficult to believe that these dirty tricks were either conceived or engineered by the innocents at Woburn or by the small Section D group which was attached to Department EH. However, they could certainly have originated in the fertile mind of Leonard Ingrams, who was EH's liaison officer at the Ministry of Economic Warfare.

In due course the members of the Consultative Committee received encouraging news about Hitler's horoscope.

> Mr Peake has been good enough to take this matter in hand and I expect the most carefully worked-out horoscope shortly, but owing no doubt to the hideous nature of the sidereal revelations it has not yet been completed. It is interesting to note that the publication of horoscopes has now been forbidden in Germany. This should increase interest in documents of this kind.

'Mr Peake' was probably Charles Peake, a member of the Foreign

Office who later (1947) became British Ambassador at Belgrade. He was then the FO's Chief Press Adviser at the Ministry of Information. It is unlikely that the MoI kept a file with the title 'Astrologers to be consulted at times of national emergency' but Mr Peake may have encountered Louis de Wohl, of whom more anon, who did his best to frequent Establishment circles.

The committee also listed a number of rumours which had been approved for dissemination, typically from selected bars in Lisbon, Stockholm, Ankara and other neutral capitals. Thus a rumour invented at Woburn and launched at Zürich could find its way back to London and be published in a slightly different form in the *Daily Mirror*. Under the heading *Ruses de guerre* the committee considered '. . . the recent suggestion for investigating a whistling device which, if dropped from the air, will emit short, sharp screams as unearthly as possible. This, it is suggested, would strain the nerves of the enemy population during bombing raids or even when British aircraft passed over.' A few weeks later the German dive bombers were making terrifying noises in France.

Life continued peacefully at Woburn until 9 April 1940 when the Germans invaded Denmark and Norway. A month later on 10 May Hitler's armies entered Holland, Belgium and Luxemburg. Eight days later the Germans reached Amiens. The RAF had not dropped any leaflets since 23 April, thus the Germans were denied the opportunity of actually *reading*, in a leaflet printed by HM Stationery Office in a *Fraktur* typeface, a translation of Churchill's famous declaration made in the House of Commons on 4 June: 'We shall fight on the beaches, we shall fight in the fields . . . we shall never surrender.'

The surviving files at the Public Record Office throw very little light on how Woburn reacted to the stirring events of the summer of 1940. However, a draft of a memorandum written by Sir Campbell Stuart on 26 May 1940, two days before the evacuation from Dunkirk began, expressed the hope that, 'With the restoration of settled conditions on the Western front, a certain amount of leaflet distribution will be possible, at any rate for the purpose of front line propaganda.'[2] By that time there was no front line in the 1914–18 sense of the expression and the RAF did not recommence dissemination until 21 July. Furthermore, Stuart had disappeared from the propaganda scene.

On 17 June 1940 Marshal Pétain announced that France had asked for an armistice, and the evacuation of the British Expeditionary Force was completed on the same day. At this stage HM Government was more concerned with the possibility that the Germans would attempt to invade the British Isles than with the reorganisation of Department EH in the light of completely new circumstances. About a week later Sir Campbell Stuart, who was just about to leave for Canada on urgent business on behalf of the Imperial Communications Advisory Board, reached an agreement with Alfred Duff Cooper, the new Minister of Information, about his department's immediate future: it was to retain its separate identity and remain on the Secret Service (financial) Vote. Stuart was to be directly responsible to Duff Cooper. The Department was to conduct propaganda to Germany and its armed forces, also to Poland and Czecho-slovakia. The concordat contained nothing to suggest that it would soon be concerned with France, Italy, Norway, Denmark, Belgium and Holland. These were still nominally MoI territories and the Department did not have the staff required to service them.

During the next few weeks Department EH operated under its own momentum, which cannot have been very great. Then Dr Hugh Dalton took charge and effected considerable changes. Dalton was a senior Labour politician whom Churchill had appointed Minister of Economic Warfare when he formed his coalition government on 14 May. After lengthy and often conflicting discussions behind the scenes Churchill had invited him on 16 July to take charge of a new and secret organisation which was to be known as the Special Operations Executive (SOE) and to 'co-ordinate all action by way of subversion and sabotage against the enemy overseas'. The Charter which defined SOE's tasks was approved at a Cabinet meeting on 22 July and it was then that Churchill is supposed to have exhorted Dalton to 'now set Europe ablaze!'

SOE initially consisted of an amalgamation of MI (R), a small sub-branch of the War Office's directorate of military intelligence, Grand's Section D and Department EH. Dalton's new secret department was divided into two branches: SO1 (formerly EH) was supposed to deal with Words (i.e. propaganda), and SO2 (formerly Section D and MI (R) with Deeds (i.e. sabotage and subversion in enemy–occupied Europe). Nominally SO1 and SO2 were two parts of a single organisation. In fact they only merged in Dalton's suite of offices at the Ministry of Economic Warfare's headquarters in Berkeley Square.

Dalton's appointment was made when Campbell Stuart was in Canada. When he returned after a brief absence he found himself unwanted. As Michael Balfour remarked, 'Campbell Stuart, who had developed the cultivation of the Establishment into a fine art, saw his influence wither as the Establishment changed. The director of Geoffrey Dawson's *Times*, who could address Neville Chamberlain's favoured adviser [Sir Horace Wilson] as "My dear Horace", realised how little time a socialist intellectual would have for him and prudently went back to Canada.'[3]

During the first few weeks of the war Department EH, under Sir Campbell Stuart, had reported to the Minister of Information (then Lord Macmillan), but in October 1939 responsibility for EH was transferred to the Foreign Office and was only partly returned to the MoI in June 1940. This was unsatisfactory because a great many lines became crossed between Dalton's SO1 and Duff Cooper's MoI, with each ministerial protagonist intent upon gaining complete control of propaganda to Germany and enemy-occupied Europe.

In the meantime Dalton made his influence felt at Woburn. Thomas Barman recalled:

> Hugh Dalton used to come down to Woburn from time to time to inspect the troops. He was a great booming bully; and even at breakfast time his manner was horribly hearty. He used to dress himself up in a sort of heavy white jersey, as worn by the best goal-keepers, and called for volunteers to go for a walk with him of a Sunday morning. Walkers became hard to find after a while; people tended to go to earth when they heard his voice and that could be heard almost everywhere. ... He was not particularly scrupulous in his methods. Many of us resented his habit of cultivating the acquaintance of very junior members of the staff in order to find out what the seniors were up to and what they were saying. 'I like to be up-to-date and well-informed of what goes on in my own Department,' he used to say with a laugh that rattled the windows in a way that church organs often do. His comments in ministerial red ink on suggestions put up to him by his office were models of rudeness.[4]

According to a note to the author by Clifton Child, 'Dalton exercised, or was widely believed to exercise, some supervision of the Woburn operations through Hugh Gaitskell, his secretary, right-hand man and political protégé, who was given a *pied-à-terre* in the neighbourhood with the tenancy of a substantial Georgian house at 6 Leighton Street, Woburn. Gaitskell himself never attempted any substantial or obtrusively obvious interference in the work being done at Woburn Abbey but he must have served as a listening post for Dalton.'

In 1940-1 nobody at Woburn can have supposed that Gaitskell, of all people, within less than a decade would be both a Minister of the Crown and a Privy Councillor.

The Dalton versus Duff Cooper battle came to an end in July 1941 when Brendan Bracken became Minister of Information. He not only had the advantage of being close to Churchill but was temperamentally better equipped to deal with the difficult Dr Dalton. At this time HM Government was at last beginning to contrive a more rational basis for the former Department EH, present SO1 and future Political Warfare Executive (PWE). In July 1941 Robert Bruce Lockhart, who had worked at Woburn in the Political Intelligence Department of the Foreign Office in 1939–40 and was to some extent familiar with the background, was appointed chairman of the small committee which helped to devise the structure of what later became PWE. Its other members were Reginald Leeper, who had been in charge at Woburn since Campbell Stuart's departure, and Brigadier Dallas Brooks. At the same time Lockhart was given the rank of a Deputy Under-Secretary of State at the Foreign Office, and was therefore made senior to Leeper who was in any case a career civil servant. On 15 July 1941 Lockhart sent a progress report to Anthony Eden, the Foreign Secretary. He wrote: 'During the past fortnight I have made a much closer inspection of a situation which has been vaguely familiar to me since the beginning of the war. I found the confusion, overlapping and lack of organisation even greater than I had believed possible.'[5]

After much discussion Lockhart and his two colleagues produced the solution which resulted in the birth of PWE. Its direction was to be in the hands of a standing Ministerial Committee: Eden (FO), Dalton (MEW) and Bracken (MoI), and the day-to-day work entrusted to Lockhart (as chairman of the Political Warfare Executive), Reginald Leeper and Brigadier Brooks. The solution was unwieldy but would serve for the time being. PWE was to assume responsibility for 'the relevant sections of the Foreign Publicity Division' of the Ministry of Information, and 'the relevant European sections of the BBC', plus 'the secret department hitherto known as SO1'. PWE's formation was formally announced to the Prime Minister and about forty others on 20 September 1941 (see footnote 4 on p. 20). According to the secret document which was circulated at that time, 'Since PWE is a secret department, its cover will continue to be the Political Intelligence Department of the Foreign Office', whose address was 2 Fitzmaurice Place, W1, even if its members were located at Woburn.

So there was the PWE in charge of all those 'relevant sections' and an existing secret department, but with an imprecise knowledge of who was doing what, and where and why. Its ignorance applied particularly to the BBC and certain intelligence-gathering and distribution activities which were duplicated at Bush House (the BBC's European services headquarters in the Aldwych) and at Woburn. A small sub-committee was then appointed under the independent chairmanship of Sir Leonard Browett, a distinguished civil servant, with instructions to unscramble the gigantic confusion which then prevailed. Sir Leonard was assisted by the Hon. David Bowes-Lyon (brother of HM the Queen), who represented 'the Secret Department in the Country' and J. B. Clark from the BBC.

The so-called Browett Report,[6] which was given a very limited circulation early in November 1941, recommended that staff engaged in black propaganda ('secret broadcasting') and the production of white leaflets, i.e. typesetting and design, should remain at Woburn, while all those concerned with the other aspects of the preparation of white propaganda and, in particular, work in connection with the BBC should be moved to London. Hence the decision that PWE's headquarters should be located on the three upper floors of Bush House, in the same building as the BBC's European Service. Thus early in 1942 Woburn Abbey was evacuated when a great many people were brought back to London. PWE retained possession only of the Riding School which provided office accommodation for the staff administering the small clandestine broadcasting teams, now known as Research Units (RUs), whose members lived and worked in a dozen or more private houses in the Woburn district. Under Dalton's influence the Department's black side had proliferated to a modest extent since October 1940, and by February 1942 sixteen stations were recording material for broadcasting at a common recording centre in the Woburn area. Furthermore, the RUs' activities were absolutely outside the control of the BBC and, as in the past, were classified 'Most Secret'.

The Browett Report reveals the Department's rate of growth since early in September 1939 when Sir Campbell Stuart's staff amounted to about twenty individuals engaged on the production of white propaganda (i.e. the so-called 'aircraft leaflets') – there was little or no 'black' worthy of the name in those days and no clandestine broadcasting. By August 1941 no fewer than 213 people were working at Woburn, or 438 if the 'messengers, maintenance staff, drivers, household domestics and cleaners' are included. In August 1941 the Military Wing at 2 Fitzmaurice Place had a staff of forty-seven, excluding messengers, drivers, etc.

In February 1942 Dr Dalton reluctantly moved from the Ministry of Economic Warfare to the Board of Trade. As Michael Balfour remarked, 'He could not be kicked out but he could be kicked upstairs.' Lord Selborne, his successor at MEW, did not inherit his responsibilities for propaganda, and Eden and Bracken divided their PWE work, with Eden taking decisions on policy and Bracken on administration. PWE's

Executive Committee (Lockhart, Brooks and Leeper) also disappeared a month later when single executive responsibility was vested in Lockhart who, as Director-General of Political Warfare, became solely responsible to the two Ministers. He was knighted in January 1943. Leeper, who had directed the Woburn organisation during a particularly difficult period in the Department's history (July 1940 to August 1941) remained there in charge of clandestine broadcasting but with diminished status and responsibilities. He eventually returned to the Foreign Office early in 1943 and his departure freed the increasingly important black operations at Woburn from any close supervision.

Dalton went to the Board of Trade (taking Gaitskell with him) three months after I joined the Department. I was hardly conscious of his previous connection with PWE and suspect that very few of my contemporaries had detailed knowledge of the recent power struggles at the summit. Since I was only interested in 'printing' and neither concerned with nor affected by departmental politics it never occurred to me that Lockhart's promotion to Director-General simply meant that it was the Foreign Office which now effectively controlled PWE. Michael Balfour explained the position in a footnote on page 92 of his *Propaganda in War, 1939–1945*:

In practice Eden's other responsibilities prevented him from giving as much attention to PWE as Bracken did. But it would be a mistake to infer that, as a result, the Department's contacts at official level were chiefly with the MoI. That may have been as far as administrative matters were concerned but on questions of propaganda policy and content, the Ministry had no staff who were competent to talk about PWE's territories, whereas the FO naturally had.

When I mentioned my surprise at the apparent puerility of the manœuvres of Dalton, Eden and Bracken to Clifton Child many years later he explained the past with admirable clarity.

Dalton, Eden and Bracken were at times clearly jockeying for control of what they could make into a very influential (and personal) power-sustaining machine in post-war British politics. There was a lot, career-wise, at stake for them: this machine could conceivably become comparable with that which Goebbels had built up to satisfy his ambitions and to sustain his personal influence and position in the Third Reich. ... Propaganda at that time still, of course, enjoyed the mystique which had surrounded it in World War I; and the control of it was still very much worth fighting for.

Robert Bruce Lockhart's minute to Eden of 6 March 1942 indicates the ferocity of the political infighting:

I understand from a member of the Executive that at today's meeting of the Labour Party the future of PWE will be considered. I am informed that the following points were down for discussion.

The Labour Party have a strong interest and a strong belief in political warfare and have a claim to be represented on PWE. They are determined that Mr Bracken, whom they describe as 'the Tory thug', shall not have control.

They would be content if you were to assume full responsibility with a Parliamentary Under-Secretary to run PWE for you. They did not want a Committee of Three. If you do not wish to accept this task, they would like a separate Ministry with a separate Minister.

These views, I imagine, are sponsored by Dr Dalton. How far they will command the support of his colleagues I cannot say. But I am told the opposition to Mr Bracken is strong, and that Major Attlee, who has been shown copies of Mr Bracken's letters to Dr Dalton, will represent this opposition to Mr Churchill. I shall probably be able to receive a full account of what actually happened.

On the same day the Foreign Secretary merely scribbled a laconic 'Thank you' on the minute. The 'Tory thugs' at the FO and MoI had won the battle.[7]

1   FO 898/6

2   FO 898/3

3   Michael Balfour, *Propaganda in War 1939–1945*, p. 90

4   Thomas Barman, *Diplomatic Correspondent*, 1968, p. 110. Robert Bruce Lockhart criticised Dalton's constant visits to Woburn and the BBC in a note to Brendan Bracken. 'He seems to have more time at his disposal than either yourself or the Foreign Secretary.' FO 898/286 (8 September 1941) quoted by Cruickshank, p. 26.

5   FO 898/9

6   FO 898/10

7   FO 898/10

# 5

# Enter Richard Crossman

Two major personalities emerged in the German political warfare area: Richard Crossman in the spring of 1940 and Sefton Delmer a year later. Both resembled virtuoso orchestral conductors, although their respective styles and interpretations could not have been more different. Unlike Delmer, Crossman was only peripherally concerned with black operations but was nevertheless running a clandestine broadcasting unit before Delmer arrived on the scene and immediately created a new conception, at least in PWE, of the possibilities of black psychological warfare.

Crossman's background was academic. Such was his brilliance as an undergraduate at Oxford that he was elected to a Fellowship at New College before taking his degree. Regarded as too young to start teaching at the age of twenty-two, he was sent to Germany to continue his study of Aristotle's doctrine of the soul. Up to that time (1929–30) he had taken no great interest in politics and his first political associations were with the communists in Germany. Indeed he became friendly with the brilliant Willi Münzenberg, then the controller of the German communist press.

Returning to Oxford Crossman began to study Plato and Karl Marx in parallel. At this time Marxism was not recognised as a philosophy at Oxford and he claimed to have been the first Oxford don to master Marx's early philosophical work. Simultaneously he introduced a minor revolution in the teaching of Plato by treating him not, as had been done for fifty years, as the spiritual father of British democracy, but as a politician *manqué* who, in a period of democratic decline, sought salvation in the totalitarian state.

In 1934 Crossman was elected to the Oxford City Council and became leader of its small Labour group. Meanwhile he was spending part of every year in Germany, making a close study of national socialism and broadcasting about it on the BBC. This brought him into touch with the small group of socialists headed by Ernest Bevin (the trades union leader who became Minister of Labour in Churchill's wartime coalition government) and Hugh Dalton, who were opposed to the Labour Party's

54

prevalent pacifism and urging a policy of rearmament. While Dean of his college in 1937 he fought a parliamentary by-election in Birmingham during a vacation. The election overran the beginning of term and when he returned to Oxford H. A. L. Fisher, the Warden of New College, told him that he must choose between practical politics and their academic study. Some months later he resigned his Fellowship and was soon appointed Assistant Editor of the left-wing *New Statesman and Nation*.[1]

Many years later Thomas Barman, who was already in a fairly senior position at Woburn when Crossman arrived there in May 1940, wrote, 'It has been said of him that he is a great stirrer-up of hornets' nests. I do not agree. Crossman, it seems to me, is a hornet's nest all to himself.'[2] Robert Walmsley recalled Crossman's arrival at Woburn:

> One day in the early spring or summer of 1940 the Departmental security authorities received serious news. Dick Crossman had been heard proclaiming in some public waiting-room that he had been asked to help in controlling [on behalf of Department EH] the German broadcasts of the BBC but he was damned if he would take £1000 a year for sitting on his behind and making suggestions which the BBC ignored. But Crossman survived this affront to the Department's rule of secrecy. And for the rest of the war he continued to survive an almost unending series of outrages to the *amour propre* of his chiefs or his Department's code.

His old friend and mentor Dr Dalton soon encountered Crossman at Woburn. Dalton recalled that he found 'the atmosphere heavily charged with personal rivalries', also that 'not everyone liked him or respected his judgment, nor did all his seniors find him an easy subordinate, but I regarded him as one of our best propagandists to Germany'. Thus in August 1940 Crossman was made head of the German department at Woburn. Dalton said that he engineered this appointment 'after some highly-strung discussion', while Crossman stated that it was made 'against the furious opposition of Foreign Office officials'.[3] However, I am inclined to believe that both the discussion and the opposition probably only involved Reginald Leeper, whose previous Foreign Office training had not equipped him to deal with anyone remotely resembling Richard Crossman.

Thomas Barman's and Robert Walmsley's recollections of Crossman at that time are strikingly similar:

> *Barman*: His argumentative spirit was a heavy cross for his nominal superiors in the Enemy Propaganda Department. An order or a reprimand would automatically become the occasion for a great debate that Crossman

would invariably win on points. When his superiors had an order to give they used to call him on the telephone, give the order, put the receiver down very quickly and hope for the best. Others would appeal to senior officials in the Foreign Office for support when it looked as if Crossman was on the point of trampling them down.

*Walmsley:* His masters, in those early days, tried like the Lilliputians, to bind him with silken threads, but with less success. Indeed, they had practically no success at all. In the unceasing departmental war of Crossman *contra mundum* victory seldom fell to the big battalions ... Once I was astonished at the bitterness of his comment on Rex Leeper. I had remarked that after all a propaganda department was unlikely to get a much better head and Crossman ejaculated with venom in every word: 'An – almost – illiterate – civil – servant!' Certainly Crossman used every means of circumventing Leeper's authority and once, in my presence, even told Leeper that he was ready to disobey his instructions.

Walmsley also recalled a half-jesting prophecy which Reginald Leeper made about Crossman in 1940: 'There goes a future Prime Minister of England – Conservative, of course!'

While Crossman was involved in running one of the Department's earliest clandestine broadcasting stations, the very 'pale black' *Sender der Europäischen Revolution* from 7 October 1940 until 22 June 1942, he left its German socialist operators very much to their own devices. In fact, I do not believe that he ever had very much personal interest in, let alone talent for, subversive operations and black propaganda – 'the only aspect of war at which we achieved real pre-eminence', as he wrote in 1973.

Crossman's status as head of the German section was confirmed when the Department was completely re-organised and became PWE in the autumn of 1941. However, his appointment was by no means automatic. On 28 August 1941 Leeper wrote to Robert Bruce Lockhart:

Crossman is a difficult selection but he is much superior to [Hugh] Greene and [Leonard] Miall in the BBC. They both eat out of his hand. Brendan [Bracken] will only accept C. if we stop most of his socialist stuff on the BBC and that we must do. C. has now got to be controlled as he never was by the MoI. If he doesn't accept control, he must go.[4]

Crossman survived 'control', in spite of some perilous interludes, until May 1943 when he went to Algiers in order to try, at least, to resolve a muddled and unsatisfactory situation on the joint Anglo-American political warfare front. As Michael Balfour charitably remarked, 'He found an alternative outlet for his great abilities as a propagandist (or educator) in the Mediterranean at the time of the Italian surrender and (after an interval of illness in the winter of 1943) with SHAEF [Supreme Headquarters, Allied Expeditionary Force] in London and Paris.'[5] In any case he never effectively returned to PWE.

1   The information about Crossman's early career is largely based on the short autobiographical contribution he wrote for Daniel Lerner's *Sykewar: Psychological Warfare against Germany, D-Day to VE-Day*, New York, 1949.

2   Thomas Barman, *Diplomatic Correspondent*, 1968, pp. 119–20.

3   Hugh Dalton, *The Fateful Years*, 1957, p. 380, and Daniel Lerner, *Sykewar* (as above).

4   Communicated in a letter to the author by Michael Balfour who transcribed the passage from a document at the PRO.

5   Michael Balfour, *Propaganda in War, 1939-1945*, 1979, p. 95 n.

# 6

# Clandestine Broadcasting
# – Otto Strasser

In a report written in December 1938 which summarised the unsatisfactory propaganda arrangements at the time of the Munich crisis, Sir Stephen Tallents observed, 'There may be lessons to be deduced from the success with which the apparently mobile [short-wave] *Deutsche Freiheitsender* [German freedom station], the secret opposition radio station, continued its operations in spite of the vigilance of the Gestapo.' However, the Gestapo was well aware that the station, which was operated by German refugees with the knowledge of the French government, was static and located on the outskirts of Paris. Today, four decades later, the Gestapo would possibly contrive a subterfuge for bombing it out of existence, but at that time peacetime terrorist activities were less common than they are now. In any case the use of short-wave radio for subversive broadcasting was then a very new development.

The first identifiable short-wave clandestine station was the one operated for Otto Strasser in Czechoslovakia in 1934–5.[1] Indeed, its story contains all the ingredients for an exciting television thriller. Strasser had been one of Hitler's early and prominent followers but he fell out with the *Führer* in 1930 and severed his connection with the Nazi Party. He was both a German nationalist and a socialist but certainly not a National Socialist in the accepted sense of the word. Soon after Hitler achieved power on 30 January 1933 Strasser formed a loosely organised opposition group known as the *Schwarze* (i.e. Black) *Front*. However, many of his followers were arrested and Strasser quickly went underground. In May 1933 he learned that the Gestapo was on his trail and after a number of hair-raising escapes reached Vienna where he lived under a false name, using an equally false passport. There, with the help of friends, he produced *Der Schwarze Sender* (a periodical), of which thousands of copies were smuggled across the frontier into the Reich. He then moved hurriedly to Prague where he continued his underground propaganda activities. Contacts in Germany supplied large quantities of printed matter rate postage stamps. These were used to frank envelopes which were overprinted with the addresses of the German Medical Association, the League of National Socialist Lawyers and similar official bodies. The envelopes were stuffed with anti-Hitler propaganda booklets, printed on thin paper and with camouflaged covers ('Recent Advances in Cancer Research' cannot have reached many medical men), and then smuggled across the frontier for bulk mailing from large towns such as Leipzig.

The use of the official mail for the dissemination of subversive propaganda was by no means a recent invention. During the 1850s French refugees resident in London, members of the *Commune Révolutionnaire*, had employed the same technique to attack the Emperor Louis Napoleon in France. However, Otto Strasser seems to have been the first to use a short-wave radio transmitter for clandestine propaganda purposes. This technique, which was certainly new in 1934, became possible when his friend Rolf Formis arrived in Prague.

Formis had formerly been the chief engineer at the Stuttgart radio station but was in trouble with the Gestapo when they suspected that he was personally responsible for the apparently fortuitous technical hitches which prevented the transmission of an important speech by Hitler. Formis was able to bluff them on this occasion but was arrested when he staged a repeat performance. He managed to escape and eventually reached Prague after a long and adventurous journey.

In his autobiographical *Mein Kampf*, 1969, Strasser mentioned that Formis had been the first German to receive a licence for amateur short-wave radio transmissions. He said, too, that he was greatly surprised when Formis proposed that a short-wave transmitter would provide an effective method for spreading the anti-Hitler gospel and added that he could build the necessary apparatus at a remarkably low cost. He had most of the components at Stuttgart and it was merely a matter of arranging for someone to bring them to Prague. So Formis built his transmitter and showed it to Strasser on the latter's thirty-seventh birthday on 10 September 1934.

The apparatus was taken to a country inn at Zahori, a resort village about thirty-five miles south-west of Prague on the river Moldau. With the approach of autumn the holiday visitors had left and the landlord was glad to accept Formis as a permanent resident who needed peace and quiet for his alleged scientific work. Formis installed the transmitter in an attic above his bedroom with a lead to the microphone which was actually in his room.

The *Schwarze Front*'s clandestine broadcasts on the 48-metre band began in September 1934. In Prague Strasser made gramophone records for broadcasts – the magnetic tape recorder had not yet been invented – and periodically delivered them to Formis. The latter was also kept supplied with German newspapers and periodicals and regularly listened to German broadcasts. Thus, well informed about events in the Reich, he was able to contribute his own abrasive commentary. With the exception of Strasser's recorded talks everything was transmitted live and Formis was regularly on the air for three periods of about an hour between 7pm and 3am.

Strasser's *Schwarze Front* station was active for about four months. Then there was trouble. Two Gestapo agents, a man and a girl, arrived at Zahori and discovered Formis. They even found an excuse to photograph him together with the girl – it was one of those 'Rolf and Irma on the terrace' pictures. When the film was developed in Berlin it was soon realised that the friendly gentleman at Zahori was none other than Herr Formis, the short-wave radio expert. The couple reappeared on 23 January 1935, this time accompanied by a third Gestapo operative who remained outside in their Mercedes until the landlord and the establishment's waiter had retired to bed. When all was quiet he entered the house by a rope ladder, then the action began. The girl tried to drag Formis into her room where the two gunmen were waiting. Either Formis, who had a revolver, managed to shoot her or she was hit by a bullet intended for him. One or other of the male assassins killed Formis. They then poured petrol over his lifeless body and attempted to incinerate it. They managed to get the badly wounded girl out of the house via the rope ladder and drove off at high speed in the direction of the border. She died inside Germany on the way to a hospital at Dresden.

Strasser continued his fight against Hitler almost single-handed. The Gestapo made a number of unsuccessful attempts to abduct him and bring him back to Germany. He left Prague and went to the vicinity of Zürich, but on 1 October 1935 he transferred himself to Paris because the Germans were demanding his extradition from Switzerland. He was able to install a second transmitter in the villa of Robert Trenkle, a former German police captain, at Le Cannet, near Cannes. Trenkle could operate the transmitter but had little political experience so Strasser sent Heinrich Grunow, his right-hand man in Prague, to take charge of the broadcasts. Grunow was later arrested by the French and handed over to the Gestapo after the armistice. Trenkle remained at liberty until the Germans occupied southern France and the Gestapo found him. He and Grunow were subsequently beheaded in Berlin.

Strasser miraculously escaped from France after the French defeat and reached Portugal where the German military and press attachés, armed with an alleged extradition warrant, tried to find him but failed by a hair's breadth. Finally the British spirited him on board an American vessel – he never learned how they found him – and ensured that he was disembarked at Bermuda. He was to remain in Canada, virtually silenced and ignored, during the war years.

I asked Clifton Child why the Department had left Strasser to languish in Canada and had not brought him to Woburn to work in the Delmer organisation, although I must confess that I had previously wondered if the Strasser-Delmer 'mix' would have worked. Child had become familiar with Strasser's name when he was working in the Political Intelligence Department of the Foreign Office (1941 until he joined Delmer in March 1943). In a letter to me he wrote:

> The Churchill Government and especially the Foreign Secretary [Eden] had the same animus towards Strasser as they did towards any native German opposition to Hitler, preferring to bring Nazi Germany to its knees through such instruments as the Lindemann Plan[2] and unconditional surrender. Admittedly, Strasser was a gadfly for many of us, particularly because of his scatterbrained antics in Canada. The wartime censorship of his mail gave us an insight into these; he apparently never knew that we were reading so much of his correspondence. Some of my FO colleagues obsequiously followed the Ministerial line on Strasser. His name did occasionally crop up at MB [Delmer's operational HQ near Woburn 1943–5], and of course copies of his 'censored' correspondence flowed in some quantity through our intelligence-gathering machine, but I do not recall Delmer ever expressing an opinion about the man.
>
> Strasser, with all his pretensions and alleged 'contacts', was so remote from the German scene of that time that it was a very prudent course to ignore him. He never came up to Delmer's standards as a 'black' practitioner anyway.

1   The material for this chapter is based on Otto Strasser's *Mein Kampf*, 1969, and two biographical studies by Douglas Reed: *Nemesis—The Story of Otto Strasser*, 1940, and *The Prisoner of Ottawa: Otto Strasser*, 1953.

2   The 'Lindemann Plan' can roughly be described as bombing civilian as opposed to exclusively military targets and hence destroying the lives and homes of German workers. In any case the RAF could not guarantee to hit military targets so the bombing was always to some extent indiscriminate.

# 7

# The Concordia Büro – Berlin

Whether the Germans ever studied Otto Strasser's subversive broadcasting operation as a model for future activities of this kind, under wartime conditions, for example, is unknown. The German Propaganda Ministry's initial experience with clandestine broadcasting was gained during the Spanish Civil War when a special unit was sent to Spain.[1]

In relation to the Second World War, during which the Germans operated a number of *Geheimsender* (i.e. secret stations, abbreviated *G-Sender*), an early reference to this kind of subversive propaganda work is to be found in the minutes of Dr Goebbels's daily ministerial conference held on 30 October 1939.[2] Alfred-Ingemar Berndt, director of the Propaganda Ministry's broadcasting division, was told to consult the appropriate department in Joachim von Ribbentrop's Foreign Office and the *Oberkommando der Wehrmacht* (OKW, High Command of the German Armed Forces) about the organisation of a bogus French communist station, i.e. one which would purport to be operating on French territory, and also an allegedly Irish one.

During the war dozens of short-wave G-stations (British, German and Soviet Russian) were on the air at various times, all pretending to be what they were not. Short-wave transmissions had a number of advantages. By comparison with long- or medium-wave broadcasts they were surprisingly inexpensive to operate and mobile transmitters could be used to reinforce static installations in combat areas. Furthermore, if correctly beamed according to the season of the year, the range of a short-wave transmitter could extend to several thousand miles. For instance, in February 1940 *La Voix de la Paix* ('The Voice of Peace' – German but pretending to be in France) was actually broadcasting from Warsaw, and a year or so later the British *Gustav Siegfried Eins* station was picked up by short-wave enthusiasts across the Atlantic. One peculiarity of the wartime clandestine stations was that while they could be heard in the immediate vicinity of the transmitter they began to be inaudible only a few miles away. This was because the transmissions were directed upwards to the stratosphere and followed their original path until they reached the Heaviside layer whence they were deflected earthwards. However, short-wave radio could play strange tricks and there was one instance involving British broadcasts which should have been heard in Norway and for which no evidence of reception was received until the necessary technical adjustments had been made at the transmitter.

The policies of the wartime G-stations varied enormously, depending upon whose interests they hoped to serve. The quality of their output was inevitably conditioned by the available background intelligence material and how effectively or imaginatively it was exploited. While it was possible to broadcast programmes which appeared to be of local origin, i.e. transmitted by a local group working underground and improbably still undetected by the authorities, even listeners who were not over-endowed with critical faculties would soon have realised that someone was taking them for a ride.

The G-stations of all nationalities almost invariably broadcast on short-wave. However, during the war years only a relatively small proportion of the civilian population in western Europe possessed radio sets capable of receiving short-wave transmissions. On the other hand many members of the armed forces could listen on short-wave, even if illicitly, by using receiving apparatus which was certainly not supplied for their private enjoyment. In the majority of cases an individual first discovered a G-station by a process of random tuning and was intrigued by what he heard. Then this or that item of information, or more likely misinformation, would be conveyed to a friend – in the case of German listeners in strict confidence of course – who would then tell someone else. Given the speed with which 'latrine' gossip could circulate, the right kind of story was liable to take wings surprisingly fast. It was not necessary to gain a regular captive audience as long as someone was listening and above all talking.

A second important factor was that members of the armed forces were far more mobile than civilians: they were often posted from one unit to another, exchanged information (or misinformation) with friends and casual acquaintances encountered in services canteens, and returned home for brief periods of leave. In the process of repeated dissemination an attractive subversive story would be embroidered, distorted and exaggerated to the point where the original version was no longer recognisable. While subversive propaganda will not win battles it is clearly a useful weapon in the context of psychological warfare.

When Alfred-Ingemar Berndt was instructed to attend to the organisation of the first German G-stations on 30 October 1939 neither he nor anyone else had any experience in the clandestine broadcasting field. There was no further reference to the project at Dr Goebbels's daily conference until 27 February 1940 when Dr Ernst Brauweiler, Deputy-Director of the Propaganda Ministry's foreign press section, was requested to concern himself with the affairs of two French-language stations. One of them, *La Réveil de la Paix* ('The Awakening of Peace), had already been broadcasting since at least 21 December 1939, whereas '*La Voix de l'Humanité*' – *Humanité* was the title of France's leading communist newspaper – was not in action until April, some weeks before the German armed forces began their campaign on the western front. By 27 February the 'New British Broadcasting Station' had already been on the air for a couple of days. Nothing more was heard of the proposed Irish station (discussed on 30 October 1939), probably because there was no one available who could speak as if he were a native of Dublin or Cork.

The new G-stations were operated in Berlin by the so-called Concordia Büro, whose staff worked in 'a heavily-guarded villa adjoining the *Rundfunkhaus*' (main broadcasting studios) in the central Charlottenburg district.[3] The *Reichsrundfunkgesellschaft* (the German equivalent of the BBC) provided the technical facilities and the Propaganda Ministry was responsible for the personnel. Ribbentrop's Foreign Office was represented by a liaison section in which Kurt-Georg Kiesinger (Chancellor of the German Federal Republic 1966-9) played an important role. It may be mentioned in passing that the wars waged by Goebbels and Ribbentrop respecting their spheres of influence were far more virulent, not to say comic, than those fought by Dr Dalton and his ministerial rivals at the Ministry of Information.

From February 1940 onwards the daily conference minutes reflect the intense personal interest taken by Dr Goebbels in every phase of the operational short-wave propaganda campaign which was being orchestrated to coincide with the German military operations in the west. Indeed, he was in far closer control of the day-to-day working of his ministry than his counterpart in London. However, his attention was frequently diverted by matters unconnected with what was happening on the field of battle. Thus on 21 June 1940 he complained that too much music by Mozart was being broadcast, and unfamiliar works at that, while Schubert was being neglected. And on the previous day he demanded information about the members of the Wannsee (Berlin) golf club and proposed to despatch people who 'looked like golfers' to have a look at the place. A few days later two very senior Propaganda Ministry officials were told to join the club in order to discover what was going on there.

On 17 May 1940, when the Germans occupied Brussels and the British Expeditionary Force began to retreat in the direction of the Channel ports, Dr Goebbels issued the first of an almost daily series of directives which instructed the French G-Stations to 'create panic' – this theme was particularly emphasised – in France. Rumour material was fabricated, for instance, that the French government was about to make a hasty retreat from Paris although it did not actually leave for Tours until 11 June. Yet another, which was intended to start a run on the banks, was that when the Germans occupied successive towns they would seize all bank deposits. Next, it was to be suggested that all German-Jewish refugees, of whom there were many in France, were members of a German 'Fifth Column', hence spies, and therefore to be mistrusted. As soon as the French armies were clearly on the run, the 'create panic' theme was replaced by another which was intended to persuade listeners to demand 'peace *now!*'

*Radio Humanité*, the communist station, was also active by this time. On 30 May Dr Goebbels demanded to see its scripts because Dr Brauweiler was complaining that they were both boring and excessively doctrinaire. On 2 June it was decided to enlist the services of Ernst Torgler to assist the *Humanité* team. According to the minutes the latter's members, who were French communists, could only appeal to intellectuals and not to what were described as 'primitive mass instincts'. Torgler, who had once been the leader of the communist faction in the Reichstag, had been one of the defendants in the notorious Reichstag Fire trial but was now under Goering's protection. Wilhelm Kaspar, Torgler's friend and former colleague in the Reichstag, was extracted from a concentration camp to help with the work.

On 4 June, ten days before the Germans entered Paris, Goebbels ordered an intensification of the radio campaign. Medium- and long-wave broadcasts, masquerading as if from French transmitters and far more widely heard than any short-wave transmissions, were emitted by the powerful Cologne and Leipzig stations. A mobile transmitter calling itself *Camerade du Nord* ('Friend of the North') was in evidence, and *La Voix de la Bretagne* ('The Voice of Brittany'), which was probably mobile, was also heard in June. It broadcast in French but used Breton slogans. Its tendency was strongly separatist and emphasised that the hour of liberation for the Bretons would soon arrive.

On 12 June Goebbels claimed that the effects of his propaganda activities were beginning to be evident. Subversion was to continue and the provision of genuine news items was only of secondary importance. Thus the G-stations were told to attack hypothetical French circles which wished to defend Paris at all costs, and 'demonstrations in favour of peace' were to be encouraged. Two days later the instructions were to concentrate henceforth upon the peasants and lower middle classes because the capital had been 'finished off'. Furthermore, the communist station was to stop using typical Soviet platitudes and concentrate upon socially divisive arguments on the lines of 'Who will pay for all the destruction? Who will guarantee the payment of pensions? The burden of taxation will be insupportable, etc.' Then on 18 June the propagandists were told to take a tough line with the French, who must be sternly discouraged from supposing that the Germans would henceforth adopt a 'kiss and be friends' policy.

To sum up, Dr Goebbels's *G-Sender* propaganda methods during the French campaign were more operational than black, as Delmer later understood black techniques. Dr Goebbels and his acolytes often adopted an identifiably *menacing* tone towards their French listeners. This was something that the British black propagandists never did and could *never* do. They never threatened the ordinary German soldier or civilian, even if in their role as hypothetical Germans they might castigate their military and political superiors and, of course, their British enemies at Churchillian level.

On 23 June the French language G-stations were instructed to appear to carry on normally for a few more days and then unobtrusively disappear. Dr Adolf Raskin, director of foreign broadcasting at the *Reichsrundfunk-gesellschaft* was given forty-eight hours in which to draft a plan for the organisation of the English-language G-stations, the policy for each of them and to state who was to be responsible for the broadcasts. So far there had only been one English G-station, namely the New British Broadcasting Station which had been transmitting on three short-wave frequencies for about 1½ hours daily since 25 February 1940. However, two more were to go on the air without delay and 'Caledonia' (Scottish Nationalist) began to broadcast daily for half an hour on 27 June and was followed by 'Workers' Challenge' (left-wing 'revolutionary') on 7 July. It was supposed that a daily fifteen minutes of incitement to revolt would be sufficient.

The New British Broadcasting Station's signature tune was 'The Bonnie Bonnie Banks of Loch Lomond' and it concluded its transmissions with 'God Save the King'. According to a monitoring report dated 31 August 1942:

It has produced many 'stunts', including the purported revelation of General Ironside's report on the difficulties of repulsing invasion, a report on the proceedings at a secret meeting of the British government at which the station's activities were supposed to have been discussed, revelations of German invasion plans, first aid hints (in the course of which the opportunity was taken to describe in a very gruesome manner the type of casualties which would result from German air-raids), and code messages to alleged supporters in this country.... Its general character is Fascist.[4]

Department EH and its personalities were the subject of the NBBS's kind attentions in July 1940. The BBC's monitoring service made a transcription of a particular broadcast and a copy of the document reached Valentine Williams, who expressed his irritation in a letter to Colonel Brooks.[5] He suspected that it had been given a wider circulation than was actually the case. The broadcaster described the events which followed his fictitious exposure of the proceedings of a high-level meeting at Department EH. Major-General F. G. Beaumont Nesbitt 'of the War Office' (he was actually Director of Military Intelligence) was supposed to have accused Sir Campbell Stuart of having indiscreetly shown a copy of the previous meeting's minutes to an unauthorised person or persons. The General was confident, however, that none of the others present had 'leaked'. The General said that he would urge Scotland Yard and the BBC to trace the NBBS's exact location in England and concluded his remarks with 'a magnificent peroration spiced with military and Indian oaths'. According to the transcript:

> Conferences had already been held in an unassuming little office in Oliver House, Cromwell Road, South Kensington, where Colonel Kell (identified as the Chief of MI5), supported by his henchman Captain Butler, a man of weak intellect, thrashed out the matter with Major-General Nesbitt. It was finally decided that the Number One sleuth of MI5 should be set on the trail. This turned out to be Lt.-Col. Hinchley-Cooke ... who boasts of having served as an artillery officer in the German army.[6] It is our intention to keep Lt.-Col. Hinchley-Cooke under close observation and we hope to let you have a report on his endeavours to track us down within the next three weeks, providing that he is not under the protective custody of the German Army of Occupation by that time.

All this was great fun and the liberal inclusion of the names of identifiable individuals was on the correct black lines. Whether many people apart from the BBC's monitor heard the broadcast is, of course, unknown. The Battle of Britain and the first large-scale German air-raids began on 10 July 1941 and my guess is that few British citizens were taking the trouble to listen to the NBBS's offerings.

'Caledonia' was first heard on 18 July 1940, disappeared at the end of October and was revived on 8 February 1941. The speaker, who had a pseudo-Scots accent, appealed to Scotsmen to make a separate peace from the English by whom, he said, their native land had been exploited for far too long. He dealt at length with the German air-raids on Clydeside and the problems of the workers there. The station was not heard after 21 July 1942.

'Workers' Challenge' was active from 8 July 1940 until at least May 1944. According to a monitoring report: 'The announcer employs material copiously interspersed with foul language to attack capitalists in general and Churchill, Stafford Cripps (until May 1942 "Workers' Challenge" approved of him) and the Cabinet in particular. At one time it called upon the workers to stop the war immediately by withdrawing their labour but now (1942) was urging them to demonstrate for the creation of a Second Front in support of Russia.'

Finally there was Concordia's 'Christian Peace Movement' station which was first heard on 15 August 1940 and ceased to operate in April 1942. 'The broadcast often took the form of a religious service. It opened with a hymn and contained Bible readings, prayers and a long, involved and ill-reasoned address from the speaker. He dwelt on the horrors of aerial bombardment of the civilian population and, using the text "Blessed are the peacemakers", appealed to all true Christians to refuse to do anything to assist the war and thus force the Government to make peace.'

The Germans had far more problems with their English G-stations than they ever experienced with those which broadcast to the French. Firstly there was an endemic shortage of suitable staff, and secondly a lack of good background intelligence to provide the basis for provocative talks. Thus on 8 August 1940 Dr Goebbels proposed a new co-operative system for producing material and Dr Raskin was told to consider how he could enlist a larger circle of regular contributors. However, it appeared impossible to induce panic in the British by the German military victory in France, and they even appeared to be impervious to the threat of imminent invasion. Whereas Dr Goebbels was constantly issuing instructions for the French G-stations, he had far less to say during the late summer and autumn of 1940 as far as operations against the British were concerned.

While Dr Raskin was in nominal charge of the Concordia Büro it was Dr

Erich Hetzler, his assistant, who was largely responsible for its day-to-day operation. He had spent thirteen years in England, including a brief period at the London School of Economics, and had latterly been an England specialist on von Ribbentrop's staff.[7] It happened that he had encountered William Joyce (soon to be famous in Great Britain as 'Lord Haw-Haw' on the official English-language service) very soon after the latter arrived in Berlin at the end of August 1939. By 11 September he had found employment as a news-reader. After first pledging him to secrecy Hetzler told Joyce about Concordia's proposed English-language operation some months later and enlisted him as a part-time scriptwriter for the New British Broadcasting Station. His output for the NBBS and the other English-language G-stations was formidable. According to J. A. Cole, his biographer, who later interviewed some of Haw-Haw's former colleagues in Germany, 'The themes for the day noted, Joyce took a formal leave and walked smartly back to his office where, for an hour, he dictated fluently, very much as if he were addressing a meeting impromptu and had to keep going. Observers estimated that he did as much in that hour as any two script-writers in a day.'[8] Indeed, Joyce is said to have produced about nine-tenths of all the material used for Concordia's English-language stations. He continued to work for the NBBS until the last days of the war.

The NBBS undoubtedly had a small following among former members of Sir Oswald Mosley's British Union of Fascists, which ceased to exist when Mosley was imprisoned under the 18B Defence Regulation at the end of May 1940. In October 1941 Dr Hetzler circulated a translation of a report received from a certain A.T. – he was certainly not a German since he wrote in English, possibly from Eire – together with some recent cuttings from London newspapers. A.T. said that he had been in London early in 1940 and listened to the NBBS in spite of poor reception. He mentioned that its wavelengths and broadcasting times were then being advertised by means of gummed stickers which could be seen in telephone boxes and London buses, also 'all along Whitehall and above all in the post office in Parliament Street'. He claimed that he used to mail a dozen or more stickers together with his periodical *The Voice of the People*[9] to subscribers in Scotland and Wales. Some of his contacts believed that Captain Archibald Ramsay, a pro-German Member of Parliament (he was imprisoned at the same time as Mosley) spoke on the NBBS, and since he was obviously in England the NBBS must also be there. T.A. said that he left England at the end of May 1940 and did not know if Scotland Yard had succeeded in tracking down the station.

Scotland Yard knew that the NBBS's transmitters were outside Great

Britain but the dénouement of this episode did not come about until 16 October 1941 when Messrs Wilfred Snape and Joseph Thumwood, resident in south London, were both sentenced to three years' penal servitude at the Old Bailey for offences under the Defence Regulations for 'conspiring to produce and distribute matter concerning enemy radio'. At the trial, 'Thumwood, who was formerly a district leader in the British Union of Fascists for Kennington, declared in the witness box that his leader – Sir Oswald Mosley – had asked them to carry on a peace campaign ... The splitting-up of the Fascist ranks [when Mosley was arrested in May 1940] put a brake on Snape's propaganda machine for a time. Men who had so far escaped police attention were enrolled in an organisation called the British Union of Freemen ... Special Branch officers are still searching for a man who is thought to have played an important part in the subversive propaganda machine.' – (*Daily Mail*, 17 October 1941.)

On 17 October Dr Hetzler circulated a report of the earlier police court proceedings extracted from the *Daily Telegraph* of 3 October and claimed that the NBBS had a sizeable staff of helpers in England. He said, too, that the defendants had stated that they were convinced that the NBBS was actually operating in this country.

1   There is a brief reference to the Propaganda Ministry's activities in Spain during the Civil War in Willi A. Boelcke, *Kriegspropaganda 1939-1945. Geheime Ministerkonferenzen im Reichspropagandaministerium*, 1966, p. 166. His reference N[ürnberg] G[ericht] 1558 summarises a German Foreign Office document dated 29 April 1938 which merely reveals that the Ministry's secret radio station was no longer required.

2   All the references in this chapter to the daily ministerial conferences are from Boelcke's *Kriegspropaganda* (see above).

3   See J. A. Cole, *Lord Haw-Haw and William Joyce: The Full Story*, 1964, p. 135.

4   FO 898/52. PID Research Units, Underground Broadcasting Stations, description and reports on. Part 2 contains brief information about nearly two hundred clandestine stations (British, German, Russian, French, etc).

5   FO 898/6, 7 July 1940.

6   Colonel W. Hinchley-Cooke was involved in the production of a British propaganda leaflet at the time of the Munich crisis and had links with MI6 (see p. 29 above). His name cannot be found in the official Army lists between 1910-45.

7   There are references to Dr Hetzler in J. A. Cole's biography of William Joyce (see footnote 3 above). He is identified as head of Concordia's English section in Reimund Schnabel's *Misbrauchte Mikrofone: Deutsche Rundfunkpropaganda im Zweiten Weltkrieg. Eine Dokumentation*, Vienna, 1967, p. 93. The location of the documents

reproduced by Schnabel is not revealed, although I suspect that they are in the German Democratic Republic. Furthermore, the book was clearly intended to discredit Kurt-Georg Kiesinger, who was Chancellor of the German Federal Republic at the time of publication, by throwing light on his wartime employment in von Ribbentrop's ministry. The author took care to exaggerate his importance in the Concordia organisation (see p. 91).

8　See J. A. Cole (note 3 above).

9　Not available at the British Library.

# 8

# Early Clandestine Broadcasting
# at Woburn

Department Electra House did not react to the Concordia Büro's G-stations until May 1940. The late Terence Harman told me that when the fighting in France was beginning to reach a critical stage Sir Campbell Stuart sent him on an urgent mission there where, with the help of the *Deuxième Bureau* (the French equivalent of MI5), he was able to contact a certain Herr Spiecker. The latter returned to Woburn with him and became known as 'Mr Turner'. According to some notes made in 1945, which appear to have been based on information received from Terence Harman and Ralph (later Sir Ralph) Murray:

> Mr Turner's career had been chequered and included having been a leader of a German *Freikorps* [i.e. one of the paramilitary formations which countered the communist uprisings in Bavaria and Silesia in 1919], a friend of the brothers Strasser and *Polizei-Präsident* of Danzig. He may be classed, therefore, among the unsuccessful thugs who had fallen foul of the Nazi Party instead of joining it. For some months he was provided with the means of broadcasting to Germany on short-wave from what was commonly known as the '*Bahnhof*'. Mr Turner, however, did not feel comfortable after the Nazis had reached the channel ports and by the end of 1940 had transferred himself to the USA.[1]

Far from being an 'unsuccessful thug' Dr Carl Spiecker (1888–1953) had been a member of the civil service (with particular experience in the field of press relations) during the era of the Weimar Republic. In 1930 he was the head of a section in the Ministry of the Interior which kept an eye on radical movements, e.g. the National Socialists as well as the communists. It was rumoured that he had provided Otto Strasser with financial support. In any event he was obliged to emigrate to France in 1933. In Paris he was a prominent member of the *Deutsche Freiheitspartei* (German Freedom Party), a loosely organised group of social democratic

72

German refugees and a strongly conspiratorial organisation which smuggled leaflets into Germany for underground dissemination before the frontiers were closed at the outbreak of war in September 1939. According to Werner Röder, during 1938 the DFP briefly operated a short-wave transmitter (for clandestine broadcasting purposes) on board a fishing vessel in the English Channel but no specific information is available.[2]

From the autumn of 1939 until the approach of the German troops in June 1940 Spiecker and his associates ran an allegedly mobile transmitter which broadcast on short wave to Germany. It was actually a static installation situated just outside Paris. This operation was backed by Jean Giraudoux, the French playwright who had been appointed Minister of Information. Douglas Reed, who wrote a British biography of Otto Strasser, learned about the DFP broadcasts from Strasser whom he visited in Paris late in 1939 when he was collecting material for his book *Nemesis: The Story of Otto Strasser*. Reed wrote:

> When I was in Paris, talking about this very book, the air was fouled every night by something called the *Deutsche Freiheitssender*. ... This dishonest fake pretended to be operating from within Germany. Every night you could hear the speaker telling how the Gestapo were close behind him, but tomorrow, no matter what the Gestapo did, he would pop up in Cologne, or in Hamburg, or in Breslau, or somewhere else. And anybody who cares to, and has not been in Germany, may believe this, if he be credulous enough. To anybody who knows Germany, and the closeness of the Gestapo net, the thing is farcical. 'Liberty Radio', when I was in Paris, was operating from Paris, and the Germans must have laughed themselves into fits when they heard it.

A number of writers have supposed that Willi Münzenberg, the gifted German communist and anti-Nazi propagandist – he was responsible for the notorious *Brown Book of the Nazi Terror*, 1933, and had already severed his connection with the Moscow Stalinists – was responsible for the DFP station but in fact he merely supplied scripts and advice.[3] There are some who believe that his *Brown Book* did infinite harm, especially to some of his fellow Jews. The objection to it is that it misled many of the 1930s generation and became a weapon in the hands of those who claim that stories of Nazi wartime infamy and deportations, etc. can be regarded as an invention of propaganda.

Thus Dr Spiecker, who was a thoroughly respectable individual, arrived at Woburn and broadcast from the *Bahnhof* for the first time on 26 May 1940. Far from leaving England when the Germans reached the

Channel ports he remained in this country until after Rudolf Hess's arrival in May 1941 when he left for Canada.

Nothing is known about the discussions at Woburn which led to the organisation of the first of what were initially known as 'freedom stations', although it was not long before they were called Research Units or RUs. My own hypothesis is that at that time the new secret broadcasting activities were in many respects a measure induced more by a sense of despair than by the hope that they would do any particular good. The RAF had not dropped any leaflets since 23 April, relations with the BBC's European Service had not improved and a week before Dr Spiecker arrived at Woburn the Germans were already in Amiens and looked as though they would be going much further – without any difficulty. Indeed, the day he made his first broadcast very appropriately coincided with a Day of National Prayer in the United Kingdom.

As for the urgent necessity to bring Dr Spiecker from Paris, it must be remembered that he was at least supposed to be an experienced broadcaster and that most of the German *émigrés* in this country had been interned in the Isle of Man as potential Fifth Columnists. Given the fact that it is likely no one knew where or how to find any other suitable German microphone voice, the proposition that its owner should be brought to anywhere as secret as Woburn was probably unthinkable. My own impression is that Dr Spiecker's *Das wahre Deutschland* ('The true Germany') station cannot be regarded as a vigorous and confident answer to the Concordia Büro's NBBS but, rather, as a wildly pathetic gesture of defiance.

Under the prevailing circumstances in May 1940 it would have been a waste of time for Sir Campbell Stuart to consult Duff Cooper (MoI) or the BBC about secret broadcasting from the Woburn district because countless objections would have been raised. Thus he very sensibly spoke to Colonel Richard Gambier-Parry's boss, who was now Chief of the SIS. Gambier-Parry, who was Menzies' Controller of Wireless Communications, could provide the necessary technical staff and transmitting facilities without tangling with either the MoI or the BBC.

Dr Spiecker's broadcasts were already in progress when Sir Campbell Stuart was about to leave for Canada towards the end of June 1940. For the purpose of confidential telegrams he devised a personal code which concealed the names of those Cabinet ministers and senior officials whose views were likely to affect the future of Department EH. Soon after his departure there was a monumental row.

Sir Walter Monckton, Director General of the MoI, had become aware that Dept. EH was engaged in secret broadcasting to Germany, or, in the language of Sir Campbell Stuart's code, that 'Father kept a farm', of which he had been kept in ignorance. Sir Walter had up till then believed that under the Charter he was himself responsible for all broadcasts to Germany and 'Topsy' (as he was referred to in the code) was unquestionably angry.

On 10 July Mr Valentine Williams wrote to Sir Walter Monckton, offering to explain to him in confidence the nature of these broadcasts, but Sir Walter Monckton was not appeased and replied the next day that he would have no further concern with the work of Dept. EH and that he was explaining to the Minister of Information and to the Secretary of State for Foreign Affairs his reasons for refusing to co-operate in future. This would produce a deadlock. Sir Campbell Stuart was appraised of this turn of events by code in a telegram which ended: 'Family very worried generally. Surmise attempt to break Father's [Sir Campbell Stuart's] lease.' In another cable Sir Campbell Stuart was warned that 'the Vicar' (Mr Duff Cooper) might seize upon the situation to force through a plan affecting Father's position. Sir Campbell Stuart cabled back that Mr Williams was to consult Gladwyn Jebb [later Lord Gladwyn, then Dr Dalton's chief assistant for SOE work at MEW]. But it was clear from a further cable that Sir Campbell Stuart was fully occupied with his other activities.[4]

In the meantime Dr Dalton arrived on the scene as the minister in charge of the newly created Special Operations Executive and was obviously pleased to be able to add secret broadcasting to his still very modest armoury of covert activities. According to the writer who recorded the anecdote printed above, Dalton supposed that, 'Black activities, such as secret broadcasts, might play a large part in helping to prevent Germany from exploiting the economic resources of the countries which she had recently occupied.' This was wishful thinking, but no matter. At that time, soon after the retreat from France, Dalton and a great many others were liable to clutch at straws. In fact an irrational belief still prevailed – although it was not to endure for much longer – that the Nazi regime would soon be incapable of supporting the economic strains imposed by the war. Indeed, even on the eve of Dunkirk, Dalton was predicting revolt in enemy-occupied Europe within six months.

The new Special Operations Executive, of which the former Department EH was a component and for which Dalton bore ministerial responsibility, was supposed to organise 'subversion' in Germany and the occupied territories. Dalton's conception of subversion was that it was something which 'concerned Trades Unionists and Socialists in enemy and enemy-occupied countries, the creation of Fifth Columns, of explosions, chaos and revolution'.[5] It is not surprising, therefore, that when a second clandestine station began to operate in the Woburn area in October 1940 it called itself '*Der Sender der Europäischen Revolution*'.

Mr Harold Robin was in charge of the technical side of all the Department's secret broadcasting operations throughout the war. Whereas all who were employed in Department EH and its successors were essentially amateur propagandists until we had learned our trade, Robin was already a professional wireless technician before the outbreak of hostilities in September 1939. Thus, a brief account of his early career is a part of this story.

Harold Robin was born in London on 7 May 1911 and educated at Oundle, a well-known public school which provided instruction in elementary engineering workshop practice for boys who were more interested in lathes than in Latin. From Oundle he went to London University's City and Guilds College and studied Communications Engineering, which at that time meant 'telephones and telegraphs'. Robin was far more interested in 'wireless', a subject which, he said, was not then taught with any particular expertise. When he left C & G in 1933 he immediately found reasonably well-paid employment in the Standard Telephone Company's laboratories where the designs for American domestic radios were adapted for manufacture in Great Britain. Three years later (1936–7) he moved to Philco, another American firm, whose similar products were selling well in this country.

Philco's sales manager was Richard Gambier-Parry, an extrovert Old Etonian (*b*. 1891), who played an important role in this story and in Robin's future career. He had served throughout the First World War in the Royal Welch Fusiliers and the Royal Flying Corps and later (1926–31) found his way to the BBC's Public Relations Department. He was already at Philco when Sir Stephen Tallents went to the BBC as Controller of Public Relations in 1935. In 1938 Gambier-Parry introduced Robin to his friend Peter Hope, who had a Cambridge B.Sc. degree. The two young men were contemporaries, both in their late twenties. Hope had recently acquired a concession to operate a small 'commercial' radio station in Liechtenstein on condition that he provided a local service. Robin was not only invited to run the station at Vaduz but also to build its first transmitter. He made most of the latter's components at his father's house in south London and in due course took them to Liechtenstein where a small building had been erected by a local labour force to accommodate the studio and a ten-kilowatt transmitter; it required a power supply equivalent to 10,000 watts. Hope and Robin soon went to Berlin to order a 50-kW transmitter from Lorenz; they evidently hoped to compete with Radio Luxemburg which was at that time attracting a large audience in Great Britain, especially at weekends, with its popular music and lively advertising jingles. 'Luxemburg' provided an attractive alternative to the BBC.

Peter Hope was based in London and he and Robin kept in touch by using their own $\frac{1}{4}$-kW transmitters, hence avoiding the cost of telephone calls. This radio link was unlicensed and illegal. Indeed, there were soon complaints from radio hams who were accustomed to chat together on far less powerful instruments and there were indignant protests that pirate broadcasters had invaded the 49-metre short-wave band.

It was fortunate that Hope and Robin could communicate by radio because when the international telephone circuits were constantly overloaded during the last week in August 1939 Hope made contact on 29 August and said, 'Drop everything and return to London at once!' Robin drove non-stop to the nearest Channel port, arrived in London and saw Hope, who told him to report to Colonel Gambier-Parry without delay. Philco's sales manager was now in charge of the SIS's wireless communications. Robin met Gambier-Parry, signed a copy of the Official Secrets Act, and was immediately instructed to build an additional short-wave transmitter for an MI6 outpost at Woldingham, Surrey, where a few Czechs and Poles were already sending coded messages in morse to their native lands.

Then Gambier-Parry said that a transmitter was needed in the west country, i.e. away from the *Luftwaffe's* presumed target areas. The *Luftwaffe* had so far been inactive but precautions were necessary. They drove to Cirencester - it was Gambier-Parry's birthplace so he knew the district well - in Robin's enormous Lincoln Zephyr automobile (he told me that it was a glorious youthful folly) and cruised around the local countryside keeping their eyes open for a large open field in which the relatively high (100-ft) masts for the transmitter could be erected. A suitable site was found at Renscombe - it had been used by the Royal Flying Corps during the First World War - and the farmer agreed to rent it to the gentlemen from London for use by HM Government. Robin remained in Cirencester where a local builder contrived a simple, partly prefabricated building to house the transmitting station. It was also necessary to arrange for a supply of electric power and the necessary Post Office telephone lines. A caravan served as a studio. By the time the masts were erected Gambier-Parry had acquired three small RCA transmitters from the USA ($\frac{1}{4}$, $\frac{1}{2}$ and 1-kW). They were mainly used for sending lengthy and non-secret news bulletins in morse to South America. These originated in the Ministry of Information which now occupied the University of London's Senate House building. A skilled morse operator sat in a small room in the Senate House tower and the material was relayed by telephone wire to Renscombe.

In the meantime (end of 1939?) Gambier-Parry established himself at Whaddon Hall, a requisitioned or rented stately home a few miles to the west of Bletchley Park, where the Government Code and Cypher School's 'pupils' – they included many distinguished mathematicians and other gifted individuals – were already wrestling with the German 'Enigma' cyphers. GC & CS was an SIS outpost. When the work at Renscombe was completed Robin moved to Whaddon Hall where the Selby-Lowndes family butler – he must have been at least an honorary member of the SIS – would bring Robin an early morning cup of tea and solemnly ask: 'Which suit are we wearing today, Sir?' Harold's invariable reply was: 'My tweed jacket and grey flannel trousers, please,' because with the exception of his black dinner jacket the extent of his wardrobe was limited. However, evening dress was obligatory for the pre-dinner glass of sherry and the evening meal (black ties for the gentlemen and a long dress for the lady).

Lisa Towse, Gambier-Parry's personal secretary and later his wife, was also a member of the Whaddon Hall party. She spoke and wrote excellent French and with Gambier-Parry's encouragement wrote the scripts for a hitherto unknown British clandestine station which called itself *Radio Beaux Arts*. Whether Sir Campbell Stuart, Department EH's chief, knew about Miss Towse's propaganda activities, is not known. She periodically drove herself to Renscombe to broadcast.

Early in 1940 Robin was asked to build another short-wave transmitting station not too far from Whaddon Hall. The necessary large field was found at Gawcott, a village about two miles south of Buckingham, where two American 7.5 kW transmitters were installed. It is possible that Dr Spiecker's broadcasts were generated from Gawcott but I cannot be sure of the actual location of the studio. A similar transmitting station was established at Potsgrove, a village close to Milton Bryant and not far from Woburn Abbey. From March 1943 Delmer's expanding broadcasting activities were located at Milton Bryant (known as MB).

The recording centre known as 'Simpson's' was probably first used late in 1940 when the Department's secret broadcasting activities began to increase very rapidly. 'Simpson's' was in fact Wavendon Tower, a large house (but not in the stately home class) in the rural village of Wavendon. The latter is now part of the 'new town' called Milton Keynes and Wavendon Tower accommodates the offices of the Milton Keynes Development Corporation. With its additional wings and large car parks, what was once an extremely private place is now a very public one. The cover name 'Simpson's' derived from the fact that the next village on the road to Bletchley happened to be called Simpson. Wavendon Tower was acquired when Harold Robin and his colleague Cecil Williamson were told to 'go out and find another house, somewhere close to Woburn'. The local ordnance survey maps showed the location of all the larger residences, most of which were occupied by members of the 'gentry' class. Cecil Williamson, who acted as 'front man', would accost a sometimes surprised owner and enquire if he or she would be willing to rent their home to a small party of very respectable civil servants. Sometimes the answer was an indignant 'certainly not', but the Marler family, who owned Wavendon Tower, were happy to oblige. Major Marler was in the army and his dependants preferred to live in Scotland at a convenient distance from the nearest German soldier, not to mention the *Luftwaffe*'s increasingly disagreeable intrusions. According to Harold Robin, Wavendon Tower was 'a beautiful place with a large garden and extensive lawns'. Four recording studios were organised, one of them in the billiards room. The recorded broadcasts could have been relayed to the transmitters at Gawcott and Potsgrove by the Post Office's telephone wires, but for security reasons it was decided to transport the discs by road. Any local vicar who happened to understand German would have been shocked beyond measure if a crossed line had made it possible for him to hear Delmer's first station's intimate revelations of the sexual aberrations of a number of the *Führer*'s leading henchmen.

As soon as 'Simpson's' was ready for operations Harold Robin moved there from Whaddon Hall. Two recording technicians and the three well-spoken young ladies who carefully supervised the arrivals and departures of the secret broadcasters – known to them as 'The Funnies' – also took up residence. They were soon joined by Colonel Gambier-Parry and Lisa Towse, who left Whaddon Hall for the less patrician but nevertheless agreeable ambience of Wavendon Tower. Moreover, since Great Britain and her Allies were not doing particularly well in the war against Germany, it was no longer necessary to 'dress for dinner'.

The material for a coherent history of PWE's clandestine broadcasting activities does not exist and the researcher must glean whatever he can from the very miscellaneous collection of papers now available at the PRO. In this book I have concentrated upon the stations which broadcast to Germany, the German armed forces in the occupied territories and the U-boat crews, because these were not only our most important targets but at the same time the recipients of the very best we had to offer in the way of subversive ideas. In the latter context we also eventually arranged for an increasingly regular supply of instructive 'black' reading matter. In fact 'the black game' was almost exclusively played against the Germans, although their collaborators in other countries were also attacked regularly.

I have failed to find any document which explains the policy behind the expansion of the secret broadcasting stations during 1940-1 when twenty stations began to broadcast during a period of almost exactly twelve months. The most plausible reason is that the Department found it convenient to develop an independent apparatus for propaganda which had no connection with either the BBC or the RAF. Its relations with the BBC were still unsatisfactory and the RAF could not be depended upon to drop its white propaganda leaflets whenever and wherever it was required. Thus the whole RU organisation was under the Department's exclusive control even if depended upon Gambier-Parry and Co., who were employed by the SIS, for all its technical broadcasting facilities. Again, since the Research Units were enveloped in a cloud of secrecy, any detailed knowledge of their organisation was restricted to a handful of individuals. Even the people attached to the many RU teams knew nothing about similar activities outside their own secret cabbage patch. The security aspect was maintained even more effectively when Woburn Abbey was vacated early in 1942 and scores of the PWE's employees returned to London.

There were good reasons for the remarkably tight security. Most of the broadcasters had relatives in Germany or the occupied territories, against whom reprisals could be taken, and their identities and the nature of their work had to remain secret. Indeed, from 1943 onwards Sefton Delmer's unit included a number of prisoners of war from the German army, navy and air force. Apart from these considerations a number of the RUs were operating in close harness with resistance organisations in the occupied territories. It was particularly important, too, that the Germans should never obtain any information about the British propaganda machinery, particularly its personnel, which they could use in their own propaganda. Thus the complete secret broadcasting organisation in 'The Country' had to be protected against ill-informed chatter and speculation. In any case PWE was a secret department and in those days its existence, likewise that of SOE, was never mentioned in public or to outsiders.

Once the RU operation got under way in the autumn of 1940 it became the equivalent of a cottage industry with the 'home workers' bringing their products (broadcasting scripts) to the 'factory', i.e. 'Simpson's', where they were recorded on sixteen-inch glass-based discs of American manufacture and played at 33⅓rpm.[6] The latter were then despatched to one or other of the transmitting stations where Gambier-Parry's technicians 'delivered' the finished product to whomever in Europe happened to be fiddling with the tuning dial of a short-wave set and received it by chance or, alternatively, knew which wave band to select and the right time at which to listen.

The teams, most of them very small, of script-writers and broadcasters, were accommodated in requisitioned private houses in villages in the Woburn area and were under the control of a British 'housemaster' who supervised their work and daily life. A wife was often available to look after the domestic side. The elaborate 'Special Security Precautions for Research Units', drafted on 26 July 1941 by Colonel P. R. Chambers (Indian Army, retd.), the Department's Security Officer, indicate the extent to which RU personnel were required to lead segregated existences.

English villages are usually friendly places but, according to this document, 'Enquiries from neighbours or callers should be discouraged, but when a reply is unavoidable, it should be stated that the house is in Government occupation and the residents are engaged in research work for HMG.'[7] Furthermore, the 'researchers' were expressly forbidden to visit their local pub or the Bedford Arms at Woburn, nor were they allowed to use the telephone or send telegrams without permission. No letters could be posted locally but were sent to London for mailing, while all incoming letters had to be addressed to a post office box number in London. Occasional leave was permitted but, 'Heads of houses should use their judgement to see that all residents whose English is poor and who are at all likely to attract attention or suspicion do not travel by train,' i.e. from Bletchley.

Whether or not life was tolerable under these conditions depended upon individual temperaments and the personality of the 'housemaster'. I recall the relaxed atmosphere at Sefton Delmer's extremely black German *Gasthaus*, 'The Rookery' at Aspley Guise, where the researchers worked with great application but still found time for the perpetration of hilariously funny practical jokes.

Twenty RUs began to broadcast during the period of twelve months following November 1940. Nine more were started in 1942 and a further sixteen in 1943 but many of them were replacements for stations which had outlived their usefulness. In October 1943, when Ritchie Calder (PWE's Director of Plans) called for a detailed report covering the whole RU activity, twenty out of the twenty-four RUs which then existed were actually broadcasting. No new RUs were started in 1944 and only one (*Hagedorn* for Germany) in 1945.

Whereas the BBC's European Service was a large and to some extent bureaucratic apparatus and hence not particularly flexible, RUs could be started and eliminated without any trouble. Some of them had very brief existences, for example, a station vaguely described as 'Italian Socialist' lasted for only five weeks early in 1941 and *Radio Rotes Wien* (for Austria) was on and off the air in less than two months later that year.

Until Delmer's German team took exclusive possession of their own custom-built studios at Milton Bryant (MB) early in 1943 all broadcasts were recorded at 'Simpson's'. The speakers were taken there by car and the times of their arrival and departure were carefully regulated so that the members of different teams were never allowed to meet or see one another.

The RUs, which had begun in a very modest way with Dr Spiecker's one-man business in May 1940, inevitably provided good reasons for the development of a 'RU empire' in Bedfordshire with its own 'managing director' (Reginald Leeper until early in 1943), and a small army of script-writers, broadcasters, supervisors, intelligence officers, radio technicians, transport fleet, administrators and, for the 'secret houses', cooks and bottle-washers. Furthermore, in 1942 the whole RU business was effectively separated from PWE's constantly expanding organisation in London.

1  F & CO document

2  For Dr Carl Spiecker see the important *Biographisches Handbuch der deutschsprachigen Emigration nach 1933*, Vol. 1, 1980. The mobile transmitter on a fishing vessel is mentioned in Werner Röder, *Die deutschen sozialistischen Exilgruppen in Grossbritanien 1940-1945*, 1973, p. 73. For his functions in the Ministry of the Interior and supposed connection with Otto Strasser see Dieter Fricke (ed.), *Die bürgerlichen Parteien in Deutschland*, Vol. 2, Leipzig, 1970, p. 252.

3  See Babette Gross, *Willi Münzenberg: eine politische Biographie*, 1967, p. 308.

4  F & CO document

5  Hugh Dalton, *The Fateful Years*, 1957, p. 367, quoted in David Stafford, *Britain and European Resistance, 1940-1945*, p. 29. Professor Stafford has provided an excellent account of Dalton's current views on subversion.

6  F & CO document

7  FO 898/7

# 9

# The First Research Units
# November 1940

Dr Spiecker's broadcasts from the *Bahnhof* had begun on 26 May 1940 but five months were to pass before the *Sender der Europäischen Revolution* first went on the air on 7 October 1940. It was followed during the next fortnight by:

> *Frats Romun* (Romanian), 10 November 1940–20 July 1943[1]
> *Radio Inconnue* (French), 15 November 1940–10 January 1944
> *Radio Italia* (Italian), 16 November 1940–15 May 1942
> *Radio Travail* (French), 17 November 1940–21 May 1942

The fact that these stations all began to broadcast at much the same time indicates that the Department had received a directive to employ secret broadcasting for the purposes of subversion. Indeed, a paper on 'Subversive Activities in Relation to Strategy', dated 25 November 1940 – it was SOE's first general directive from the Chiefs of Staff – shows that according to current thinking, 'Subversive activities should be given preference over the [organisation of] secret armies in the occupied territories'. Under the heading 'Subversive propaganda and other subversive activities' it was stated that 'these can play an important part against German economic life and morale.' However, as Professor David Stafford emphasised in his *Britain and European Resistance 1940–1945*, 1980, the British still believed that, 'When looking ahead to the eventual defeat of Germany, the blockade and the strategic air offensive were still seen as the two major weapons of war.' This belief was to endure for a long time although it was manifestly ill-founded because Germany survived the blockade by exploiting the occupied territories, and the success of the strategic air offensive is debatable.

That left subversion, which was constantly discussed, although I am inclined to doubt whether those who talked about it had any very clear idea of its techniques. After all, subversion was an activity outside the experience of those who proposed its use, and this applied equally to the

Department's first subversive propagandists at Woburn. The latter were also handicapped by their initially poverty-stricken situation as far as background intelligence material was concerned. However, even if it had been available in 1940 it is unlikely that anyone would have known how to exploit it to the best advantage.

The task presented to the black propagandists in 1940 was to weaken German morale and to encourage the still embryonic resistance movements in Europe. My own belief is that most of the subversive outpourings broadcast during the twelve months following November 1940 were a waste of human effort and the electricity required to transmit them. However, there is evidence to suggest that Sefton Delmer's *Gustav Siegfried Eins* station was attracting a modest (and sometimes even appreciative) audience in Germany by the end of 1941.

### Sender der Europäischen Revolution, 10 November 1940–22 June 1942

On 31 August 1940 Reginald Leeper presided at a meeting at which vague plans for an 'International Communist station to broadcast in German' were discussed. F. A. Voigt, formerly the *Manchester Guardian*'s correspondent in Berlin, Richard Crossman and Ralph Murray were asked to produce a suitable plan. A document dated 6 September records the following decisions:

> In accordance with Mr Voigt's memorandum, it was agreed that it would be desirable to divide the present Freedom Station into two units:
> (a) A unit containing Mr Turner [i.e. Dr Carl Spiecker], whose policy would be that of a patriotic German loyal to 'Das wahre Deutschland'.
> (b) A unit composed of revolutionary socialists whose theme should be revolutionary Europe and whose appeal should be specially directed towards German industrial workers. This unit should not be left-wing in the sense that it is either communist, social-democratic or trades unionist, but revolutionary in the sense that it gave a lead to new groups of industrial and black-coated workers, disillusioned by the old parties and disappointed by the National Socialist regime. It would, of course, have a European outlook as contrasted with an international outlook in the bad old sense of the word.
> It is hoped that its policy might be found closely to conform to that of [future] secret stations putting out European revolutionary propaganda in other languages, but it was thought wiser to keep it first a purely German station.[2]

Paragraph (b) is such glorious twaddle that it would be charitable to suggest that it merely reflects careless drafting. However, the 'revolu-

1   Denis Sefton Delmer in *c*. 1960

2     2     Harold Robin in New York City (1941) when he was supervising the Aspidistra transmitter's technical specification

3   Leonard Ingrams
4   Dr Leslie Beck
5   Donald MacLachan in *c*. 1962

6   Wavendon Tower (Simpson's). The buildings at the rear did not exist during the war years.

7   Excavation in progress for Aspidistra at Crowborough (Summer 1941)

8  The Aspidistra site completed and camouflaged with turf and trees
9  One of the Aspidistra control panels

10

10 'The Sergeant', i.e. Frank Lynder (*left*), in Germany in 1945

11

**Volksgenossen!**

**Macht euch keine Sorgen um den Führer !**

Wenn wir auch alles verlieren – Ein Fern-Flugzeug oder Groß-U-Boot ist immer noch da, ihn nach Japan oder Argentinien zu retten.

**Seid guten Mutes!**

11 Gummed sticker (1945): 'Volk comrades! Don't worry about the Führer. If *we* go down the drain [colloquial translation], a long-distance aircraft or large U-boat is always there to rescue him to Japan or the Argentine. Be of good cheer!'

# ALLE SABO TAGE

12   An example of punning gummed stickers produced in many versions. *Alle Tage* means 'every day'. They were liable to appear in the cloakrooms of places frequented by the Germans and were an unwelcome reminder of the presence and activities of the Resistance movements.

Gültig für freie Urlaubsreisen einen Wehrmachtfahrschein

## Kriegsurlabsschein

Der ...........................................................................................
                                    (Dienstgrad,              Zuname)

von ..........................................................................................
                                          (Tru        )

ist vom ..............................194..... bis einschl. ..................................... 194 ............... Uhr beurlaubt

nach ....................................................... näch Bahnhof .....................

nach ....................................................... näch Bahnhof .....................

nach ....................................................... näch Bahnhof .....................

Er reist auf kleinen Wehrmachtfahrschein. Die Jnanspruch      e von Wehrmachtfahrkarten oder Fahrkarten des öffentlichen Verkehrs für die im Wehrmachtfahrschein bezeichn      trecke ist verboten.

Ueber die umstehenden Befehle ist er belehrt worden.

Ausgefertigt am.............................. 194....

...............................................................
(Truppenteil)

(Dienststempel)

...............................................................
(Unterschrift, Dienstgrad, Dienststellung)

Lager-Nr. 63 b Heß, Braunschweig-München

13   German soldiers travelling on leave needed a variety of documents which were always liable to be inspected by the *Feldgendarmerie* (military police). The military pass illustrated had a rather limited utility.

Der Normalverbraucher
und Reichswohnungskommissar

**Reichsleiter Dr. Robert Ley**

im „Angriff" vom 12. Oktober 1943:

„ . . . Wir Nationalsozialisten kennen
keinen , Diplomatenhaushalt'. Jeder,
ob Reichsminister oder Reichsleiter,
muß genau so von seinen Karten leben
wie der einfache Arbeiter, Handwerker
und Beamte. Aber selbst die Normal-
karte reichte, für alle, denn ich pro-
biere sie täglich aus, da a u c h i c h
zu den Normalverbrauchern
g e h ö r e."

(Siehe umseitig)

15

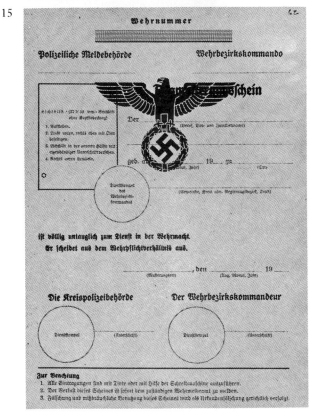

14   The dissipated Dr Robert Ley, the Reichskommissar in charge of housing, indignantly denied that he received coupons for additional food rations. 'I am a normal consumer!' he exclaimed, but the regular broadcasts from *Gustav Siegfried Eins* claimed that he was not! We issued the illustration shown here as a post card.

15   Forgery (greatly reduced in the illustration) certifying that the holder had been officially released from service in the German armed forces. It required a photograph and three rubber stamps with the appropriate signatures. The original was printed in black over a pink background.

tionary socialists' required to run the new station could not be found and by 28 September, 'the proposed communist German station had been transformed into a left-wing station but had not begun operations owing to the difficulty of recruiting staff. ...' Broadcasters for the European Revolution station were eventually found, probably by Crossman, and settled at 'Dawn Edge', always known as 'DE', a sedate house at Aspley Guise, a few miles from the Abbey. Crossman was appointed as 'housemaster' and was in nominal charge of the work, although the team insisted on preserving a large measure of independence.

The 'European Revolutionaries' were identified with the *Neubeginnen* coterie of independent left-wing German socialists. This was one of a score or more small German *émigré* political groups which fought interminably among themselves about which could claim to be *the* official anti-Hitler opposition. They appear to have been more tolerated than heeded by the Foreign Office, but eventually a fair number of them found employment with the BBC and, I believe, in PWE. The individuals who lived with Crossman and his wife at 'Dawn Edge' included Fritz Eberhard (i.e., Hellmut von Rauschenplat, b., 1896), Waldemar von Knoeringen (1896–1971), Richard Löwenthal (b. 1908), and Paul Anderson (i.e. Harald Müller, b. 1908) and his wife Evelyn. They were all highly educated left wing political scientists and hence spoke the same language as Crossman.

Their station, which broadcast daily on 31.3 metres, was 'grey' rather than black since it did not attempt to give the illusion that it was broadcasting from inside Germany. It hoped to reach listeners there who would accept its admonitions to 'go slow' gently rather than violently, sabotage transport and generally offer passive resistance to the demands for increased output and greater energy in the prosecution of the war. The *Sender der Europäischen Revolution* ceased to broadcast on 22 June 1942 when, according to Werner Röder (pages 186–7), the team showed itself unwilling to express itself more energetically in favour of the Allied war aims.


## THE EARLY FRENCH RUs

Two French clandestine stations began to broadcast about a month after the German *Sender der Europäischen Revolution* commenced operations in October 1940: *Radio Inconnue* on 15 November and *Radio Travail* two days later.[3] Whereas the German station was little more than the BBC in sheep's clothing, the offerings from *Radio Inconnue* were distinctly subversive. The BBC carefully avoided making personal attacks on

Écoutez les Voix Connues
de la Radio Inconnue.

Tous les Jours (Avec la
permission de la Gestapo et
de la Police) sur 30.77 mètres.
à 8.0ʰ, 12.30ʰ, 20.0ʰ.

Les Chevaliers sont là!

Sticker for use in France advertising *Radio Inconnue*

Marshal Pétain although Maurice Schuman, who was the official spokes-man for the so-called Free French, was allowed to do so. The reason for the BBC's reticence was that the British were anxious not to underline the difference between the British and the American attitude to the Marshal, since the Americans clearly expected far more from him. Indeed, for a long period the British could never be sure that Pétain would not transfer himself to North Africa and turn against the Germans. Although this possibility became increasingly remote, the situation could have been politically embarrassing and far more so if the BBC had been attacking him publicly as a renegade and traitor to France. Finally, in 1940–1 the majority of Frenchmen still respected the Marshal as the hero of Verdun and as a father figure who was doing his best to protect them against the rapacious Germans who had quickly initiated a policy of economic exploitation in France. However, in the secret broadcasts which purported to originate inside France, there were no limits to the infamies of which the Marshal, the Vichy government and many well-known *collaborateurs* could be accused.

The small team of script-writers and broadcasters which served both the French stations were accommodated at the Old Rectory at Todding-ton (TOR), a village about four miles south of Woburn. It will now possibly never be known who recruited the people concerned, although it was probably Dr Leslie Beck, a mysterious figure whose role in the obscurer corridors of wartime Anglo–French relations was undoubtedly more important than most of his colleagues in PWE's French Section realised.

Dr Leslie Beck (1906–78),[4] Chief Intelligence Officer of the French Section and of its RUs, was one of the Department's most formidable characters. Small in stature, he had been a Jesuit novice but was never ordained. As a young man he taught in India before proceeding to the Sorbonne (*Diplôme supérieur en philosophie, doctorat et agrégé*) and thence to Campion Hall, Oxford, and an Oxford D.Phil. His great love for France began during his Sorbonne period (1930–4). He was an authority on Descartes and immediately before the war was a lecturer on philosophy at Magdalen College, Oxford. Like Richard Crossman he was a considerable 'educator', one of his great achievements being to impress upon the Americans, whose ignorance of France and the French could be alarmingly naïve, that a *French* government was going to take over in France after the Liberation and certainly not AMGOT (Allied Military Government Occupied Territories). PWE sent Beck to the USA in November 1943 where he accomplished an excellent public relations mission for the Department seven months before D-Day. According to a contemporary report from David Bowes-Lyon:

> Besides successfully conducting negotiations on particular matters he had a variety of contacts. Field-Marshal Dill, for example, had Beck to lunch privately ... Dill was clearly impressed because shortly afterwards General Macready [US Army] asked to see Beck and spent an hour and a half listening to his analysis of the French underground. General Donovan had Beck to dinner alone – a rare honour. The Charlottesville School of Military Government invited Beck to lecture there and to address their special seminar on France. [The Chancery of the British Embassy in Washington] arranged for him to meet the head of the French desk in the State Department at lunch; the next day another member of the State Department asked to see him, obviously because the first one had reported what good value Beck was. He had lunch with Walter Lippmann and breakfast with Edgar Mowrer and got them both a bit straighter on France. He did not confine himself to the illustrious; he got right down to the working desk in OWI and OSS [the Office of War Information and the Office of Strategic Services] ... Galantière, head of the French desk of OWI, has spoken to me enthusiastically about the benefit to his section's work of Beck's visit.[5]

After the war the British Government awarded Beck the Order of the

British Empire, and the French the Légion d'honneur. I suspect it was the latter that he prized most.

A Mr Graham and a Miss Maxwell – both names are pseudonyms – were responsible for all the work for *Radio Inconnue* (script-writing and broadcasting) until Mr Graham's young daughter arrived after a perilous journey from France in the autumn of 1942. She, however, only helped at Toddington for a few months. I am tolerably certain that these three individuals were all British citizens with a perfect command of the French language. It is unlikely that we will ever learn about the circumstances which brought an ex-miner from the Lille district (plus wife and children) to Toddington where he was known as *L'ouvrier* (the workman). Until 29 July 1941 he was the only speaker on *Radio Travail* and Mr Graham wrote his scripts for him.

There was a little trouble just before Christmas 1940 when Dr Beck, who was in overall charge of TOR (although he clearly did not live there), discovered that *Radio Inconnue* and *Radio Travail* were planning a joint broadcast on Christmas Eve in order to celebrate the festivity. This naïve undertaking would have destroyed the illusion that the two stations were operating in different parts of France.

The domestic problems which prevailed at the Old Rectory were not without their comic side although they were taken very seriously at the time. The British, who were bourgeois, ate in the dining-room and spent their few leisure hours in the drawing-room. *L'ouvrier* and his family, who were working class, were relegated to the kitchen. This class-conscious distinction worked well enough until a French trades union official, who was an educated man, was enlisted as an additional speaker for *Radio Travail*. He clearly preferred the company of the bourgeoisie at mealtimes and in the *salon* afterwards to that of his proletarian compatriots and this caused ill-feeling. Then *l'ouvrier* had a row with Mr Graham about the scripts given to him for broadcasting. This must have been a violent altercation because Mr Graham, by now convinced that the ex-miner and his wife were extremely dangerous, contrived to effect their immediate transfer to separate prisons. They were soon liberated, but not without considerable trouble, thanks to the combined exertions of Colonel Chambers and Dr Beck.

It might be asked why *Radio Inconnue* and *Radio Travail* were not staffed by French broadcasters of the same quality as those already employed by the BBC. The answer is that they could not be found. Furthermore, since the abortive naval raid on Dakar (23–25 September 1940) the security of the Free French was doubted and the clandestine broadcasting activities at Woburn were classified as 'Most Secret'. The existence of *Radio Inconnue*, which was kept going until January 1944, was never divulged to General de Gaulle nor anyone else in Free French circles.

*Radio Inconnue* gave few indications of its location but purported to be in the Paris area. Its speakers used the language and ideas of the *petite bourgeoisie* and addressed themselves almost entirely to that class. The station's principal targets were usually Marshal Pétain personally and the Vichy regime. After 21 June 1941, when the Germans invaded Russia, *Radio Inconnue* became increasingly 'operational', advocating slashing the tyres of German vehicles and sundry forms of passive resistance. On 3 July 1941 the station broadcast details of an imaginary organisation called 'Les chevaliers du coup de balai' (The knights of the sweeping broom), implying that its members, armed with symbolical brooms, would henceforth harass the Germans in France. On 28 August 1941 Paul Colette, a ship's stoker, sprayed bullets into a gathering of notables present at a barracks at Versailles – the occasion was a review of the new *Légion des volontaires contre le bolchévisme* – and wounded Pierre Laval and Marcel Deat, both of them notorious *collaborateurs*. *Radio Inconnue* immediately suggested that Admiral Darlan and Fernand de Brinon should be regarded as high on the list for assassination.

The rumour that Pierre Pucheu (a representative of the French steel cartel and Vichy Minister of the Interior) and Yves Bouthillier (Minister of Finance) had a corrupt association with the *Banque* Worms was launched in July 1941. Both men were accused of being implicated in the famous 'Synarchie' conspiracy, of which details were broadcast on 19 November 1941. According to a contemporary summary of an unpublished text:

This secret society (*La Synarchie*) has a very real existence. Its programme has three completely clear aims: 1. To direct the policy of the Vichy government in such a way as to ban all socialist tendencies; 2. to suppress any socialist movement which could weaken the position of certain financial groups; 3. to safeguard certain Franco-German interests which were arranged before hostilities began in 1939.

Its chief is *le Sieur* Jacques Leroy Ladurie, a director of the *Banque* Worms, and his principal assistant is *le Sieur* Yves Mouthillier. The directing committee includes Jacques Barnaud (Director of the *Banque* Worms), Francois Lehidoux (formerly a leading figure in the French automobile industry and connected by marriage with the Renault family, Minister of Industrial Production), René Belin (a member of the Vichy government who formerly belonged to the anti-communist wing of the

CGT trades union organisation), Pierre Pucheu [as above], Henri Du Moulin de la Barthète (Pétain's *chef de cabinet*) and Jean Bichelonne (Lehidoux's successor and Albert Speer's opposite number in France).

The following extract from the minutes of a meeting of PWE's Executive Committee held on 10 March 1942 (it was attended by Leeper and Brooks and two very senior representatives from SOE) suggests that the British were as much puzzled by the famous 'Synarchie' myth as many French citizens. The story, with many embellishments, received very wide publicity in France in 1941-2. Indeed, PWE's top people appear to have been inclined to believe that it might have been based upon the inspired inventions of *Radio Inconnue*.

The Committee had before them a paper on Synarchy which had been forwarded by Mr Jebb [later Lord Gladwyn] for consideration by PWE. The Secretary read a minute from the French Section pointing out that the description of the movement in this paper closely corresponded, even down to its details, with the general story that had been put out by an RU. It seemed likely therefore that the basis of the paper was in fact the rumours spread by one of the French RUs.

It was agreed that there was no objection to SOE telling their agent that an RU was probably responsible for the information, but that any concrete evidence of the real existence of such a movement (apart from the suggestion of the RU) would be extremely valuable.[6]

In fact the fascinating legend was undoubtedly invented at Vichy by Henri Martin, the head of Pétain's special security police, and was intended to discredit precisely the same people whom *Radio Inconnue* attacked, i.e. Jacques Leroy-Ladurie *et alii*, known to their opponents in France as the 'Worms gang'. Furthermore, post-war judicial enquiries cleared Worms & *Cie.* of all charges of economic collaboration.[7] *Radio Inconnue* operated until January 1944, and many of the rumours it originated were refuted in the French press.

The Vichy French's reply to *Radio Inconnue*, first monitored in December 1941, was *Radio Révolution*. It occupied studios in the Grand Casino at Vichy and according to an intelligence report its staff included 'two Jewish actors, one of them a *pensionnaire* of the *Comédie Française* ... who denounced with great vehemence the lies uttered by the Jews at *Radio Londres*'. The material broadcast by *Radio Révolution* was said to be 'lively and amusing', with witty parodies of speeches by Churchill and de Gaulle. The latter was accused of being the author of scripts broadcast by *Radio Inconnue* and personally responsible for its frequent incitements to murder. While *Radio Révolution* purported to be a clandestine station its broadcasts (on both medium and short wave) were mainly intended for listeners inside France and letters intended for it couldbe mailed to post-office box numbers at Nîmes and later Brive (Corrèze). According to an intelligence report, many of them were abusive.

*Radio Travail* offered rather more serious fare to its audience in France than the irrepressible *Radio Inconnue*. The ex-miner from Lille invariably prefaced his broadcasts with the words: '*Écoutez, c'est un ouvrier du Nord qui vous parle!*' The station was intended to reflect the revolutionary traditions of republican France and, as befitted its location in the occupied northern *départements*, regularly attacked the Germans. After the German invasion of Russia considerable attention was also paid to the possibilities of passive resistance and sabotage. The speakers – for by then the trades union organiser had joined the team – disassociated themselves from both communism and de Gaulle's Free French movement and distinguished between the German working class and the Nazis. The station appeared to be excellently informed on the subject of French internal politics. Indeed, it claimed to have an informant who was actually a member of Admiral Darlan's cabinet at Vichy although this was a pardonable exaggeration. When *l'ouvrier* departed the ex-trades union organiser continued alone. *Radio Travail* ceased to broadcast on 21 May 1942 because there was insufficient information on the subject of organised labour in France and because the trades union man tended to express himself in pre-war formulas and language.

A third French RU, *La France Catholique*, began to broadcast on 1 July 1941, probably with the knowledge of General de Gaulle's organisation and undoubtedly at the suggestion of Dr Beck. It is likely, too, that Captain Lagrave, the French priest who was at first its only speaker, knew nothing about the operations of the two other French RUs and lived at a safe distance from Toddington's Old Rectory. The RU's purpose was to encourage a spirit of resistance among Catholics in France and to assist priests there by providing material for their sermons. In his opening remarks Father Lagrave stated that he was speaking with the sanction of his Bishop. Twice weekly there were prayers of a strongly propagandist character, e.g. 'for our children who are starving' and 'for our prisoners in captivity in Germany'. It was stated that these prayers were offered in response to a request from the Pope. Although German broadcasts suggested that *La France Catholique* broadcast from the Vatican, in order to provoke an official denial, the Vatican, although aware of its existence, never denounced it. On 15 August 1941 Mr d'Arcy Osborne, the British Minister to the Holy See, was asked to enquire whether the Vatican could supply 'any information about a short-wave station calling itself *La France Catholique* which is occasionally heard in Great Britain'. A month later Mr Osborne reported that the Vatican knew nothing about it but his Jesuit friends in Rome thought that the station, which was clearly audible there, might be based in Hungary. The Vatican's attitude was probably influenced by the genuinely religious atmosphere of the broadcasts and the fact that the station gave many talks on such subjects as Catholic missionary work and religious instruction which contained no propaganda element.

However, *La France Catholique* was certainly employed for clandestine propaganda. Comparisons were made between the methods of Hitler and Satan. Firms working for the Germans were advised to continue operating in order to provide employment but nevertheless to produce goods of poor quality. Collaborators, including priests, were told that the day would come when they would have to stand trial as traitors.

The station was closed on 14 May 1942 when Captain Lagrave insisted, as a matter of conscience, that he should be allowed to join the Free French air force. He was trained as a pilot but returned to PWE on a part-time basis in 1943, this time with Captain Florent, another French priest, who recorded broadcasts when his colleague was not available. André Gillois, who arrived in England in September 1942 and was soon in charge of yet another French clandestine station (*Honneur et Patrie: le poste de la Résistance française*), recalled that Father Florent used to lunch with him – they lived in adjoining houses in the Woburn district – and invariably brought an ample supply of communion wine. Father Florent, who had a reserve commission in the Free French air force, served throughout the 1944–45 campaign in north-west Europe and then retired to a monastery. His colleague Lagrave, on the other hand, went to Brazil where he found himself a wife. *La France Catholique* was broadcasting until 14 May 1944.[8]

After the German invasion the Russians also entered the religious broadcasting field with *La Voce Christiana* (in Italian), which claimed that Soviet Russia was a defender of the Christian faith! Similar stations operated in the Polish, Spanish, French and German languages. They were under the direction of the pious Herr Richard Gyptner (1901–72), who was on the staff of the Comintern, the Soviet organ whose role was to spread the communist gospel in countries outside Russia. He returned to Germany together with Walter Ulbricht and other future leaders of what became the German Democratic Republic in 1945 and was Vice-President of the East Berlin police (*Volkspolizei*) in 1951–3, and subsequently the GDR's ambassador in Peking and Warsaw. When he died in 1972 it is unlikely that masses were said in Rome for the soul of this particular recipient of the Golden Banner of Work and the Karl Marx Order.[9]

## THE EARLY ITALIAN RUs

According to a contemporary assessment, 'For the first year of the war with Italy secret broadcasting (i.e. in Italian) was spasmodic, unplanned and amateurish.'[10] The first Italian RU, *Radio Italia* - locally known as 'Wop 1' - went on the air on 17 November 1940 and was followed in June 1941 by *Radio Libertà* ('Wop 2'). *Radio Italia* specialised in saying disagreeable things about the Germans and *Radio Libertà* revealed an intimate knowledge of Mussolini's private life alleging, for example, that he had married his half-sister. For a time *Radio Libertà* only broadcast at week-ends owing to the absence of suitable speakers and there were occasions when Signor C—, at one time the station's only artiste, refused to broadcast because of a 'fit of temperament'. An attempt was made to classify *Radio Libertà* as the mouthpiece of a group of young and disillusioned *Fascisti* but nothing useful emerged. It ceased to exist on 27 November 1941.

Both the Italian RUs tried various 'operational' themes which were intended to deplete the availability of certain articles which were in short supply. Thus listeners were exhorted to buy and hoard radio valves, any available metals and the copper sulphate needed for spraying vineyards. The station's value as a medium for such benevolent advice was questioned when an economic analyst pointed out that Italian agricultural and industrial workers owned less than four per cent of the receivers available in Italy for the reception of short-wave broadcasts.

On 17 November 1941 the gentleman who supervised these obviously futile activities circulated a lengthy document which included the following dramatic passage:

> On 17 November the stenographers on the fourth floor in the Via Vittoria Veneto at Rome, tuning their sets through the 41-metre band, were startled by a new apparition on the ether ... It was a memorable day in Italian history ... Deafened by years of Fascist propaganda Italians were at last hearing the authentic voice of Italy.

However, the fortunate Italians were not to hear the 'authentic voice' for very much longer because *Radio Libertà* was closed down ten days later and PWE happily dispensed with the services of the writer of the self-congratulatory memorandum. The Department's clandestine Italian service could record at least one success: *Radio Italia* managed to deceive the head of its mission at Cairo. His monitors heard it in February 1941 and, unaware of recent developments in secret broadcasting at Woburn, supposed that it *must* be a freedom station operating in Italy. A few days later the head of mission sent a telegram to the effect that *Radio Italia* had been definitely located on 20 February in the neighbourhood of Brindisi. Nobody bothered to disillusion him.

I have found it preferable not to inflate this book by attempting to study the later French, Dutch, Belgian, Norwegian, Danish, Czech, Polish and 'Balkan' RUs. However, a complete list of all PWE's Research Units with, where available or necessary, condensed information about the forty-eight short-wave stations operated by the Department between 1940–45 will be found in an Appendix.

1   This and other operational dates are from F & CO documents.

2   FO 898/9

3   My information about the French RUs is largely based upon F & CO documents.

4   Dr Beck's widow kindly supplied certain biographical details.

5   F & CO document

6   FO 898/27

7   See Richard F. Kuisel's excellent study 'The Legend of the Vichy Synarchy' in *French Historical Studies*, Vol. 6, 1970, pp. 365–98.

8   See André Gillois, *Histoire secrète des Français à Londres*, 1973.

9   For R. Gyptner, see *Biographisches Handbuch der deutschsprachigen Emigration nach 1933*, 1980.

10   F & CO documents were extensively used for this section.

# 10

# Denis Sefton Delmer

In January 1946 Robert Walmsley, who had been one of the Department's founder members and was then at the beginning of his post-war career at the Foreign Office, wrote a brief account of his wartime experiences. In it he expressed the hope 'that the history of Delmer's unit is being written separately and given as much importance as at least the whole of the rest of PWE'. Much later, in a letter written to me on 15 August 1973, he remarked: 'Delmer was the nearest thing to a genius which PWE produced. In fact, in his particular line he *was* a genius.'

Although I was in frequent contact with Delmer from the spring of 1942 onwards I did not see a great deal of him because I worked in London and Delmer spent practically all his time in what we called 'The Country'. Indeed, it was not until the late 1950s, when he was writing *Black Boomerang*, the second volume of his memoirs, that I began to see him fairly regularly. Thus Mr Walmsley's recollections are particularly valuable because he was actually on the spot when Delmer arrived at Woburn early in 1941 and witnessed his emergence as the Department's black propagandist *hors concours*. Here are some extracts from his *aide-mémoire*:

Crossman differed widely from that other formidable personality, Sefton Delmer, whom I also came to know well, more intimately indeed than it was possible to know Crossman. Delmer, who created vastly more than Crossman ever did, whose mind ranged in fields where Crossman never felt at home, and who had a far wider range of opposition to overcome, made friends of those who might have stood in his path. In this he was helped by a genial and Rabelaisian nature and by a Falstaffian corpulence which so easily became the subject of confidences. But above all Delmer possessed a true modesty and humility of soul. He believed, certainly, in his own power, but never in his own infallibility. He could behave far more violently than Crossman, browbeat his subordinates with a fury and persistence of which Crossman would never have dreamed, but he remained open to conviction and he never gave the impression of despising those who disagreed with him. Furthermore, on his own ground his judgment was extraordinarily good. In all these ways he differed profoundly from Crossman.

I think Delmer joined in May 1941. At that time there were weekly meetings in Leeper's room attended by Delmer, Crossman, Voigt and myself. . . . These meetings often degenerated into long tirades by Voigt against the methods of British propaganda. It was not always clear whether Voigt was tilting at black or white propaganda, or at whom for what, but although he was rather wearisome to Delmer and Crossman I think he made useful contributions, even if only by clarifying the issues. He was, however, totally unsympathetic to the idea of anything but the whitest of white propaganda and seemed unable to distinguish between propaganda to different audiences. At these meetings Delmer used to assume an attitude of innocence and modesty and Leeper used to enjoy his bland descriptions of the early broadcasts of *Gustav Siegfried Eins*.

It was fairly clear from the outset that Delmer and Crossman were incompatible, not only in character but in their approach to propaganda. Delmer, however, never gave Crossman (his titular superior)* any reasons for suspecting 'disloyalty', and the only effect of the incompatibility (I believe) was to slow down the taking over by Delmer of all black propaganda. In case it is not recorded elsewhere, it is easy to forget that at first Delmer controlled only one small black station [*Gustav Siegfried Eins*] and that his control of black leaflets and of Crossman's 'European Revolution' station (really the BBC in sheep's clothing) came at rather a late stage. Delmer never asked to control anything extra until it seemed not only ripe but over-ripe.

The relations of my own intelligence unit with black propaganda were of course much closer from 1941–3 than after the move to London. Although Delmer almost at once set up his own intelligence section in the country, I myself was a regular visitor at his house, and I think a good many of his standard 'lines' first saw the light over the remains of his cellar at RAG ['The Rookery', Aspley Guise]. He was not only an indefatigable but an unceasing worker, and after dinner, from nine until one or two in the morning (at least on my own frequent visits) discussions on new projects and new themes were broken only by intervals of listening to his own station or even rival ones.

On the use of refugees, Delmer always had a low opinion of the BBC staff (except its most able member whom he enticed), but maintained that there were excellent refugees to be used if you knew where to find them. In support of this he had himself acquired an astonishingly good team

*Crossman was not Delmer's 'titular superior'. According to a minute dated 27 May 1941, four days after Delmer's GS1 station first broadcast, it was decided that, 'Mr Crossman and Mr Delmer should in future be jointly in charge of the German Department, which should remain a unity, serving both the BBC and SO1.' (FO 898/4) Crossman now became the German region's 'front man', *vis-à-vis* the BBC in particular, while Delmer's equal status remained a closely guarded secret. It simply meant that he could not be trampled on by Crossman!

from the point of view not only of talent but of character. Even so, in spite of anything he may say himself, it was his training which made them what they were.

The more one reflects, the more one appreciates Delmer's complete singleness of purpose and untiring application to work. I have seen him squatting on his vast settee at RAG reading through a paragraph of a talk, not once or twice but literally dozens of times, muttering crossly to himself as he did so, then sending the wretched writer off to change a few words and repeating the same process with the same talk about once an hour for three or four hours on end. Or, stopping in the middle of a sentence, a worried wrinkle would appear on his large brow and, retrieving at least one of his shoes and giving his braceless trousers a heave, he would stump rapidly out of the room to impart a brilliant new idea to one of his writers, probably by that time in bed.

I do not know whether his hold on his refugees was strengthened or shaken by exhibiting in his sitting-room a trophy – a shield bearing the words '*Hier sind Juden unerwünscht*' ['The presence of Jews is undesirable'] – allegedly captured in Germany by C. E. Stevens and smuggled out in a motorcycle side-car.

Denis Sefton Delmer – always known as Sefton Delmer, to his friends as Tom Delmer and to members of his staff who could not claim familiarity as Mr Delmer – was, as Robert Walmsley has suggested, temperamentally the antithesis of Richard Crossman. His particular speciality was the blackest of black propaganda, with the Germans at the receiving end and no holds barred. Its purpose, as Lord Ritchie-Calder suggested in 1973, was to 'confuse and disturb them and soften them up'. Furthermore, as Richard Crossman wrote in the same year (see page 3 above), he played it 'as a game'. Those who never knew Delmer might suppose that his undoubted talents as a black operator might be indicative of some kind of twisted personality. However, this was not the case and Clifton Child, who worked closely with him during 1943–5, remarked to me thirty years later, 'Tom was one of the most honest men I ever met.'

Other contemporaries with whom I have discussed Delmer mentioned his ability to maintain a very high standard of discipline. When necessary he could be discouragingly aloof. Thus Child: 'One tended to avoid Tom at MB. It was never advisable to approach him with silly questions; he expected one to solve one's own problems.' It was Child, too, who emphasised 'Tom's fabulous security', meaning a discretion which gained the respect of the Director of Naval Intelligence and other senior individuals in the intelligence world. In fact he was able to ignore the very existence of PWE's inflated Directorate of Intelligence because he had his own alternative – and considerably more effective – lines of communication.

Frank Lynder who, as a very young man, was one of the small group who lived with Tom and his first wife Isabel at that fascinating house at Aspley Guise, told me that the experience was by far the most memorable and rewarding of his youthful years. After the war he was to become a successful journalist. 'Tom taught me how to write,' he told me. 'He was a first-class teacher . . . but impatient!'

Delmer was a hard and exacting taskmaster but drove himself to the very limit. He had less reason to hate the *Führer* and all his works than those who worked as much with him as for him. There were very few British subjects in his team and Aspley Guise and the large studio compound at Milton Bryant resembled German enclaves in the Bedfordshire countryside. If he was single-minded in tending what Grand Admiral Doenitz once described to Hitler as 'that poison kitchen',[1] although naturally unaware of who was in charge of it, it was because the work appealed to two of his most conspicuous qualities: a demand for perfection and a highly developed sense of humour. There must have been times when he exasperated his long-suffering team almost beyond the limits of endurance, but readers of *Black Boomerang* will notice the generous praise he gave them. He was, in fact, the most modest of men and, as Robert Walmsley remarked, 'in his own line a genius'.

Delmer's own intimate experience of Germany and the Germans was a vitally important factor. The son of Australian parents, he was born in Berlin where his father was a member of the English faculty at the University.[2] Soon after his birth on 24 May 1904 he was registered as a British citizen by the British Consul General in Berlin. Delmer *père* was interned at Ruhleben in August 1914 but his wife and the children remained at liberty and Tom continued to attend a local *Gymnasium* (grammar school). The family was repatriated in May 1917 and Tom attended St Paul's School in London. From there he won a scholarship to Lincoln College, Oxford, where he read Modern History and rowed in the college crew at Henley. He was, of course, bilingual in English and German and could imitate the accents of both Berlin dustmen and Prussian officers.

His father returned to Germany after the war. He had briefly represented the *Daily Mail* in Switzerland but in 1919 he joined the Allied Control Commission and Tom spent most of his school holidays in Germany. Before taking his final examinations at Oxford he was undecided whether to follow in his father's footsteps as an academic, try for admission to the diplomatic service or become a journalist. At the time he left Oxford his father was working in Berlin as a local correspondent for a number of British publications and already had a connection with Lord Beaverbrook's *Daily Express*. In August 1927 Tom was in Berlin doing odd journalistic chores for his father. An unexpected encounter there with Lord Beaverbrook, who clearly liked and encouraged him, led to his immediate employment by the *Daily Express* and he became its Berlin correspondent in 1928. He spent the next five years there and personally encountered many of the leading Nazi personalities including Hitler.

Lord Beaverbrook transferred him to Paris in 1933 and promoted him to Chief European Correspondent in 1937. Thus he covered the Civil War in Spain during three strenuous months in 1938 where he met two men who were later to play an important role in his wartime work. In September 1938 he hurried from Spain to Berlin and arrived there on the day that Mr Chamberlain was conferring with Herr Hitler at Berchtesgaden. He left immediately for Prague where he met Miss Unity Mitford, who was wearing a swastika badge which, she told him, was a personal gift from the *Führer*. During the twelve months before the outbreak of war in September 1939 he was present at times of crisis in almost every European trouble-spot. On 23 August 1939, the day when the German–Soviet non-aggression pact was signed in Moscow he was on the Polish border close to Katowice, and was in Warsaw when the first German bombs fell there. He escaped through Romania and eventually made his way back to London where his next employment was as a British war correspondent attached to the French army. On 14 June 1940, when the Germans entered Paris, Tom and two other British war correspondents had left the city at the last possible moment only a few hours earlier. They reached Bordeaux after a nerve-wracking journey by road and at the mouth of the Gironde boarded an ancient P & O passenger ship which brought them back to England ... and for Tom a period of boredom and uncertainty. He was thirty-six years old and weighed seventeen stone, so enlistment in a Rifle Brigade regiment, for example, was clearly impracticable.

He hoped to find employment in one or other of the intelligence services but did not succeed. In *Trail Sinister*, the first volume of his autobiography, he mentioned that the fact that he had been born in Berlin and had known so many of the leading Nazi bosses was held against him. In those days MI5's right hand did not invariably know what its left one was doing because a few weeks before Tom arrived back in London it insouciantly allowed Kim Philby to find a niche in Grand's

Section D which, after all, was a branch of the SIS. However, Tom had the good sense to contact Leonard Ingrams, an international banker whom he had known well during his Berlin period.

Leonard Ingrams was among the select few of my friends whom I knew to have something to do with the cloak-and-dagger side of the war and he looked the part of the mysterious Mr X. to perfection. He was tall and athletic . . . and his eyes and mouth had just the right expression of drawling sardonic pity for the world around him. . . . Leonard had been one of my special friends in Berlin where he was known as 'The Flying Banker' because of his habit of piloting himself around Europe in his private Puss Moth on his business trips for the Chemical Bank of New York.

According to Tom's account in *Black Boomerang* he was invited to lunch at Boodle's Club in St James's Street where he was introduced to Valentine Williams, Reginald Leeper's deputy at Woburn. After the meal there was a whispered (!) conversation in an unoccupied card room upstairs and Williams offered him an unspecified job, at the same time explaining that MI5's vetting process might take time and he would have to be patient. Weeks passed by and there was no news. Finally Ingrams hinted that MI5 had again rejected him.

It was typical of the prevailing confusion that in November 1940 MI6 (i.e. the SIS) obliquely invited Tom to do some work for them in Lisbon using his employment as a *Daily Express* correspondent as a cover. He spent his time talking to German Jews who, in return for a fat payment to the *Sicherheitsdienst* or the Gestapo, had been allowed to travel to Lisbon to emigrate to North or South America. He was surprised 'that the Gestapo should have allowed men and women to go abroad who could give so much information about such important electronic firms as Askania and Lorenz, to mention but a few'. He also realised that while his articles for the *Daily Express* were read by about twelve million people before being used to light a fire, those he delivered to MI6 were 'distributed to several hundred persons, read by no one, and then incinerated as secret waste'. However, the material he collected in Lisbon was to be surprisingly useful some months later.

While he was still in Lisbon a telegram arrived from Leonard Ingrams suggesting that he should resign from the *Daily Express* as an important job was waiting for him in England. He returned to London, probably in January 1941. When I read *Black Boomerang* in 1962 I was amused to discover the extent to which Tom's early experiences in the Department resembled my own. Like Tom I was recruited by Ingrams and was soon driven to Woburn in a large vehicle together with a 'goatee-bearded

Harrow schoolmaster who was an expert on Spain'. Delmer also encountered him as a fellow passenger on the occasion of his first visit to 'The Country'. And like Tom I was installed in 'a small office in a hush-hush building in a cul-de-sac off Berkeley Square', although, unlike my illustrious colleague, I was not required to wait for about two months before learning what kind of work I was expected to perform.

Delmer eventually discovered the reason for his employment when Ingrams told him about the secret broadcasting business at Woburn, at the same time expressing his complete contempt for Crossman's *Sender der Europäischen Revolution* with its 'appeals to the workers to shake off the Fascist yoke and all that stuff'. Ingrams explained that what was now needed was a new right-wing RU and that Delmer would be in complete editorial and political control of it. 'The Germans under you will say and do what you tell them to do,' he emphasised. 'No more nonsense about freedom and independence.' He was referring to the working conditions demanded by the 'revolutionary socialists' who ran the left-wing station of which Crossman was nominally in charge. As a true-blue Tory, Ingrams was deeply suspicious of Crossman's socialist ideas and supposed that he might be obstructive, although his fears on that score were groundless.

That was the beginning of the station which would soon become well known as *Gustav Siegfried Eins*, signaller's German for 'George Sugar One'. But what did those cabalistic initials signify? *Geheimsender* 1 (Secret Transmitter 1)? Or perhaps *Generalstab* 1 (General Staff 1)? Ingrams sardonically suggested that *Gurkensalat* 1 (Cucumber Salad 1) was the probable answer.

1   According to Frank Lynder.

2   The biographical information in this chapter is largely based on the German translation (*Die Deutschen und ich*, 1962) of Delmer's *Trail Sinister*, 1961, and *Black Boomerang*, 1962. I have preferred to use the German version because it contains some material which is not available in the original English editions.

# 11

# Gustav Siegfried Eins

The concept was Delmer's although the preliminary details were discussed at length with Leonard Ingrams who was able to persuade Leeper that what was required for the Germans was more a robust dose of subversion than the political idealism of Crossman's 'revolutionary socialists', who addressed their remarks to a vague audience of 'good Germans'. There were still some at Woburn who believed in an effective left-wing opposition to Hitler. I do not believe that either Ingrams or Delmer had any particular views about 'good Germans' but, rather, were in favour of a determined effort to corrupt or undermine the unquestioning loyalty of any German who happened to listen to GS1.

During April 1941 there were oblique references to 'the new Research Unit' (i.e. GS1) in the minutes of the German Section's weekly meeting and from these one merely learns that 'arrangements were proceeding for obtaining the personnel'. Finally on 22 April it was revealed that, 'This station should primarily be an operational one, i.e. spreading rumours, etc. It would be a station voicing the grievances of the man in the street in Germany and should give special emphasis to the corruption of [Nazi] Party officials. Questions of personnel were being considered. It was agreed that the work of the new station would be of greater importance than D[awn] E[dge], i.e. the *Sender der Europäischen Revolution* since it would specialise in black propaganda.'[1]

This is the first reference to 'black' propaganda that I have found in the PWE documents and am inclined to suppose that at that time the adjective 'black' was meant to imply something rather shocking. On 6 May 1941 it was reported that 'Mr Sefton Delmer was choosing the necessary team,' also that 'the necessary accommodation would not be available for two or three weeks'. However, by Sunday 12 May 1941 Delmer and his wife Isabel were already installed at 'Larchfield' (LF), a modest villa at Aspley Guise, a few miles from Woburn Abbey and within a stone's throw of the house inhabited by Crossman and his socialists.

Rudolf Hess, Hitler's Deputy *Führer*, had unexpectedly parachuted into

Scotland during the night of 10–11 May. HM Government was so completely taken by surprise that no effective use was made of the dramatic event's propaganda possibilities. The BBC kept strictly within the limits of what it was allowed to say, which was very little. GS1 was not yet ready to broadcast so, greatly to Delmer's regret, was unable to make an immediate contribution to the confusion which prevailed in Germany. Hess, on his side, was saying nothing of the slightest interest.

Valentine Williams,[2] Leeper's deputy at Woburn, talked to Delmer about an ambitious plan to fake a complete page from the *Völkischer Beobachter*, the official Nazi Party newspaper. This was to contain a bogus account of current reactions in Germany to Herr Hess's flight and be planted on him, no doubt in order that it might persuade him to talk. However, in view of the technical difficulties involved they contented themselves with making a line reproduction of a couple of pages from the *VB*'s issue of 21 May, which was the latest to have arrived at Woburn, and inserting a brief forged paragraph in the bottom right-hand corner of one page. It read: 'Stories in the foreign press to the effect that Hess's wife and 4-year-old son are in the custody of the Gestapo are the malicious inventions of enemy propaganda. At the present time Frau Hess and her son are in a mental hospital in Thuringia.'

This was followed by a faked article alleged to have been published in the *Daily Telegraph* on Friday 20 June. Only three copies were printed under conditions of the greatest possible secrecy at a printing firm at Luton, not far from Woburn Abbey. This contained a *fictional* account of an interview which Hitler was alleged to have given on 23 May at Berchtesgaden to Mr John Cudahy, formerly US Ambassador in Belgium. Hitler's alleged remarks were not quoted, but merely what a Dr Paul Schmidt was supposed to have told Mr Cudahy.

> Dr Schmidt, head of the Foreign Office Press Department, repeated the request that he had made to me ... that under no circumstances should I mention the name of Rudolf Hess.
> 'If he hears a mention of that arrogant braggart Hess,' Schmidt had said, 'he flies into a rage and then there is no talking to him.' ... Schmidt, like other intimates of Hitler's circle, had taken great trouble in the talks I had with him to impress upon me that Hess was mentally deranged. Rudolf Hess, he said, had long been suffering from an incurable disease which had now affected his brain. His small son Wolf-Ruediger had inherited his father's malady and was now undergoing treatment in a mental institution.

My unexciting account of those probably time-wasting forgeries differs in every respect from Delmer's in *Black Boomerang*. The fakes were

**Landesgruppenleiter der AO. in Berlin**

Berlin, 20. Mai.

Die Hoheitsträger der Auslandsorganisation der NSDAP. aus 30 Ländern traten in der Reichshauptstadt zu einer Kriegstagung zusammen. Diese Tagung ersetzt die in Friedenszeiten in Stuttgart, der Stadt der Auslandsdeutschen, abgehaltenen Großkundgebungen der AO., bei denen Tausende von Auslandsdeutschen ihr Bekenntnis zur Heimat ablegten.

Auf dem ersten Arbeitstag sprach der Leiter der Auslandsorganisation der NSDAP., Gauleiter Bohle, über Haltung

und Tätigkeit des Auslandsdeutschtums im Kriege.

**Ministerpräsident Siebert beim Duce**

Rom. 20 Mai.

Der Duce empfing am Montagnachmittag im Palazzo Venezia den Präsidenten der Deutschen Akademie, Ministerpräsident Ludwig Siebert.

Der neue japanische Botschafter in Vichy. Der neue japanische Botschafter, Graf Kato, hat am Montagnachmittag dem Staatschef, Marschall Pétain, sein Beglaubigungsschreiben überreicht.

---

**Landesgruppenleiter der AO. in Berlin**

Berlin, 20. Mai.

Die Hoheitsträger der Auslandsorganisation der NSDAP. aus 30 Ländern traten in der Reichshauptstadt zu einer Kriegstagung zusammen. Diese Tagung ersetzt die in Friedenszeiten in Stuttgart, der Stadt der Auslandsdeutschen, abgehaltenen Großkundgebungen der AO., bei denen Tausende von Auslandsdeutschen ihr Bekenntnis zur Heimat ablegten.

Auf dem ersten Arbeitstag sprach der Leiter der Auslandsorganisation der NSDAP., Gauleiter Bohle, über Haltung

und Tätigkeit des Auslandsdeutschtums im Kriege.

**Der Angehörigen von Rudolf Heß**

Eine Richtigstellung

Berlin, 20. Mai.

Die Nationalsozialistische Parteikorrespondenz teilt mit: „ Berichte in ausländischen Blättern, denen zufolge die Gemahlin und der 4-jährige Sohn von Rudolf Heß sich im Gewahrsam der Geheimen Staatspolizei befänden, sind böswillige Erfindungen der feindlichen Propaganda.

Frau Heß ist zur Zeit mit ihrem Sohn in einer Nervenheilanstalt in Thüringen."

THE VOELKISCHER BEOBACHTER (21 MAY 1941)

*Above:* The bottom right-hand corner of a genuine page reproduced from a poor-quality microfilm made at Freiburg i. Br. in 1981

*Below:* The same area reproduced from the SO1 (PWE) forgery made at the *Luton News* plant late in May or early in June 1941. The text of the 'misinformation' we concocted for Rudolf Hess will be found on p. 103 above. The comparative clarity of the new *Fraktur* typesetting (nine lines, bottom right) will be noticed. However, the headline *Der Angehörigen von Rudolf Hess* should read *Die Angehörigen* etc. It is unlikely that Hess even bothered to read our 'offering'.

produced by the late John Gibbs at the *Luton News* printing department and what may well be the only surviving copies, which I have seen, were acquired by Mr Reginald Auckland, the founder of the Psywar Society (see page 20n. above). Indeed, I do not believe that Delmer can ever have seen a copy of the bogus *Völkischer Beobachter* because he, of all people, would have noticed and corrected one horrendously silly misprint.

Before I discuss the early history of GS1, I must refer to a document headed 'Decisions taken – week-end 24–25 May 1941', which was circulated to a few insiders at Woburn four days after GS1 began to broadcast. According to these minutes it had been decided that:

> Mr Crossman and Mr Delmer should in future be jointly in charge of the German Department, which should remain a unity, serving both the BBC and SO1; that Mr Delmer should be responsible to the Director [i.e. Reginald Leeper] for all the S[pecial] O[perations] work carried out by the Department [meaning black propaganda], while Mr Crossman should be responsible to the Ministry of Information for the BBC work. . . . It was, however, decided that Mr Crossman would continue to direct the D[awn] E[dge] Research Unit [i.e. the *Sender der Europäischen Revolution*] while, on the other hand, Mr Delmer would continue to broadcast on the BBC programme.[3]

My impression is that the fact that Crossman and Delmer were now co-equal chiefs of the German section was unknown outside a very small circle because it would have been impracticable to inform all and sundry that Delmer was in charge of certain very secret operations. When I arrived at PWE in November 1941 I supposed that Crossman was in sole charge of the German section. However, the new arrangement relieved Delmer of the necessity of having to report to Crossman. Delmer was so discreet that it was not until many years later that I learned that they were mutually antipathetic.

The minutes of that week-end meeting also contain another interesting item, namely that, 'The training of SO2 [the later SOE] propaganda agents should be done in conjunction with Mr Philby.' Kim Philby's transfer from SOE to the SIS did not take place until September 1941. During his Section D and SO2/SOE period (June 1940–September 1941) he was of no great use to his Russian friends whereas once in the SIS he was ideally placed to carry on his traitorous activities on their behalf.

According to a friend who had some knowledge of the much later inquest, 'Philby clearly did more damage during the 1941–5 period than has commonly been accepted. . . . Amongst other things he attempted to sabotage SIS operations and did his best to undermine (for the benefit of the Russians) the usefulness of SIS agents abroad. He did this by exposing them to capture by the Nazis.'

On 8 June 1941, when GS1 had been on the air for about a fortnight, Delmer defined the aims of his station in a memorandum for Leonard Ingrams which the latter forwarded to Leeper. According to Delmer:

1   The objective of L.F. [i.e. Larchfield, Delmer's house at Aspley Guise] is subversive. We want to spread disruptive and disturbing news among the Germans which will induce them to distrust their government and disobey it, not so much from high-minded political motives as from ordinary human weakness (for which, however, we shall be delighted to supply a high-minded political excuse).

2   We are making no attempt to build up a political following in Germany. We are not catering for idealists. Our politics are a stunt. We pretend we have an active following to whom we send news and instructions. The purpose of this is to provide ourselves with a platform from which to put over our stuff. We therefore make no attempt to provide our listeners with a political programme.

3   Our listeners are intended to feel they are eavesdropping on the private wireless of a secret organisation, whose members presumably know what the programme of the organisation is. What the listener learns of this programme he picks up by studying the news that we put over. He finds that we are anti-communists who once thought Hitler pretty good, fought alongside him in fact, but are now appalled at the corruption, godlessness, profiteering, place-hunting, selfishness, clique rivalries and Party-above-the-law system which the Party has. *Gustav Eins* is appalled at the left-wing swing in social politics which is coming under the aegis of the Hitler–Stalin hook-up [that sentence was written shortly before the Germans invaded Russia] and which is going to give the Party bureaucrats even greater power.

4   GS1, by its organisation, is able to get plenty of news from everywhere inside Hitler–Europe, news which all tends to show directly or (preferably) indirectly, that every man for himself is the axiom every intelligent German should be following.

5   We have already put over directly and by implication:

That *Wehrmacht* soldiers, the best element in the *Volk*, are being bumped off in *Himmelsfahrtkommandos* [i.e. suicide squads, latterly in Crete], while the SS Party-police are being given cushy jobs at home to make Germany safe for the Party.

That the Party's *Blockwarte* [Nazi small fry who kept an eye on the inhabitants of a small district or a few streets] are keeping back the news of soldiers' relatives killed in air-raids.

That it is ridiculous to fire-watch in factories while your own home is burning down through lack of a fire-watcher, and your children burned to death.

That while the Party bosses go off to Dubrovnik and other nice safe places for their holidays, they ask us ordinary Germans to stay at home and be bombed during our holidays.

And masses of stuff proving the corruption of the machine and the selfishness of its leaders. We concentrate our attacks on the lesser-known local leaders.

We shall be putting over a line on food-racketeering which is intended to make people buy and sell even more in the black markets than at present.

We have told of the passive sabotage the population of the Vorarlberg [in western Austria] have been carrying on against the unpopular Nazi leaders, in the hope that this may appeal to some of our listeners and be carried out by them.

The mysterious Herr Gustav Siegfried Eins, *der Chef* (The Boss), was the product of Delmer's imagination combined with memories of certain German prototypes whom he had met in his Berlin days. *Der Chef* was not a disillusioned Nazi satrap because his kind had never joined the Nazi Party. Before Hitler achieved power on 30 January 1933 he and those like him had thought of Hitler as an Austrian–Bavarian demagogue rather than as a serious statesman. It is uncertain whether they knew that President Hindenburg had once described the future *Führer* as a 'Bohemian Corporal'. However, Herr Eins and his friends soon became critical of much that was associated with the National Socialist 'revolution', its contempt for the rule of law as exemplified by the murder of General Schleicher at the time of the alleged Roehm *Putsch* in June 1934; the Party's ambivalent attitude to the Christian religion; the stories (which quickly circulated) of the secret 'prisons' where Party sadists tortured their captives and of the first concentration camps. Furthermore, they had no faith in the incredible gang of apparent nonentities, seldom seen without their Party uniforms, who had assumed power in the Reich: hard-faced men who appeared to be living in a far more impressive, even ostentatious, style than *der Chef* had ever permitted himself. There was a smell of corruption in the air and *der Chef* sniffed it with a mixture of contempt and dislike. Thus his prototype could have been a modest Prussian landowner, frugal in his habits and with a distinguished record as a soldier during the First World War. He was never a wholehearted supporter of the Weimar Republic (because he regretted the downfall of the monarchy) but was nevertheless an immensely patriotic German.

In the spring of 1941, when the concept of *der Chef* was evolved, there was no question of attacking Hitler personally because for the average German he still remained their wonder-working *Führer*, who had led and inspired the German army to achieve those impressively quick victories in Poland and France. Not only had Germany's unwillingly admitted defeat in 1918 been redeemed, but also the shameful Treaty of Versailles. Shortly before the beginning of the Russian campaign (22 June 1941) most Germans still implicitly believed that Hitler would give them a complete and final victory and make them literally the masters of the whole of Western Europe. It would then only remain to teach the obstinate British a well-deserved lesson.

*Der Chef*, then, in Delmer's view, would represent the voice of a hitherto unidentified opposition, namely patriotic Germans. They were not necessarily identical with the 'good Germans' in whose existence some at Woburn still believed, but others who had become increasingly concerned by the manner in which Germany was being run, *not* by the *Führer* but, rather, by his corrupt and self-seeking Party functionaries. The latter naturally included Himmler's SS.

However, early in May 1941 at Aspley Guise there was not even a 'voice' to represent *der Chef*. It is true that Corporal Peter Seckelmann, who was in a Pioneer Corps bomb disposal unit, had been identified but MI5 was taking time to 'vet' him. Furthermore, his 'adjutant' had not yet been found, let alone appointed. In those days every high-ranking Nazi was invariably accompanied by his adjutant, in uniform of course, who carried his briefcase and acted as a combination of personal assistant and messenger boy. The Corporal's adjutant was required to make the formal announcement that *der Chef* was about to broadcast.

It remains to explain why Herr Gustav Siegfried Eins was to be known as *der Chef*. During the 1932-3 election campaigns Delmer had often accompanied Hitler in the latter's privately chartered aircraft when the future *Führer* travelled the length and breadth of Germany on his marathon speech-making tours. Delmer had noticed that Hitler's inner circle invariably spoke of him as *der Chef*.

Thus, early in May 1941 GS1 lacked *der Chef*, the latter's adjutant and, most important, an audience in Germany and among the German armed forces outside the borders of the Reich. The audience would have to be created. I am uncertain whether or not Leonard Ingrams's research analysts at the Ministry of Economic Warfare had any clear idea of what proportion of the German civilian population could receive short-wave broadcasts. Apart from the fact that after the outbreak of war the Germans were forbidden to listen to enemy broadcasts, the inexpensive receivers of recent manufacture were the co-called *Volksempfänger* (people's radios), which were designed for the almost exclusive reception of the official *Reichssender*, the German equivalent of the BBC. On the other hand many members of the German armed forces had access to short-wave receivers.

Delmer hoped that it would not be too long before someone, who might be anywhere in Germany or enemy-occupied Europe (and soon in Russia), might be idly fiddling with a tuning dial and then listen, with bemused fascination, to a voice whose owner appeared to talk with impressive authority and offer all manner of astonishing revelations. Furthermore, this '*Chef*' chap, whoever he was, appeared to have excellent sources of information inside Germany. Surely the station could not be British because *der Chef* was apt to describe Mr Churchill as 'that flat-footed drunken old Jew'!

Members of all armed forces are great purveyors of what used to be known as 'shit-house gossip'. Delmer hoped, and not without justification, that *der Chef*'s intriguing stories – they were to combine a brilliant mixture of truth and falsehood – would soon be circulating in barrackrooms, canteens and even in such obscure villages as Peppenhochstadt near Uchfeld when young Sepp came home on leave. And since individuals were often posted from one unit to another, the good news would soon circulate that if one tuned in on the 30-metre waveband at exactly seven minutes before the hour one was liable to hear the most amazing stories. *Der Chef* appeared to be particularly well informed about the black market deals and sexual misdemeanours of quite obscure Party functionaries in every part of the Reich and, indeed, even in the Occupied Territories. In fact their names were often recognisable to listeners from the same locality.

Delmer recalled from his *Daily Express* days that the public denunciation of vice sold more copies because people liked to read about it. He was, too, fascinated by the concept of a sort of 'psychological judo', meaning that if he could demonstrate that many people on the home front were behaving in an antisocial manner (e.g. avoiding military service, fiddling extra rations, operating on the black market) and remaining undetected except of course by the omniscient *Chef*, then there was no reason why the military should not follow their example. Delmer's view was that clandestine propaganda as such was a complete waste of time unless it persuaded its recipient to '*do* something', e.g. sell *Wehrmacht* property to civilians, grab a handful of leave passes from the Battery Office and give them to friends in need ... indeed, almost anything was possible provided that one remained undetected. *Der Chef* never made such outrageous suggestions in specifically clear terms, but his accounts of the corruption which was endemic elsewhere was always liable to give his listeners a few good ideas.

Finally, *who* was *der Chef*, who appeared to be running a small, loosely-knit and apparently secret organisation with such excellent sources of information? A German *émigré*, known to both Frank Lynder (the Sergeant) and myself, who spent the whole of the war years in Sweden, later informed Lynder that he had written many of the broadcasts himself. Furthermore, there were rival 'authors' in both North and South America, although their claims can be ignored because they were utterly false.

The original GS1 team was very small. Leonard Ingrams produced the 'voice' which was to represent *der Chef* sometime in April 1941. It belonged to Corporal Peter Seckelmann, known at Aspley Guise as Paul Sanders or more often simply as 'the Corporal'. He was born in Berlin in 1902 and had earned his living there as a journalist and writer of detective stories. When he arrived in London in 1937 he started a small literary agency. In March 1940 he enlisted in the Auxiliary Military Pioneer Corps (later the Royal Pioneer Corps) and served in France. The AMPC was a dumping ground for the younger so-called 'enemy aliens' who wanted to serve in the British army, although most of its personnel was British. Whatever their nationality they did a lot of rough work as 'hewers of wood and drawers of water'. There were two Companies which included many German intellectuals who could have been more usefully employed elsewhere. In fact with the passage of time a more effective use was made of their intelligence and particular skills.

Delmer described his original encounter with the Corporal in *Black Boomerang*:

> When I first met him in April 1941 he was in a bomb disposal squad risking his life day after day to dig out the *Luftwaffe*'s time-bombs. Not content with this hazardous job, he had volunteered to be parachuted behind the German lines in one of the cloak-and-dagger commandos of SOE. That was how Leonard Ingrams had come across him, and Leonard passed him on to us. I liked him enormously, this man with the observant eyes and aristocratic hawk nose. His voice seemed to me just right for *der Chef* as I envisaged him, virile and resonant with just that slight trace of a German drawl which I had found so often in the speech of *Junker* officers of the Kaiser's guards regiments.

The Corporal arrived at Aspley Guise in mid-May 1941 and immediately began to rehearse the first GS1 scripts, which Delmer himself had written. Delmer was anxious to start the GS1 broadcasts without delay because Hess had already arrived in the country and opportunities were being lost. The Corporal had no previous microphone experience and at first found it difficult to adjust his voice for broadcasting purposes. He lacked confidence in himself and Delmer, who was not always the most patient of men, had to exercise a lot of patience to prepare his pupil for the first GS1 transmission, which took place on 23 May 1941. Unfortunately the adjutant was still missing – his vetting by the security people proved to be a slow business – and he does not appear to have arrived until the end of July.

Delmer's account of the first GS1 transmission in *Black Boomerang* was reconstructed from memory but no doubt represents a sufficiently accurate account of what was said.

*Der Chef*, in that first broadcast, began very soberly by announcing his call sign and then dictating some code signals.

'Here is *Gustav Siegfried Eins* ... here is *Gustav Siegfried Eins* ...' he repeated monotonously for about forty-five seconds. And then 'calling Gustav Siegfried 18, here is a message for Gustav Siegfried 18 ... calling Gustav Siegfried 18, a message for Gustav Siegfried 18 ...' There followed a message in a number code. It was not a high grade cypher and when broken and decoded by the monitors of the Reich Central Security Office, as it was bound to be, I reckoned it would produce quite an acceptable flurry in the Gestapo dove-cotes all over Germany. For the message said: 'Willy meet Jochen Friday row five parquet stalls second performance Union Theatre.' There were hundreds of Union Theatre cinemas all over Germany, and I fondly imagined leather-coated Gestapo thugs attending every one of them on the look-out for 'Willy' and 'Jochen'. The Gestapo with their radio detection instruments would be quick to fix our signal as coming from Britain. They could not ignore the possibility that Willy and Jochen were British agents, and that the message to them was genuine.

Then, at last, code dictation done, it was time for *der Chef* to launch into his special address. He was answering queries, he said, which had followed his last message. (Of course there had been no previous transmission, but I thought it a good idea for him to talk as if there had been several, in order to cause trouble for the German Security monitors. They would be accused of having missed them.) In that message, so the Chief let it be understood, he had warned that this obscenity of a dilettante Deputy *Führer* was about to do something idiotic and he ordered his comrades to lie low because of the witch-hunt which was bound to follow the fellow's folly. He had been off the air himself for a few days as a consequence. But now the coast was reasonably clear again and he could answer the queries.

'First, let's get this straight,' rasped *der Chef*, 'this fellow is by no means

111

the worst of the lot. He was a good comrade of ours in the days of the Free Corps. But like the rest of this clique of cranks, megalomaniacs, string-pullers and parlour Bolsheviks who call themselves our leaders, he simply has no nerves for a crisis. As soon as he learns a little of the darker side of the developments that lie ahead, what happens? He loses his head completely, packs himself a satchel full of hormone pills and a white flag, and flies off to throw himself and us on the mercy of that flat-footed bastard of a drunken old Jew Churchill. And he overlooks completely that he is the bearer of the Reich's most precious secrets, all of which the obscenity British will now suck out of him as easily as if he was a bottle of Berlin White-Beer.'

Dramatic pause.

'I must however deny one thing that some of the lickspittles in the *Führer* headquarters are putting around,' *der Chef* went on, 'namely that the fellow flew to Britain under orders of the *Führer*. That I am convinced is quite out of the question. The *Führer* would never have authorised a man with such an intimate knowledge of our operational plans to go into enemy country. And that is proved, too, by the drastic way the *Führer* is dealing with those who have, by their negligence, permitted this grave blow against the future of our fatherland to be stuck, namely the security snoops, who, if they had been anywhere near as good as they say they are, would have stopped the poor idiot in time. Unfortunately, however, that supreme obscenity of a Reich Security Chief, to get himself out of the mess, has seen fit to arrest a number of men – leaders of industry, leaders of the *Abwehr* – true German patriots, all of them, men of the deepest national devotion and fatherland-loyalty, men whose one fault was that they misjudged the nerve strength of this so-called deputy leader and placed before him, in the last days of April, the grave misgivings which, owing to the hedge of liars and lickspittle sycophants that surround him, they had been unable to place before the *Führer* himself.'

There followed a list of alleged arrestees. But the amazing thing is, that though we invented them all, several of the men we said had been arrested, it turned out later actually had been detained on suspicion of having been initiates of Hess's schemes.

A certain Dr Jahncke, for instance. I remembered having heard of him as the top espionage expert in Hess's office. So we put him on the list. And to my great pleasure, when I visited Germany after the war, I learned that the Chief had not misled his listeners. Nor did I have the slightest idea that when I got the Chief to talk of 'a grave crisis' and 'dangerous developments ahead' Germany was in fact on the verge of the most dangerous development since 1939 – Hitler's invasion of Russia.

The Chief finished off his transmission with an undramatic: 'That is all for now. I shall be repeating this – all being well – every hour at seven minutes to the full hour. *Immer sieben Minuten vor voll!*'

112

Delmer was greatly relieved when *der Chef*'s adjutant finally arrived in June 1941. The man whom he called Johannes Reinholz in *Black Boomerang* was a 'genuine German Conservative' who had worked with the right-wing opposition to Hitler. Not only was he able to write *der Chef*'s scripts, according to Delmer very efficiently, but was most convincing when, acting the role of adjutant, he dictated the bogus code messages before introducing *der Chef*. Delmer recalled that, 'His metallic baritone and his clipped accent, pregnant with generations of heel-clicking, goose-stepping, command-barking Pomeranian forebears gave just the right military tone to the station.' Furthermore, working with Reinholz gave the Corporal a confidence he had lacked when he was on his own with Delmer. In fact, according to Delmer, 'With every transmission he was growing more and more into the role of *der Chef*.' Finally, to Delmer's great delight the Corporal asked if he might be allowed to write a piece on his own. Delmer described it as 'a masterpiece, caustic, witty, even moving'.

It must be remembered that unlike the other RU transmissions *der Chef*'s broadcasts resembled small-scale theatrical productions and even minor details of presentation were discussed and rehearsed.

The small team (Delmer, the Corporal and Reinholz) which operated GS1 during the station's early months had plenty of imagination but insufficient first-class intelligence material upon which to base their often inspired inventions. The intelligence position improved with the arrival of Max Braun (known locally as Herr Simon), a Rhinelander who had been a prominent social-democrat politician and journalist at Saarbrücken, where Delmer had first met him. He had narrowly escaped being murdered by Nazi killers in December 1933 and hurriedly crossed the border into France. When the Saar territory was reunited with the Reich after the plebiscite in 1935 he was active in the heterogeneous group of German exiles in Paris who were doing their best to organise an *émigré* anti-Nazi opposition. There was a similar concentration of activity in Prague until it collapsed after the Germans dismembered Czechoslovakia in March 1939. Braun then came to England (date unknown) and was interned like so many other Germans on the Isle of Man. It is probable that he arrived at Aspley Guise in August 1941, because it was then that Delmer and his team moved to a larger house, namely 'The Rookery'. Max Braun, with the aid of his lawyer brother Heinrich, now took charge of the 'intelligence department', one of his tasks being to read even obscure local German newspapers with very great care. He also initiated the huge card index which contained the names and other particulars of thousands of Nazi Party functionaries and other Germans. It was to provide invaluable background material for the GS1 broadcasts and those of Delmer's later stations.

According to Delmer his best outside source of intelligence material was Leonard Ingrams at the Ministry of Economic Warfare because Ingrams had a sound instinct for the kind of material he could exploit. Valentine Williams, who was still Leeper's deputy at Woburn during the summer of 1941, was prepared to show Delmer the transcripts of material 'bugged' at the Combined Services Detailed Interrogation Centre but not without making rather a fuss about allowing him to read them. These CSDIC documents contained a record of just the kind of often harmless chatter which was to provide GS1 with literally priceless background material.

The resourceful Mr Delmer then proceeded to organise his own supply direct from the source. The Naval Intelligence Division at the Admiralty was the first of the major intelligence directorates to realise that Delmer could be a useful ally. Indeed, from 1943 onwards Delmer's organisation might fairly be described as one of NID's operational outposts. The RAF Intelligence Directorate began to employ him a little later, but Military (Army) Intelligence was slower off the mark.

When PWE's intelligence intake was completely reorganised at the end of 1942 with the establishment at Bush House of a large and no doubt grossly inflated Directorate of Political Warfare Intelligence, Delmer was able to ignore its existence. As Robert Walmsley remarked: 'In the case of Delmer's black unit, for instance, it was both unnecessary and unthinkable to have any intelligence independent of Delmer.'

On 6 June 1941 Delmer was summoned to a 'Big Meeting' at Woburn Abbey where he was surprised to see Dr Dalton (the Minister of Economic Warfare) Lord Vansittart (Chief Diplomatic Adviser to the Foreign Secretary) and certain other eminent persons whom he had not so far encountered. Reginald Leeper presided and announced that the Prime Minister had authorised him to acquaint them with a 'Most Secret' item of information, namely that Germany was expected to attack Russia on 22 June. The forecast was accurate. The regional directors were then invited to discuss the event's political warfare implications. Leeper asked Delmer how *der Chef* would react to the situation. Delmer recalled that he felt very nervous when he rose to his feet.

'*Der Chef*, Sir,' I said, 'is all for Hitler and this new war of his against the Bolsheviks. *Der Chef* will applaud and support the *Führer*'s decision.'
Lord Vansittart, sitting next to Leeper, roared with laughter, and

barked, 'Bravo, Delmer! Excellent!' But the rest of my colleagues knew nothing about *Gustav Siegfried Eins*. They stared at me in horrified incredulity.

'*Der Chef*,' I continued, 'will insist that the *Führer* combines his anti-Bolshevik crusade against Soviet Russia with a cleaning-up campaign against the Bolsheviks at home, the Bolsheviks that is, of the National Socialist German Workers Party. He calls them "*Die Parteikommune*", an interesting hybrid made up of "*Partei*" meaning the Nazi Party and "*Kommune*", the word by which the Nazis themselves used to refer to the Communists. *Der Chef* has collected a great deal of astonishing material about the *Parteikommune* which he will bring to the attention of the *Führer*.'

Now they all laughed. 'The Chief' had at least provided the comic relief of the meeting.

According to the minutes of the German Region's meeting on 24 June, two days after the German armies crossed the Soviet border, GS1 'found it easy to deal with the Russian crisis as it had adopted the line it had carefully prepared, enthusiastically welcoming the return of the Party to its straight, anti-Bolshevik policy, urging the rehabilitation of the Hess supporters and a drive against all Communists'.

The *Sender der Europäischen Revolution* team, on the other hand, found the situation altogether more complicated and was criticised for 'taking too narrow a sectarian line, particularly on the Russian issue. It was suggested that it should be advised to adopt a broader approach in its discussions, dropping the purely sectarian and certain subtle ideological issues.'

While the SER's *Politologen* were inclined to be become confused by their doctrinal doubts, Delmer and Co. were soon mildly criticised for being too 'sensational'. It is conceivable that what was said to be sensational was at the same time extremely vulgar. According to a F & CO document it was recorded that:

A year after GS1 had been broadcasting the Secretary of PWE was greeted by Sir Stafford Cripps, then Lord Privy Seal, with the words, 'I am sorry that you belong to that beastly pornographic organisation', and stated that he intended to take up the matter of GS1 with the Secretary of State for Foreign Affairs or if necessary with the Cabinet. 'To what sort of audience could it possibly appeal?' demanded Sir Stafford. 'Only to the thug section of the Nazi Party who are no use to us anyway.' In Sir Stafford's opinion our RUs should concentrate on giving messages of hope and sympathy to the 'Good Germans' on whom we should rely to rebuild Germany after the Nazis were defeated.

Sir Stafford had been outraged by *der Chef's* lurid account of a German admiral's orgy with his mistress and four sailors. So far the only source for this detailed information is the entry for 16 June 1942 in the second volume of Sir Robert Bruce Lockhart's diaries (1981). Since Cripps was unlikely to receive GS1 scripts with his morning mail I wondered how he knew about *der Chef's* story until I recalled a passage in Delmer's *Black Boomerang* (page 252). Crossman's 'European Socialists', who could listen to the GS1 broadcasts at their house at Aspley Guise, had made an English translation 'that outdid even the original' and sent it to Sir Stafford. Lockhart took the puritan Lord Privy Seal out to lunch and saved the situation.

Delmer mentioned in an article he wrote for *The Times Literary Supplement* many years later (21 January 1972) that he used pornography merely to attract an audience because PWE's 'Marxist station under the benevolent supervision of my colleague Dick Crossman, after months of broadcasting had no audience in Germany, not anyhow so far as PWE had been able to ascertain. . . . The recipe was an immediate success. One unfortunate young German woman, denounced by the *Chef* for having insulted the honour of the army by using an officer's steel helmet as a chamber pot during a sexual orgy (our intelligence claimed she was an informant of the Gestapo) is still angry with me today [1962] because of the stream of telephone calls she received from listeners denouncing her in the harshest terms.' Delmer explained that with the progress of the war and the increasing evidence of the growing number of the *Chef*'s listeners he reduced the pornography in his output to minimal proportions. Delmer continued:

> But here is the point I am trying to make: we did not use pornography because we thought it would have a deleterious effect on our German listeners. We used it simply for its listener appeal – just as some popular newspapers use scabrous stories and pictures of scantily-clad models to increase their circulation. And we took great care not to let it seem that the *Chef* himself enjoyed the bawdy details of what he revealed about the licentious sexual excesses of Hitler's 'élite'. He never sniggered over them. His denunciations were filled with the indignation and horror of a Salvation Army evangelist. He was a puritan diehard of the old Prussian army revolted by the depravity and corruption of the party functionaries and determined to expose and chastise them. Never, never did he let on that he was retailing these salty scandals to make his listeners eager to listen to his next harangue, which in all probability would be completely free of any pornography.
>
> I took an enormous amount of trouble over the *Chef*'s erotica and devoted many hours of patient research to finding ever new forms of sexual depravity to attribute to our victims in the Hitler machine. Professor Magnus Hirschfeld, on whose works, incinerated during the famous burn-

ing of the books in 1933, I depended for much detail, would I am sure have welcomed the *Chef*'s broadcasts as a sweet revenge. We also adopted the technique of the Austrian creator of an equivalent to Fanny Hill, a young woman with a name something like Mitzi Mutzenbacher. This Austrian author never allowed his heroine to consummate her erotic adventures. The *Chef*, too, was always careful to leave the end to his listeners' imagination.

Stray evidence received at Woburn indicates that many who listened to GS1 in Germany supposed that the station was located inside their own country. In September 1941 the American Embassy in Berlin reported to Washington:

The illegal broadcasting station Siegfried 1, supposedly transmitting inside Germany, operates daily on the 31.5-metre band taking to the air at 7 minutes to the hour. Using violent and unbelievably obscene language, this station criticises the actions of the Party and certain Party-favoured officers, especially the SS. Superficially it is violently patriotic and is supposed by many German officers to be supported by the German *Wehrmacht* in secret. A very large number of Germans listen to this station, and often names, dates and addresses are given in such detail that it may be assumed that the statements could be quickly discredited if no background existed.

When there is no air-raid warning, the station is heavily interfered with, but during alarms it comes in very clearly. Various explanations are given as to the ability of this station to continue operating. The most reasonable is that it is worked automatically with records and has been found several times in odd places wholly unattended. When found and destroyed a similar set is put up elsewhere. The station has been operating for about four months.[4]

GS1 even had its admirers in Dr Goebbels's Propaganda Ministry – 'good Germans', no doubt, although Sir Stafford Cripps would not have considered them as such. In this context Delmer received some interesting evidence of reception from SOE.

A German who worked in the Propaganda Ministry was having a drink in a bar in neutral Stockholm and finding himself standing next to an obvious Englishman spoke to him. 'Ach,' he said, 'even the anti-Nazi propaganda is done better by the Germans themselves than by the British. I tell you: just outside Berlin there is a man with a wireless station, who is called *der Chef* . . . Everybody listens to him. He has the support of high army officers and he reveals scandals about the Party which are most effective. Listen, I tell you some good advice. The British

Secret Service ought to get in touch with the *Chef* of GS1 and see whether they could not come to an understanding with him.'

If this man supposed that the GS1 transmitter was operating 'just outside Berlin' there were many other equally attractive hypotheses. *Der Chef* enjoyed teasing his German listeners about their topographical ignorance. Thus on 20 July 1943 he exclaimed:

> First we were a Russian transmitter then, when we had not been heard for a week, we had come crashing down on the pavement in the Friedrichstrasse [the RAF was presumably to blame] and broken our collective necks. Then later the arseholes located us in a furniture van in Holland and we were simultaneously traced to a ship off the Norwegian coast. Next, according to Dr Goebbels, we were in Scotland. It won't be long before I'm with the flat-footed Jews in American North Africa.[5]

A number of documents indicate what *der Chef* was saying at various times. It must be emphasised that certain themes and variations, such as corruption on the home front, were repeated time and again because GS1 did not have a permanent audience whose members could be depended upon to listen to the station night after night.

On 1 July 1941 it was reported that GS1 had been advising people to send parcels rather than letters to relatives who were serving on the Russian front, but did not explain why they should do this. Delmer's guess was that having to open all those parcels would greatly increase the work of the censors. Herr Eins also encouraged 'the purging of Communist elements in Germany' and suggested that the purge was, in fact, being used by the 'Party Commune' to remove those who were its opponents. The *Partei Kommune* was GS1's blanket expression for the Nazi Party *Apparat*, meaning the vast number of individuals who were apparently exempt from military service and interfered with the life and liberties of ordinary, decent patriotic Germans.

On 15 July it was stated in a brief policy report that GS1, 'taking account of the slow progress of the Russian war and the increasing Allied air offensive against western Germany, will increase its attacks on the Party and Party corruption for hindering Germany's war effort and increase its emphasis on Hitler's personal responsibility for not taking a stronger line against internal corruption'.

On 31 July 1941 Delmer was able to report that GS1 had been quoted on Moscow Radio, furthermore, 'Russia has started a black station, broadcasting three times a week in direct imitation of *Gustav Siegfried Eins*. The station uses the character of a Nazi called Hans Weber.'

In November *der Chef* provided a heartrending account of his recent visit to Aachen and described the bomb damage caused by Allied air attacks. Several times he repeated with considerable emphasis, 'London must be bombed, London *must* be bombed!' The object of this broadcast was to draw attention to (or perhaps even exaggerate) the damage done at Aachen and to stress that the *Luftwaffe* was not bombing London. In any case the last major attack on London had been on 10–11 May 1941. The main *Luftwaffe* bombing force was then transferred to airfields close to the Russian border and London was left in peace until 27 July when there was a relatively small raid. I cannot recall any particularly memorable German *Luftwaffe* attacks on London until January 1943 and these were nothing like as heavy as those experienced in 1940–1.

A memorandum dated 15 November 1941 mentioned that *der Chef* was doing his best to sow distrust of the Italians in general and more particularly of the many Italian workers who were already in Germany. According to GS1 the latter were nobly comforting the young German *Hausfrauen* whose husbands were fighting for the *Führer* on the Russian front where, incidentally, the temperature was already becoming disagreeably cold. Thus the generals who were responsible for supplying the armies in the east with winter clothing were accused, always by name, of having miserably failed in their duty. In any case many German civilians had a good deal about which to complain. The answer? 'Write to the *Führer* and *he* will put matters right!'

My own belief is that Delmer knew in advance about the (ultimately unsuccessful) Dieppe raid which was being planned for 19 August 1942. Why else should he have sent the following note to Leeper on 15 August:

> The *Chef* is paying a visit to France next week. He will carry on his normal campaigns with special reference to the problems of Occupied France and to the German troops, airmen and sailors there. The French factories and the Germans exploiting them will also come in for a share of the publicity.... He will pour scorn on the SS for accepting the British invasion phantom as an excuse for getting out of the firing line in the East. A new departure will be that the *Chef* will broadcast from another transmitter called Gustav Siegfried 5, stationed on the 49-metre band, which will be relayed by *Gustav Siegfried Eins*, thus giving the impression of a widespread organisation and at the same time reaching listeners whom transmissions on the 31-metre band do not reach now and setting a new problem for the jammers.

On 20 August, the day after the Dieppe raid, he informed Leeper that *der Chef* 'has just started on a tour of the Western Occupied Territories.

119

He narrowly escaped capture in the recent Commando raid. A warning might have been given to him by his French colleagues.' Perhaps he now had a fictitious liaison office at Paris?

On 26 September Leeper was informed that 'GS1 has started to run a new and sinister villain in the shape of Karl Brandt, who is responsible to the *Führer* for the allocation of medical supplies between the army and civilians, and is said to have a sinister personal influence over him.' Dr Karl Brandt did rather more than settle the destination of medical supplies. Since 1 September 1939 he had been involved in the execution of Hitler's euthanasia plans, i.e. the liquidation of the inmates of psychiatric hospitals and others who were not expected to survive for long. This particular *Aktion* was a closely guarded State Secret. On 1 October 1940 Martin Bormann noted: '30,000 already dealt with, a further 100,000–120,000 due. The circle of those in the know to be kept very small.'

According to the same document, 'Another main theme of GS1 has been the *Eindeutschung* [i.e. Germanisation] of people from the East to replace the thinned-out ranks of German nationals.' The losses on the Russian front had already been depressingly large. Four months later a further 300,000 capitulated at Stalingrad.

Early in September *der Chef* 'attacked the encouragement of illegitimacy, which was destroying the "holy German family", and illustrated this by the story of the bastard of an SS man being attributed to a soldier killed on the eastern front'. Next: 'An operational script, calculated to encourage the effects of overwork, ostensibly insisted that Germans should work until they dropped. A similar script about epidemics and air-raids, under the cover of useful hygiene tips, gave information likely to cause anxiety and confusion among the health services.'

Delmer was able to make some interesting predictions on the basis of the painstaking analysis of intelligence material. Thus on 13 October 1942 he mentioned in a memorandum to Leeper that he would like to 'point out some rather pleasing coincidences which seem to show that *der Chef* is talking on the right lines':

> On 26 July he [*der Chef*] announced that on 1 October a big new scheme was to be put into operation for the mobilisation of additional housing space by forcing everyone to share such accommodation as they had with others and obliging single persons who were occupying flats to move into barracks, thus releasing their flats for others with families.
> He protested against the use of flats and residential dwellings by Party

Offices and other administrative organisations such as the 'Permanent Cake Industry', the 'Powdered Ice Litigation Industry' etc. The object of this story was to undermine the morale of troops about conditions at home and to spread a rumour which would make women hesitate to send their children away from home and go to work in factories.

Today comes the announcement that the *Reichsmarschall* [i.e. Goering] has issued a decree on the rationing of housing space to take effect from 1 November – we were just one month late. On 14 September the *Reichsmarschall* had already decreed that no more residential dwellings should be converted into offices and ordered that such as had been converted into offices already should be reconverted into residential dwellings.

It was the final paragraph of this memorandum which interested me: 'We invented our line partly on the general estimate of the housing situation [probably made by Leonard Ingrams's people at MEW] and partly on the CX report containing photographs of the name plates of government offices outside blocks of Berlin flats.' The 'CX report' came from the Secret Intelligence Service and this is the only evidence I have found which indicates that Delmer was supplied with SIS material. The source was probably the Ministry of Economic Warfare.

In October 1942 *der Chef* reported on the alleged desertions of SS troops in France and proposed that the Vichy authorities who had helped them to escape should be dealt with conclusively. He also continued to exhibit considerable sympathy for Field Marshal Fedor von Bock, Commander of the Army Group South in Russia until Hitler sacked him on 15 July. *Der Chef* found it particularly scandalous that the Gestapo had subsequently ransacked von Bock's daughter's house. That, at least, was *his* story.

GS1's theme during the week before the Allied North African landings ('Torch', 7–8 November 1942) was that the German troops' retreat in the western desert was 'due to ambitious plans on Rommel's part, carried out by him against the opposition of maturer generals and doomed to defeat from the start'.

During January 1943 GS1 broadcast 'stories' on the following lines for the information of German troops who were serving outside the borders of the Reich:

In spite of the manpower shortage there are still $3\frac{1}{2}$ million Party officials at home or in cushy jobs in France, Belgium, Holland, Norway, etc. They are calling up diabetics as there is insufficient insulin for civilians. Foreign workers are a menace to Germany's health and have imported venereal diseases. That is why one third of the 36,000 illegitimate babies born to

German girls by foreigners last year were born blind. French doctors deliberately send infected men to [work in] Germany so that they can pass on their diseases. Large factory owners in all danger areas have had a circular informing them that for every 100 tons of bombs dropped in their district they must lower their workers' wages by 5 Pfg. an hour. This is because of the impossibility of replacing consumption goods after air-raids.

Father Robert Graham, SJ, kindly sent me several transcripts of GS1 broadcasts which he had found in the US National Archives. They had been translated, probably very hurriedly, into illiterate English and when the monitor did not understand a particular German word or the transmission was inaudible he made an intelligent guess. When reading them, and mentally translating them back into German, I was able to visualise *der Chef* speaking as though to a few close friends, often inclined to ramble on a little, but grimly exposing a succession of scandals and evidence of corruption; he probably seldom raised his voice or became excited, but certainly did not disguise his irritation and contempt for the Party Commune and all the other arseholes (his typical word, not mine!) who were leading Germany in the direction of inevitable defeat. In spite of a growing abundance of authentic intelligence material (names and addresses, etc.) a great deal of intelligent invention was clearly required as well, and my own impression is that these inventions sounded plausible.

A number of representative and mostly condensed extracts follow.

*30 March 1943:* Employing his notorious methods the Gestapo-King [Himmler] has been collecting material for years and years which he could use as his trump card against [Admiral] Canaris [*Abwehr* chief]. Himmler thinks that the time has now come, because Canaris demanded that charges of high treason should be laid against SS *Hauptsturmführer* Schultze and Himmler means to prevent them.

The Intelligence Service has unequivocal proof that the said Richard Schultze, one of the four personal aides with whom Himmler has surrounded the *Führer*, works for the enemy and smuggles news from the *Führer*'s headquarters abroad. It has come to the *Abwehr*'s attention that a certain Frau Moeckl (M-O-E-C-K-L), who sits in Ambassador Schleier's ante-room in Paris in the rue de Lille, continuously receives antique gold pocket watches via diplomatic pouch from Schultze, which she sends to Switzerland, also by diplomatic pouch, ostensibly to have them repaired.

The *Abwehr* discovered that these beautiful old watches contained micro-photographs on which Schultze conveyed information, via Frau Moeckl, to the enemy agent Lucienne Ostranger, rue de Rome 6 at Geneva.

In order to protect his treasonable SS arsehole Schultze and to avoid a major scandal, Herr Himmler found it appropriate to topple Canaris before the latter could get the first blow in.

Next Canaris was accused of having silently consented to one of his *Abwehr* men smuggling money and jewels abroad via diplomatic pouch for some Polish Jews. The alleged smuggler was hanged and General Zeitzler decided that in the future all the *Abwehr*'s diplomatic mail must be checked by Himmler's Security Service.

This is *Gustav Siegfried Eins*. This is *Gustav Siegfried Eins*. The Chief has been your speaker. We return every hour until 5 am.

Frau Moeckl probably existed, but the rest was almost certainly invented. The central theme was corruption and entirely correct hints at rivalry between Canaris's *Abwehr* and Himmler's *Sicherheitsdienst* (Security Service).

On 14 September 1943 *der Chef* turned his attention to current *Luftwaffe* scandals. In this instance the principal characters in the cast were General Adolf Galland, who commanded the *Luftwaffe*'s fighter arm, and Baron Guenther von Malzahn, the highly-decorated commanding officer of No. 53 Fighter Squadron. The story was that von Malzahn had been forced by Galland to admit to cowardice in the face of the enemy.

The only suitable reply to Galland's order would have been a couple of clouts on the inflated Galland's nose. That hasn't happened yet, but it will come if we continue to tolerate a pitiful [Nazi] *Kommune* favourite like this Galland, this shit-head who gave a man like Malzahn such a disgusting order. Furthermore, an order which can only be described as a typical example of Bolshevik psychology, such as only Moscow's candidates for the leadership of the *Kommune* increasingly display. Galland is one of them.

[At this point another voice read the text of Galland's written order to Malzahn. According to GS1 Galland wrote]:

'I have noted with surprise that your squadron's aircraft have latterly shown a regrettable lack of fighting spirit or courage. Not only does the number of [enemy] aircraft destroyed remain far below my expectations, but cases have been reported to me where your fighter pilots, in spite of the order to attack, have evaded the enemy formations in combat or prematurely broken off the attack. I order that the enemy must always be attacked, and that at least one enemy aircraft must be shot down even when the enemy formation is four times larger than our own. . . . If the number of aircraft destroyed by your squadron does not show a substantial improvement you will be relieved of your command and transferred with your pilots to the Russian front.' (Signed: Galland, Major-General.)

123

*Der Chef* now added his own commentary. In spite of the fact that the enemy in Italy had four or five times as many aircraft the *Luftwaffe* was failing to provide even a semblance of air-cover for the German infantry. German pilots who returned to their airfields safe and sound would have to prove that they had not been guilty of cowardice or face a court martial. And what about Sergeant Patasch of No. 2 squadron?

He took off in his ME 109 F having already flown 150 hours in it without an overhaul. After five minutes in the air he landed because the engine shook so much that he could no longer read his instruments. He was arrested as soon as he climbed out and faced a court martial.

Flight Engineer Holperich appeared as a witness for the defence and said that if anybody deserved punishment it was not the accused but those who sent men like Patasch aloft in unserviced aircraft. In fact Patasch's machine was no longer even serviceable, he said, and if Patasch had continued to fly it he wouldn't be alive. Patasch was forced to fly again but without much confidence in his aircraft . . . and didn't return.

As for General Galland, *der Chef* continued:

He's the kind of *Kommune* shit-bag who has brought us where we are today . . . It's these *Kommune* vultures, men with his type of mentality, who have lost the war for us – the very war we went into with the most justifiable hopes, the best weapons, the biggest superiority in armaments and a fanatical will to sacrifice ourselves.

Our entire air-defence aircraft, flying personnel, fuel, *Flak* [anti-aircraft guns], have all been generously thrown into the Mediterranean in order to defend the traitor country Italy. Italy has had it, our air defences have been shot to hell. The enemy can destroy our industry in the entire Reich from Italy and England. I'll say it again. It's those [Nazi] shits who have lost the war for us . . . It's the shitters who stand behind Heinrich Himmler in his plot to betray us and make our Fatherland a branch of the United States of Soviet North Europe.

I'll say it again. If one of the conditions imposed upon us is that we throw out these crappers and establish a [constitutional state?] which rests on our old traditions; if that is a prerequisite for peace and for an understanding with the nations of the West and defending our country against the menace of the East – then, in God's name, let's get on with it. With that kind of deal nothing is lost.

GS1's objective? To destroy confidence in the *Luftwaffe*'s leadership. Sergeant Patasch had undoubtedly been shot down and his body identified by the British. With luck one of his friends or even his parents might have heard the broadcast.

On 5 October 1943 *der Chef* adumbrated upon the activities of Mr Arpad Plesch, the Hungarian-born financier, who died at the ripe old age of eighty-five in 1974 and whose remains were interred in Monte Carlo Cathedral. It is likely that Leonard Ingrams and the Ministry of Economic Warfare's files supplied some of the Plesch material for this broadcast, and what was not precisely known was invented. The story was that Plesch was acting for a small group of members of the Nazi *Kommune* who were illicitly exporting huge sums of foreign currency. Plesch invested the money in his own Endowment Fund St Alberto at Lausanne for them. A member of the Office for Foreign Trade already had thirty-six million Swiss francs to his credit in Herr Plesch's 'Fund'.

*Der Chef*, however, mainly dealt with the less impressive defalcations of Herr Party Comrade Franz Metzger, of Hohenzollernstrasse 13 – the monitor missed the place name – in the Rhineland. The older housewives at H— would remember Franz Metzger's grocery store but now he was in the gun-barrel manufacturing business, and furthermore supplied barrels which were highly unreliable. According to *der Chef*, 'Hardly a day goes by without one of Herr Metzger's shit-barrels bursting at some place on the front. In other words every day German soldiers die, sometimes one, sometimes two, sometimes even the whole gun crew, because a faulty shell bursts prematurely in the barrel and the bursting gun-barrel knocks everybody's head off or tears his guts to pieces.'

The story of how and why Herr Metzger's barrels burst with such horrible frequency was then developed with a wealth of technical details (e.g. shortage of the right metal alloys for casting them) and was continued with an account of his corrupt relationships with a whole row of 'protectors' in the armaments industry and above all the Party. 'They all stick together like tar and feathers so that the Metzgers grow fat, regardless of whether or not a few chaps lose their lives at the front because of burst barrels.' However, in spite of the fact that Party Comrade Metzger had more than a million Swiss francs lodged in the care of Herr Plesch, he would never see them again. 'He should have remained in the grocery business. The remaining clients of the charitable Israelite in Lausanne should, however, start putting their wireless earphones on – their turn will come next!' – meaning exposure by *der Chef*.

*Der Chef* continued to broadcast his exhortations and inventions until 18 November 1943 when Delmer decided that the time had come to employ the Corporal's talents, which had matured, in another capacity. So it was necessary for Herr Gustav Siegfried Eins to disappear. The solution was very simple: the Gestapo had at last tracked him down. Listeners in Germany heard a burst of machine-gun fire and the

125

triumphant cry, 'Got you, you swine!' Unfortunately it had been forgotten that the recording was due to be broadcast again an hour later, so *der Chef* died twice.

An annotated anthology of GS1 broadcasts would make fascinating reading. For instance, what is one to make of the report dated 6 September 1942 which suavely revealed that *der Chef* had been discussing 'Ursula von Hohenlohe and her Berlin orgies'? Very little, I suppose, except for the hypothesis that the well-thumbed copy of Krafft-Ebbing's *Sexualia Psychopathia* in that extraordinary house at Aspley Guise had been consulted.

1 FO 898/4

2 Valentine Williams, who had been a pre-war founder member of Department EH, was soon to disappear from the Woburn scene. At the end of July 1941 he was 'exiled' to New York with a somewhat vague Charter as the Department's representative at the future SOE's local office. At that time Woburn was still SO1 and 'Baker Street' SO2. My hypothesis is that Leeper wanted him out of the way when the formation of PWE was being discussed. Mr Williams surfaced again in London in 1942; he interviewed Malcolm Muggeridge when the latter was recruited by the SIS. (See the second volume of Muggeridge's autobiography *The Infernal Grove*, 1973.) When I arrived in November 1941 David Bowes-Lyon was Leeper's deputy at Woburn with a specific responsibility for black operations. Sir Duncan Wilson, who succeeded Crossman as head of PWE's German Region, told me in 1978 that Bowes-Lyon had come from MEW, so could have been Dr Dalton's nominee although Leonard Ingrams was undoubtedly consulted.

3 FO 898/4

4 F & CO document

5 The quotation is from a US Federal Communications Commission monitoring report. On 16 May 1943 Walter Adams, writing as a member of the British Political Warfare Mission from the British Embassy at Washington, complained to PWE London that the FCC's monitoring reports of our black stations, GS1 and the new short-wave 'Atlantik' one in particular, were receiving publicity in the American press. Adams hoped that the FCC could be persuaded 'not to circulate, except to an extremely limited number of recipients, the monitoring of any clandestine stations', but was not very optimistic. 'I suspect that a lot of this monitoring is, in fact, not done within the US but transmitted to FCC here by their representatives in the UK.' (FO 898/69) Since GS1, etc. could not be heard in London I imagine that the monitoring was, in fact, done in the USA.

# 12

# GS1 – Evidence of Reception

It is unfortunate that what were called 'come-backs', meaning authentic evidence of the reception of the GS1 and *Wehrmachtsender Nord* broadcasts by listeners inside Germany or by the German armed forces outside its borders, were never systematically collected and analysed. The reason was that the 'come-backs' referred to yesterday's news, whereas everybody concerned was busy preparing the next programme for recording. The following extracts are from a paper headed 'Evidence of RU Reception' which Leeper wrote on 1 January 1943. It is significant that he mentioned that 'the first real flow of reactions to GS1 did not come in until four or five months after it started', meaning not until the autumn of 1941.

The two countries from which we receive most evidence are Germany and France – Germany largely through prisoners of war, France through Frenchmen who have reached this country. Evidence from Holland and Belgium is from people who have escaped from those countries.

This is the direct evidence. The indirect form is more difficult to check, as it would require considerable additional staff. Enemy and quisling Governments are very chary of referring to our stations, but a study of the European press and broadcasting has frequently shown that answers have been given, without mentioning the source, to damaging rumours put out by our RUs. As those who study the press in PWE are not acquainted with the RU scripts, and as it would require a separate staff to read the press with this in view, evidence of this kind has not been fully sifted. In many ways these forced denials are the best proof of all that the damaging rumour has had its effect.

Under the sub-heading, 'Germany: Direct Evidence', Leeper wrote:

As regards the quality and make-up of the programmes and their acceptability in Germany, we have far more direct evidence about GS1 than any of our other programmes. It should be said without prejudice to the merits of 'the Chief' that there are certain factors in his favour. He has had a longer time in which to establish himself. He broadcasts the sort of story – interesting inside

127

news of military events or Party scandal – which spreads well, which is cast in a form easy to pass on, and which is most likely to interest the comparatively cultivated audience from which most of our evidence is derived.

Direct evidence that GS1 is heard and appreciated is considerable. Since it started in May 1941 there have been at least fifty direct reactions coming from Germany itself, from sources who have just left Germany and from members of the German armed forces serving abroad. Recent and very reliable evidence shows that 'the Chief' is discussed in the highest army circles. The great majority of our sources think that GS1 is actually in Germany. Those who are doubtful, including some well-informed prisoners of war, do not regard it as the less interesting for that, but credit 'the Chief' with well-placed news sources in Germany. Nor does the direct exposure of the station in the German newspaper *Das Reich*, some eight months ago, seem to have lessened its prestige. A Swedish newspaper, for instance, has recently quoted an exclusive story of GS1 as coming from a German source.

*Wehrmachtsender Nord:* We have good evidence from Stockholm that German soldiers in Norway are listening to this programme. [Hence the 'skip distance' problem referred to above had been solved.] Stockholm newspaper correspondents have also picked it up and reported it simply as a 'German radio station in Norway'. A Swiss who has just returned from Berlin reported that the people there were puzzled as to how the British managed to put out on the 40-metre band the *Reichsprogramme* mixed up with anti-Nazi propaganda, and the theory was that the authorities had omitted to cut some cable. If, as is probable, this is a reference to the *Wehrmachtsender Nord*, it shows that it has some listeners in Berlin even if they do not believe it to be a genuine German station. While there is practically no mention of the actual name of this programme, we have evidence that rumours put out by the *Wehrmachtsender* are circulating.

*Indirect evidence:* The official German *Mitteilungen für die Truppe*, which is the special organ of the army propaganda authorities [I faked a number of these at one time or another], has asked officers to combat rumours put out by the *Schwarzsender* [i.e. black station] and cited as nefarious examples the very type of rumour most frequently put out by the German RU. German newspapers have recently referred more than once to the enemy spreading 'most foolish but often most realistically constructed rumours' intended for 'the small grumbler' and 'hours of weakness'.

Evidence of active reaction by the German public to a rumour put out by GS1 came from the Danzig and Schleswig newspapers, both of which reported a run on clothing shops in response to rumours of an impending cancellation of clothing cards owing to a large-scale forgery.

There are frequent allusions to GS1 in the clearly incomplete PWE 'Evidence of Reception' files at the Public Record Office. Since these anecdotes tend to be repetitious I will merely refer to the reports dated July and October 1943. According to the first of them:

> A striking tribute to the size of GS's audience in Germany comes from Hans Fritzsche who on two occasions this month has found it necessary to denounce GS as a British station, and to refute its stories. On 17 July he denied the *Chef*'s statement that 47,283 persons in Germany were getting diplomatic rations: 'Every wide-awake child in the Reich knows there is only one set of rations for all Reich citizens, high or low.' He returned to the charge on 25 July and indignantly refuted the *Chef*'s accusation, made on 20 July, that Fritzsche himself enjoyed freedom from ration restrictions and, if he wanted to know the scale of rations for the ordinary German citizen, had to send his secretary to the Propaganda Ministry archives to find out.

Hans Fritzsche was a particularly well-known radio commentator and before he became fully occupied with GS1 Delmer used to broadcast impromptu answers to Fritzsche's broadcasts on the 'white' BBC. We know what *der Chef* said about Fritzsche's alleged access to 'diplomatic rations' because a monitored transcript of the GS1 broadcast of 20 July 1943 exists in the US National Archives. The document states that there was 'heavy static' that evening. The monitor's task probably wasn't easy and Mr Levitch, who provided the English translation, clearly did not take much trouble. What follows is a rough English prose version of the original German text.

> If one calls these *Kommune* shits 'arseholes' or home-grown Bolsheviks, if one exposes them as being traitors to the nation and parasites, if one tells them that by their mismanagement and self-seeking, they negate the sacrifices being made on the [Russian] front, it doesn't penetrate their thick skins.
>
> If one alludes to their feeding troughs and threatens them with public exposure to the effect that they have openly founded a Gluttons' Association in the midst of our famished and starving nation, they sweat with fear and try to defend their war profiteers' fortress.

*Der Chef*'s line was that the members of this privileged gastronomic association, 47,283 of them, were all receiving special ration cards entitling them to four times the amount of nourishment granted to workers in heavy industry. This theme, including some choice variations, almost exclusively occupied *der Chef*'s attention that evening. Many Germans enjoyed listening to him because they were never quite sure what he would say next. He continued to berate Herr Fritzsche who, he said, was able to obtain unlimited supplies of the emergency ration cards issued to citizens who were temporarily on holiday or away from home.

Perhaps this fact is not known to every clever child in the Reich, but the brethren in the Food Office know it. And Mr Schwerter there knows it too because he has always given Mr Ministerialdirektor Fritzsche and his friends as many emergency ration cards as they want, and with them they can get as much to eat as they wish, wherever they wish and whenever they wish. These cards have one great advantage, because Herr Fritzsche's purchases don't attract any particular attention in a shop. So what he buys is over and above his special rations.

He needs them, does Mr Hunger Artist Fritzsche. He fills his ministerial propaganda belly at noon at the Masurenallee [the Reich's broadcasting centre in Berlin], in the evening at the *Haus der Flieger* [*Luftwaffe* airmen's club, probably for 'Officers only'] and at home again at night.

*Der Chef* then referred to 1942 when Fritzsche apparently served for a brief period on the Russian front, presumably in one of the propaganda units.

The comrades got to know him all right when the patriotic propaganda pisser Fritzsche showed up in SS uniform to do his stint of front service ... with his own car and with his own driver. But he didn't do like the others and send food parcels home from the Ukraine. On the contrary, the dear child even received food sent to him *from home*: preserves and chocolate and tinned milk and coffee – *real* coffee! And when Herr Fritzsche had survived the Bolshevik war behind the lines for four weeks they missed him there because they never had any coffee again after that.

Herr Fritzsche can stand on his head and fart into the microphone with his arse as far as I am concerned. And he can say that we are an English or a Kirghizstan transmitter, because all that doesn't change by a single fart the fact that in the fourth year of the war there is a *Kommune* system by which diplomats and the Party bosses and their employees and other personnel receive special rations which have nothing, but *nothing*, in common with the normal rationing system.

The 'diplomatic rations' story had previously been energetically exploited in connection with the name of Dr Robert Ley, a particularly prominent (and unpleasant) Nazi leader who went to the gallows as a war criminal. Delmer was delighted when the first 'come-back' was provided by a freshly captured *Luftwaffe* officer only three weeks after the legend of Dr Ley and his extra rations was first broadcast. In *Black Boomerang* Delmer described it as 'a good little story':

The father of a kitchen maid who had recently left her employ in the Ley household had telephoned the Ley major-domo to ask for his daughter's ration cards to be sent on to her. 'This is the Palais Ley,' grandly answered the major-domo. 'We have no ration cards here. We don't bother about them, you know. Here we have diplomats' rations!'

Delmer wrote: 'We plugged the diplomatic rations racket to such an extent that Goebbels and Ley had to lay on a special campaign to counter it.' According to an article in the Berlin newspaper *Der Angriff*, (12 October 1943) which Ley controlled: 'We National Socialists do not know of any "diplomat's households" such as is natural in England and the USA. Everybody, whether he is a Reich Minister or Reich Leader, must live on his coupons like the ordinary worker . . . but even the normal rations are sufficient because I sample them daily. I am a normal consumer.' The true story was that 'diplomatic rations' were available for foreign embassies in Berlin and certain government departments which had to entertain for representational purposes. *Der Chef* returned to the Ley canard at the very end of the broadcast in which Herr Fritzsche had been the principal object of the 'great rations racket' exposure.

And with these 47,283 brethren it still continues, including at the Palais Ley, where the butler once gave an astonished answer: 'Ration cards? We have no cards here. *We* have diplomats' rations!'
And if Herr Fritzsche or anybody else has any doubts about that story being true, all they need do is contact Herr *Kreisleiter* [Nazi official in charge of a town or larger rural area] and Party member Haut. H as in Heinrich, A as in Anton, U as in Ulrich, T as in Toni. *Kreisleiter* Haut at Trambot [the monitor's phonetic spelling], Küstrin district in Pomerania. Party member Haut is a decent chap and he will gladly confirm it.

The GS1 technique, then, was to invent a good story and continue to repeat it, although with variations, until yet another and another and another replaced it. There were satisfactory indications that the method was effective. Consider, for example, the sad case of a Frau Peuckert whom a special court at Halle sentenced to six months' imprisonment early in 1944 – long after the special rations legend was first launched – for asserting in a public place that there was a special rationing system for high German officials. The source of this information is the October 1943 'Evidence of Reception' report.

According to the July 1943 report:

On 15 June [1943] the *Chef* praised Switzerland for the help she was giving Germany. This prompted the Federal President to complain to the British

Minister in Berne that considerable public unrest had been caused among the Swiss by a broadcast from the Siegfried station, believed to be associated with Allied propaganda, which had accused his country of helping the Germans. A further reference to this broadcast was contained in the *Schweizer Radio Zeitung* of 27 June in an article entitled 'Black stations trouble the waters'. Without actually mentioning GS it blamed a 'foreign black station' for having recently 'spread largely untrue accusations against Switzerland'.

A man who was employed in the *Reichsrundfunk* believed that GS was a mobile station operated from a German army truck.

There is increasing evidence of GS's audience among members of the *Wehrmacht*. A U-boat captain captured early in July had listened in on board. Another, captured in June, spoke of listening to illicit transmitters with 'wonderfully well-informed' programmes and 'stories about individuals, giving exact names and details'. Both these men had strongly independent minds. But listening is by no means confined to officers. The wireless operator has, of course, the best opportunities, and there have been one or two reports from these members of U-boat crews recently.

Particularly interesting is the case of the U-boat commanded by Mützelburg, who was accidentally killed while bathing at sea in September 1942. Several members of the crew of this U-boat, which was sunk in April, had frequently heard GS, both at home and at sea. It was clearly audible even when they were several days out. Their captain, who was not particularly Nazi, had himself listened. This U-boat had had a long and successful career, and the morale was high. On the whole they were pro-Nazi.

# 13

# Expansion at RAG
# – The *Wehrmachtsender Nord*

Delmer was already planning to expand his GS1 operation soon after *der Chef* first broadcast on 23 May 1941. A number of projects were discussed, e.g. an Austrian RU, a communist or extreme left-wing team and even an astrological unit. These were all impracticable suggestions because the necessary manpower was not available. Indeed, six months were to pass before the first new recruit, other than Max Braun, arrived at RAG, soon to be followed by three more who were to play an important role in the development of Delmer's black units.

The man whom Delmer called Ernst Albrecht in *Black Boomerang* and who was known as 'Mr Albright' at RAG, was in fact Herr Dr Ernst Adam (1900–71),[1] a former divisional general on the Republican side during the Spanish Civil War. Delmer had first met him at Madrid when he was a colonel and Chief of Staff to General Kléber, i.e. Lazar or Manfred Stern, a Russian officer of Romanian–Hungarian Jewish origin. Adam had served in the German army as a very young officer towards the end of the 1914–18 war and had subsequently earned a modest living as a schoolteacher. He also achieved a doctorate. The date when he joined the German Communist Party is not known, but the Nazis quickly seized him in 1933 and he spent a period in so-called 'protective custody' (1 March–24 April). When released he fled to France and worked in Paris as a journalist. When the Spanish Civil War began he joined the International Brigade and was quickly promoted. Severely wounded in 1938 when he was commanding a division, he returned to France where he was interned in 1940. By this time, disgusted by his experiences with the Communist Party in Spain, he severed his connection with it. From France he escaped to Lisbon, where Delmer encountered him when he was there in 1940–1. According to Delmer, SOE brought him to England and Woburn at his request.

René Halkett was the next to arrive, probably at about the same time as 'Mr Albright' in *c*. November 1941. Like 'Albright-Adam' he had served briefly in the German army during the last months of the First

World War, however, unlike the latter he was certainly never a communist nor, for that matter, a Herr Doktor. René Halkett (this was not his real name) was the talented son of a noble German family who in his youth had led a bohemian existence although on a minimal income. Stage designer, artist and writer – in 1938 Faber & Faber published his crypto-autobiography *The Dear Monster* which he wrote in excellent English – he had already left Germany before the advent of Hitler. Like the Corporal he had served in the Auxiliary Military Pioneer Corps but had already returned to civilian life when Delmer enlisted him. Frank Lynder, who knew him well, described him to me as 'a 75 per cent genius'.

Frank Lynder (*b*. 1916) arrived on 1 January 1942. Always known at RAG as 'the Sergeant' because he also came from the Auxiliary Military Pioneer Corps, he had in fact been recommended to Delmer by his erstwhile comrade-in-arms. He was the son of a Bremen bookseller and publisher and had had a brief experience in a coffee-broking firm. He left Germany in January 1938 – only his mother was Jewish but his personal position was becoming increasingly uncertain – and joined the Pioneer Corps as soon as the war began. He served in France and left via St Malo about ten days after the Dunkirk evacuation. By then he had already been promoted to the rank of sergeant. He was transferred to a bomb-disposal unit where the Corporal was one of his colleagues.

He lost sight of the Corporal when the latter 'disappeared' in April 1941 and did not connect him with the mysterious interview he had in London in *c*. November 1941 with Delmer, of whose identity he was unaware. Delmer, whom he recalled as 'a very large man with a black beard and very kind eyes' asked him a lot of questions which puzzled him and he heard nothing further until a couple of months later when he was instructed to travel to Bletchley station where a car would meet him. When he arrived at RAG there was his friend the Corporal!

Lynder told me that during his early days at RAG he lacked confidence in himself. Apart from the fact that he had no writing experience, all the others were older than himself and appeared to know exactly what they were doing and, furthermore, how to do it. Delmer had the patience to teach him how to write short scripts and the Corporal also helped him. He was soon able to establish himself as a useful member of the team and in due course became its 'German navy' specialist.

Alexander Maas[2] and his actress wife Margit – they used no local cover names – arrived a few days after the Sergeant in January 1942. They had been intercepted in Bermuda by SOE (at Delmer's request) when they were on their way to Mexico. Maas was born in 1902 and was just too young to have been caught up in the First World War. He worked in the Rhineland as an actor (1919–26) and joined the Communist Party in the latter year. He was employed as an announcer at the Cologne radio station for some years before spending a period in Moscow (October 1931–August 1932) where he worked in broadcasting. He left Germany in March 1933 and was in Spain at the end of 1935, hence before the outbreak of the Civil War in July 1936. He enlisted in the International Brigade and was already a captain by the time he was seriously wounded in the Madrid sector in November 1936. Delmer met him at about that time. Thereafter he was mainly engaged in broadcasting activities and ran a clandestine station known as *Deutscher Freiheitssender* 29.8 (its wavelength). In 1938 he became disenchanted with the Communist Party, made his way to France, resigned from the CP and found his way to the group of Germans who were active in Willi Münzenberg's milieu. Like Adam-Albright he was interned in 1940 but managed to escape to Marseilles and with British help reached Oran, whence he began his interrupted journey to Mexico.

While I spent an occasional weekend at RAG during 1942 and hence met all the individuals I have mentioned above, I knew nothing about either their backgrounds or functions. Conversely none of them knew anything about my role in PWE. A year later when Clifton Child, whom Delmer liked and trusted, joined his team he was occasionally shown one or other of my unit's productions but was never told who was responsible for them. Indeed, it was Child who said to me many years later, 'Tom's security was fabulous!' He became privy to much really secret information but never 'leaked'.

I recall my impression that RAG's residents constituted a closely knit 'family party'. The atmosphere could be very relaxed, with Delmer presiding at one end of the large dining-room table engaged in a cherry-stone spitting contest with whoever was at the other end. I remember, too, that the cuisine, although strictly based on the official wartime rations, achieved an impressively high standard. Isabel Delmer, who had spent long periods with Tom in France, understood good French bourgeois cooking and taught its essentials to Freda Maddy, RAG's cook and housekeeper, who was a willing learner. The 'household' took good care of its free-range chickens and assiduously gathered mushrooms in the local fields. At certain times of the year there was venison, which was not rationed, from the ducal estates, also hares and rabbits. Mr Maddy, Freda's husband, looked after the garden where there was a lawn suitable for what can only be described as 'rough croquet' with its peculiar local rules and conventions. Isabel Delmer grieved Mr Maddy by insisting that vegetables should be eaten young; he would have liked to grow giant marrows, etc. for exhibition at the village horticultural fête.

At week-ends, at least, there were frequently distinguished visitors, notably from the Admiralty and the Foreign Office, although the Sergeant remembers an occasional General or Air-Marshall. When I first met them in the spring of 1942 both the Sergeant and the Corporal were wearing civilian clothes (although the Sergeant later told me that they mostly wore their uniforms) but were still called by their military ranks. Frank Lynder, who was then both young and impressionable, said that his RAG experience was not unlike being a junior member of an exclusive club.

As far as I know, RAG was the only RU house where there was a lively social life, especially at week-ends, although few visitors could have known that the average working day began soon after 8am and often continued until the early hours of the following morning when Delmer was liable to produce his best ideas. However, in spite of all the hard work – Lynder told me that it could be grindingly hard – the atmosphere was lighthearted and he and the Corporal at least found time for outrageous practical jokes.

The main reason for recruiting additional staff at the end of 1941 was Delmer's plan to take the GSI operation a stage further by starting a 'genuine' German armed forces station. By now he had considerable experience of black broadcasting, knew his way round PWE and, most important, was beginning to develop a whole range of contacts in the intelligence milieu, and with the Naval Intelligence Division in particular. At RAG he now had a *Hellschreiber*, i.e. a radio-operated teleprinter machine which enabled him to 'tap', and where appropriate use the official German news agency press releases and the Propaganda Ministry's directives, often before they were even read by their intended recipients in Germany.

In the meantime GS1 was operating smoothly and did not require Delmer's undivided attention. Johannes Reinholz, *der Chef*'s adjutant, departed early in 1942 and was replaced by Frank Lynder. The latter's microphone voice may have been less effective but by this time GS1's public in Germany knew *der Chef*'s voice very well indeed.

Towards the end of 1941 Delmer operated a short-lived station called *Radio Rotes Wien*, which transmitted between 3 October and 27 December 1941. If 'Mr Albright', with his Communist Party background, was already at RAG he could have written the scripts, but they would have needed a very distinctive 'voice' with an Austrian dialect and I am unaware of the presence of anyone at RAG who could have supplied it.

Delmer's account of the aims and objectives of the *Wehrmachtsender*

136

*Nord* follows. It is undated but was probably written in May 1942. The station first broadcast on 9 May.

(1) *Nature of the RU*

The idea of this RU was given to us by a German *Wehrmachtsender*, a small station operating from Smolensk. Our station purports to be run by a German unit in Northern Norway and its object is nominally to give news of home to German soldiers in the district. We hope that it, like the true German *Wehrmachtsender*, will be picked up by curious civilians who want to know what army life and *Stimmung* [morale] is like.

(2) *Main Objectives*

The main objectives of our RU are: (a) to attack the morale of the German army by painting a gloomy picture of conditions inside Germany and (b) to convince civilian listeners that the morale of the army is affected by certain developments on the home front, to which the ordinary soldier is thoroughly opposed and that army morale is thereby lowered. This is by far the more important objective.

(3) *Material*

Material for our broadcasts is provided almost entirely by the messages of the DNB [Official German News Service] Home Service which we can tap on the *Hellschreiber* before they appear in the German Press. The character of a German army station is kept up by a large assortment of messages from the homeland to particular soldiers and of cheerful march and dance music.

(4) *Technique*

Any close student of the British Press would realise that it is easy by judicious selection from it to present a wholly gloomy picture of conditions in Britain. No doubt a large department of the German Propaganda Ministry is engaged in this task. It is not therefore wholly surprising that a similar selection from DNB items can be made, with very little doctoring, to present a black picture of conditions inside Germany.

By adding a few details or omitting a few qualifying clauses from German news items, this RU should have convinced any of its listeners that conditions in Western Germany anyhow are extremely unpleasant. The major topics of its news items are British air-raids, complete with silent bombs and new types of incendiaries, with indiscriminatory looting after the raid and inadequate arrangements for housing and feeding victims and for the evacuation of children. German factories are manned increasingly by the old and by women, while the children whom the women ought to be looking after succumb to various accidents at home. In the meantime the towns are flooded with foreign workers and with *Volksdeutsche* who speak no word of German and who take advantage of bad conditions in order to steal, sabotage and escape.

That is the impression which a constant listener might form from the carefully mixed-up news items put out by this RU. A good many of the news items are harmless in themselves and even in their context, and a great deal has to be done by implication only. A typical instance of the technique was the issue by the RU of an official denial that workers imported from North Africa were niggers. They were, it was said, only 'dark-skinned French Colonials'.

Apart from conveying a generally gloomy picture of conditions inside Germany, the RU has an important function in inducing people to look after themselves against the German rules. The usual technique is to report police court sentences, complete with details of the crime, thus suggesting new ideas of technique to anyone who is inclined to use them.

Another constant object of the RU is to ridicule and excite hatred of senior Party officials. Here a great deal is done by juxtaposition, either of news items with other news items, or of news items with appropriate music. Thus accounts of unpleasant conditions resulting from British air-raids are juxtaposed with news about the movements and junketings of the Gauleiter of the district affected. Propaganda speeches about Germany's invincible morale, or stories about the rescue of portraits of the *Führer* untouched from blazing fires, are often followed by a peculiar fragment of a German march – perhaps the most telling form of ridicule. Sheer repetition has built up certain Party personalities as supremely ridiculous or hateful. A biography of Baldur von Schirach, made up of items from the *Wehrmachtsender*, would make extremely good reading. While others fight and suffer he is reported as opening congresses of European Youth Leaders or European Foresters at Vienna, with appropriate speeches and banquets.

Along with the Party the SS is also subject to perpetual ridicule. Here again repetition is the essence of the matter. Regular listeners are accustomed to at least one item a day on the following lines: 'To add realism to the great new film of Rommel's African success now being made by Leni Riefenstehl, 5000 SS-men are indulging in unarmed conflict dressed in British uniforms on the Baltic beaches.'

In addition to news items true or false, the RU broadcasts occasional special talks by such local experts as it has available. Thus, comrades supposed to have returned from Bremen, give eye-witness accounts of British air-raids; a noted army psychologist discusses with copious and startling illustrations the prevalence of disturbing rumours; and a talk on U-boat superstitions sheds a startling light on the morale of their crews.

The RU evidently has its own recording apparatus. One of its features was the recording of a German soldiers' variety show, including a moving speech on that staple food of the German soldier, the *Bratling*, told in an unmistakable imitation of the *Führer*. A recent successful feature of this kind was the recording of an interview (taken almost verbatim from DNB) with an Italian Blackshirt leader, who had just returned from the Eastern Front and had a great deal to say about the valour of the Italian units there.[3]

\*     \*     \*

138

Delmer was never very satisfied with the results of all the effort that was invested in the *Wehrmachtsender*. There was a disappointingly long period before there was any evidence that it was even being heard by the audience for whom it was intended. The Royal Navy even sent a destroyer to patrol the Norwegian coast with instructions to listen for its transmissions but its report was negative. It then emerged that there is a short-wave phenomenon called the 'skip distance' which could prevent a station being heard when it should theoretically have been audible. Delmer remarked that the *Wehrmachtsender* at least probably had a fascinated audience in China.

The Sergeant told me that the station had its teething troubles and was not sufficiently 'slick', but that it nevertheless gave the team much useful experience for later operations. The *Wehrmachtsender* included a short naval programme. The Sergeant was put in charge of this and eventually became Delmer's local specialist for the *Kriegsmarine* [German Navy], although by that time he was working under the direct instructions of Lieutenant-Commander Donald McLachan of the Admiralty's Naval Intelligence Division. However, in spite of its apparent lack of impact the *Wehrmachtsender* was, in fact, being monitored by the German intelligence people. They were impressed by the fact that the British had a special transmitter beamed to Norway, because this appeared to confirm Hitler's conviction that we would eventually attempt a major landing there.

Delmer mentioned his own dissatisfaction with the *Wehrmachtsender* in *Black Boomerang*:

> Very soon I had come to the conclusion that it did not sound right, because like all 'black' transmissions at that time, it had to be pre-recorded. Radio news, to be news, and sound like news, I discovered then, must be broadcast live. It must be up to the minute, changing from bulletin to bulletin. But unfortunately our 'black' studios could not handle live broadcasts. And after a few weeks of experimentation I abandoned the recorded *Wehrmachtsender Nord*.

The *Wehrmachtsender* was in fact on the air for far longer than merely a few weeks. It was active for nine months and broadcast for the last time on 7 February 1943. Its immediate successor, the *Kurzwellensender Atlantik*, broadcast *live*.

1 Biographical information on Ernst Adam based on *Biographisches Handbuch der deutschsprachigen Emigration nach 1932*, 1980

2 See *Biographisches Handbuch* (as above)

3 FO 898/67

# 14

# The Minor German RUs

A complete list of all the Department's RUs contains one called *Astrologie und Okkultismus*, which was supposed to have broadcast for a brief period between 28 March and 19 April 1942. This puzzled me because Delmer did not refer to it in *Black Boomerang*, and on the black printing side there was no preoccupation with astrology until the end of 1942. Mrs Margit Maas, the widow of the late Alexander Maas, eventually supplied the answer. Originally trained as an actress she was supposed to impersonate a spiritualist medium who had received messages from deceased members of the German armed forces – their names and home addresses were supplied – for transmission to their bereaved families. Margit's problem, however, was that she found it difficult to read the scripts without occasionally laughing and thus spoiling the recordings.

She fared better as a member of a small team which operated a so-called German Workers' Station from 17 July 1942 until 23 March 1943. Either she played the role of 'Red Johanna' or that became her local nickname at Aspley Guise. These broadcasts commenced with the popular 'Lili Marlene' theme song – it was also a great favourite with British soldiers – and invariably took the line that the workers, who were referred to as 'comrades', must end this plutocratic war, seize power and conclude immediate peace. A British report dated 26 November 1942 stated that the station 'had stressed disorganisation and passive resistance of workers in Italy, and had cited two cases of successful resistance by the crews of German ships abroad'.

What little I could discover about the Workers' Station once again puzzled me because it did not appear to reflect Delmer's typically subversive line. I found the answer in a paper written by Reginald Leeper on 26 November 1942.

The Left-Wing station has a secret purpose known to very few people in PWE. By an agreement made with General Sikorski, Polish agents operating inside Poland, and even inside Germany, will take down news transmitted through this station for insertion in a pseudo-German clandestine press. The Poles already produce and distribute in Germany such newspapers. They have agreed to feed them with news supplied by us in this way. We have promised them to keep this as one of our closest secrets and only three people in Woburn know the real object of this station.[1]

Father Andreas ('the Priest') first broadcast on 15 September 1942 and continued until 28 April 1945, the day when Hitler married Eva Braun, although without the benefit of clergy. Father Andreas was a young Austrian Roman Catholic priest who had received his Order's permission to join Delmer's team. There was no question of him being asked to broadcast any of the outrageous inventions thought up by Delmer and Co. His scripts, which he wrote himself, consisted of a short religious service followed by a brief talk. He did, however, make factual revelations, based upon accurate intelligence material, in which he told the Germans about some of the infamous things which were being done in their name, e.g. Hitler's monstrous euthanasia programme, the SS *Lebensborn* groups which mated unmarried girls in order to produce a Germanic master race, and the Party's contempt for all human and moral law.

It is likely that he alluded to the resentment felt in Roman Catholic circles when the Party reduced the number of religious holidays (early in 1941) because of the loss of armaments and other wartime production. He must also have known about and mentioned the anger felt in Catholic Bavaria when, in 1941, Wagner, the Munich Gauleiter, ordered that crucifixes should be removed from schools in Bavaria. The negative reaction, particularly in rural districts, was such that the instruction was countermanded a few weeks later. Father Andreas also reported on the Party's anti-religious measures late in 1941: no less than 130 religious institutions, of which seven were in Bavaria, had been requisitioned and the Party was making strenuous efforts to diminish the church's educational and social activities, among the young in particular.

As was so often the case with Delmer's other black stations the subjects of the Priest's broadcasts were refuted in the German press. Thus on 3 January 1944 the Essen *National Zeitung* strongly denied his assertion that 'Children are only evacuated in order to enable the State to obtain full control of education and eliminate the influence of parents.' This had been the subject of many of his talks.

In order to support the Priest's broadcasts my unit produced a number of small booklets containing the texts of his brief sermons, also those delivered by such eminent churchmen as Cardinal Faulhaber. I have no reason to believe that these contained any 'unauthorised additions' interpolated by one or other of Delmer's people. Delmer himself had too much respect and affection for Father Andreas to involve him, if only indirectly, in such deceptions.

However, without informing Father Andreas, Delmer asked his contacts in SOE and OSS to instruct their rumour agents in neutral capitals that the 'Christ the King' broadcasts originated from a black radio station operated by the Vatican. The story soon travelled from mouth to mouth in Switzerland where, according to Delmer, the Father had a considerable following, and thence to Germany and Austria.

In 1977 Father Robert A. Graham, SJ, sent me the typescript of his unpublished article on 'German Catholics as a Target of British Propaganda in World War II'. He had carefully examined a number of PWE files at the Public Record Office and extracted details of rumour material which applied particularly to the Vatican, the Papacy and the home front in Germany.

PWE's Underground Propaganda Committee met weekly to examine suggestions for rumours proposed by the Joint Intelligence Committee, the Foreign Office, the Service Departments and the PWE Regional Directors. Those which were approved were then put into their final shape and forwarded to the SIS and SOE with suggestions as to where they would most effectively be disseminated. At one time my friend John Rayner acted as *rapporteur* for the UPC and I used to encounter him making his rounds in Bush House collecting material for the weekly meeting. As far as I know Delmer was never a member of the UPC and had his own rumour manufactory at RAG. Father Andreas would certainly not have been told of the UPC's existence, nor, indeed, that PWE had any particular organisation for the fabrication of rumours.

On the rumour front it was reported from time to time that the Pope would be obliged to leave the Vatican. Thus in December 1941 it was said that he would be going to South America. This story was picked up by the press throughout the world. Then in July 1943, when Rome was bombed by 700 planes from North Africa and the Middle East, it was said that His Holiness wished to leave Rome to avoid the distress of seeing the Eternal City destroyed by bombs. After Mussolini had been liberated by German parachutists on 12 September 1943 and formed a new Fascist rump government in northern Italy it was said that the Pope and Cardinals would soon take up residence in Liechtenstein. 'The report of a possible kidnapping of the Pope triggered rumours and questions in Vatican and German circles.'

In mid-November 1941 a whole series of rumours was connected with the name of Count von Galen, the courageous Bishop of Münster, whose detestation of the Nazis was well known. It was announced that volunteers had gathered round him for his protection and that a Gestapo spy among them had been manhandled by his friends. In July 1941 the Bishop may or may not have mentioned in a sermon that the mother house of the Missionaries of the Sacred Heart at Hiltrup, near Münster, had been confiscated by the Party. In mid-November 1941 it was said that eighteen missionaries from Hiltrup had been shot on the Russian front. The story of the shooting was an invention but it was true that many individuals had recently been arrested and lodged in concentration camps for distributing copies of his sermons. In May 1943 it was affirmed that, 'The real reason for the visit of Bishops von Preysing and von Galen to the Vatican is to ask the Pope if the elimination of Hitler and the SS would suffice for his peace programme, or if the inclusion of Goebbels and Goering is also necessary.'

After the failure of the attempt on Hitler's life on 20 July 1944 PWE's rumour-mongers invented a 'Catholic Action Party' which planned to make another attempt on the *Führer*'s life. On 1 September a new rumour stated that, 'Arrests of Catholic priests have followed pronouncements that the Catholic Church does not recognise the validity of oaths [of loyalty] to the *Führer*, because Hitler is considered anti-Christ.'

Father Graham recorded two rumours which appear to have surprised him. The first affirmed that Joachim von Ribbentrop, the German Foreign Minister, had 'instructed Cardinal Innitzer of Vienna to ask the Pope to canonise Hitler's mother'. The second stated that a certain Karl Meister, 'the record holder of the "Day of Fructification" [i.e. Fornication?] had ended up in a lunatic asylum'.

It remains for PWE's rumour output to be scientifically analysed by a Ph.D. candidate who would be obliged to spend many hours at the Public Record Office.

---

1   The Workers' Station cannot have been G8 (see Appendix No. 27) but was far more likely to have been P(olish) 1 (see Appendix No. 30).

# 15

# Delmer's RUs – An Independent Assessment May 1941–March 1943

I owe the long document printed below to Father Robert Graham, SJ, who copied the original at the National Archives at Washington, DC. It is taken from a file whose title is 'US Federal Communications Commission. Foreign Broadcast Intelligence Service. Secret Special Report No. 58. 22 March 1943. Clandestine Radio Stations'. The March 1943 date coincides exactly with the day on which Delmer first began to broadcast *live*, not from 'Simpson's' at Wavendon Tower but from his own new studios at Milton Bryant. It must be emphasised that a new chapter in Delmer's extraordinary career in PWE began that day.

The document itself contains an impressively accurate analysis of Delmer's RU work up to that time, although its author did not have any personal knowledge of the Delmer 'organisation' and wrote his assessment on the basis of a painstaking analysis of a long series of monitoring reports. I have never seen any PWE paper which describes Delmer's work with such clarity, hence my decision to publish the document in full, hoping that it will further illuminate much with which the reader is already at least a little familiar.

## TO GERMANY

### GUSTAV SIEGFRIED EINS
(Speaker: The Chief)

GUSTAV SIEGFRIED EINS, broadcasting in German to Germany daily for 10-minute periods from 12:52–23:52 EWT, operates on two frequencies. The musical signal, played at the beginning of each broadcast, is the second bar of a German folk song, the first bar of which is used by the official German radio. Thus the Chief begins each broadcast with music written for the words '... until you reach your cool grave ...', the continuation of 'Be Always True and Righteous ...' Before the Chief begins to talk, the announcer states mysteriously, '49 transmits simultaneously, if

144

possible.' By this device, as well as in other ways, the station tries to give the impression that the Chief speaks for a large subversive organisation with which he maintains contact and from which he receives inside information on military and party affairs in Germany. Directives are given in code to persons who are asked to copy 'the orders'.

The Chief's broadcasts, though received somewhat better than 'Army Transmitter North' are often unintelligible due to jamming and static.

### Content

The Chief is the most famous of all anti-Nazi clandestine stations. His attacks on high Party and SS officials are not merely vigorous but are based on 'inside information' not to be gained from any other radio source. While much of this information is difficult to check, the Chief has repeatedly proved to be exceedingly well informed about major personnel changes in Germany. For example, he announced the replacement of von Halder by Zeitzler as Chief of Staff several weeks before the Germans released the news.

*Attacking the Nazis:* The Chief is an enemy of the Nazi party, the Nazi bureaucracy from top to bottom, but above all, the SS. Interestingly enough, the words 'Nazi' and 'National Socialism' are never used. The Chief speaks instead of the 'commune' which, more specifically, stands for all those 'blunderers', 'war profiteers' and 'pompous asses' of the Party who 'sit in decisive and responsible administrative and executive offices and by their selfishness torpedo the efforts of the homeland and the sacrificial courage of the front'. The 'commune' is the Chief's preferred term for derogation of the SS.

The Party official is a greedy, immoral, ruthless and parasitic individual who exploits his power for selfish ends and even robs the dead soldier of his possessions; he exterminates his opponents by calumny and murder; he behaves as an incompetent coward at the front – if, indeed, he ever shows up at the fighting line. Only slightly less contemptible is the military officer who uses his Party connections to further his personal career.

*Himmler*, 'the pale Heinrich with his pince-nez', and his upstart protégés, *Zeitzler*, 'the pauper, the nonentity, the political clown', and the swashbuckling and ill-trained careerist and 'SS-general' *Rommel*, present the prototype of Commune officers in the Chief's shooting-gallery. Other Nazi leaders who come in for infrequent criticism are *Goebbels*, *Ribbentrop*, *Backe*, and SS-leader *Sepp Dietrich*.

*Hitler* himself, however, as well as *Goering*, were *at first* exempted from any attack. Such strategy apparently was dictated by the recognition that many Germans identify themselves with the *Führer*. In September 1942, however, the Chief made his first attack, though veiled and indirect, upon the *Führer*. Hitler was depicted as the victim of a band of party scoundrels who were maliciously and ruinously influencing his decisions. This was related by the Chief in a tone of apparently genuine affection and sympathy,

145

but the conclusion which he suggested was clear! The *Führer* is credulous, drugged and ill. He is unable to make competent decisions.

After this the Chief did not mention Hitler's name for some time. Instead he flew into a rage over conditions prevailing at the '*Führer*'s Headquarters' where Himmler and his clique were said to be dictating military strategy. This theme was then tied up with Rommel's fiasco by the magic appearance of a Mediterranean-SS-super-plan, called the 'Hohenstaufen-plan'.

Meanwhile the 'Commune' was shown to be interfering with official diplomacy, with armament production, rationing, labour conscription, German home-life, always for the benefit of a few Party parasites and to the disadvantage of the army and the decent average citizens, the compatriots, the German soldiers' wives, widows and orphans. Evidence was piled sky-high and used on 30 January to launch a grand assault on 10 years of the 'Commune'-regime. After this and after the fall of Stalingrad the ground seemed sufficiently prepared to attack, on 1 February, 'that man' (Hitler's name was not mentioned) by linking failures with the setbacks on the Eastern Front. The attack was still modified by an acknowledgment of Hitler's merits. But it was the kind of condescending appreciation which the old military can spare for the gifted civilian who has done his duty. The critique itself, however, was direct and strong. In content (although not in tone) it was similar to that directed against Rommel. Hitler's decisions are fatal, based on intuition instead of scientific calculation. For, 'The man [has] no military education.' In following broadcasts, after the loss of Rostov, the attack grew in intensity and wound up with the direct postulate that, 'The army needs a Commander-in-Chief who understands his business'.

Shortly afterwards the Chief found it necessary to defend his tactics against 'anxious spirits who have characterised my words as frivolous'. He modified his position by declaring that his criticism is primarily levelled against Byzantinism, i.e. against conditions bred by Hitler's entourage. A few days later the Chief withdrew almost completely, hinting at an expected change in the High Command.

*Other enemies of the Chief:* the Chief is not only anti-Nazi but also anti-French, anti-British, slightly anti-Semitic, anti-Russian and anti-Italian. With the exception of his contemptuous tirades against the Italians, his aggressiveness with regard to other nationalities is of a routine nature and never reaches the intensity of the Chief's anti-Nazi invectives. It appears that these attacks are spurious and are merely included in the script in order to conceal the Chief's true aims.

*The Chief's positive political programme:* The same holds true of the Chief's positive political programme. His aims are shrouded in vagueness. The words he uses are stereotypes whose meaning is never fully amplified. The Chief speaks of the 'fatherland', '*Lebensraum*', and of other nationalistic values. In the summer of 1942 he professed to be for a '*Rechtsstaat*',

146

and he has since taken a stand, occasionally, for an independent judiciary. His pet friend, however, is the German army. Men like Rundstedt, Kesselring, Halder, Thomas, von Kleist, von Bock have been praised by the Chief, and much of his time has been devoted to defending those generals against the measures taken by the 'Commune'. However, when the Chief shows his concern over the difficulties which Prussian generals of the old military tradition have to face in Nazi Germany, he devotes much more time to vilifying the Party role than to defending the army officers who, in the broadcasts, play the role of either the losers or the politically impotent. In short, the Chief's approach is destructive rather than constructive.

## Techniques

In a sense, the Chief shares with the 'Army Transmitter North' the technique of camouflage; his subversiveness is wrapped in patriotism. But different from 'Army Transmitter North', the Chief's attacks are direct and forceful. His language is coarse and frequently obscene. Furthermore, the Chief's broadcasts are talks – each of them being devoted to an attack on one target only – whereas, the 'Army Transmitter North' delivered many minor attacks at a time, mixing news and short commentaries with music, messages, etc. In the attempt to discredit personalities and symbols of the Third Reich (and perhaps to build up his audience), the Chief indulges freely in pornography. Many of his talks have been devoted to detailed revelations of loose living in high Nazi circles. However, this technique has been employed recently to a smaller extent.

Like the 'Army Transmitter North' the Chief has tried to spread rumours by denying them (and has in fact at times co-operated with the 'Army Transmitter North' is disseminating the same rumours). Some of them, dealing with personnel changes in high army circles, were publicly rejected in speeches by Goebbels, Goering and other Nazi leaders. (Of course, no references was ever made to the stations in these denials.) It is impossible to say whether the Chief succeeded in generating the rumours or whether he merely spread more widely rumours already circulating in Germany.

The Chief's broadcasts do not contain a running commentary on the war. Instead, they offer 'sensational' inside information which is presented as though the Chief is naturally in the know, conducting a peep show of politics. Lately, however, the Chief has increasingly commented on front-page news related to major domestic and military events.

## Audience

From the content of the Chief's broadcasts it may be inferred that the station aims at an audience which is nationalistic (imperialistic) and politically conservative. The possible disadvantage of antagonising such a higher middle-class audience by coarseness of language may be outbalanced by the advantage of attracting dissident, critical and wavering

Nazis as well as other opponents of the regime within or without the army, who may be attracted rather than repelled by this scandal-sheet of the air.

## 'ARMY TRANSMITTER NORTH'
## (WEHRMACHTSENDER NORD)

This station was first monitored by the FBIS on 9 June 1942, and it was then assumed that it had been in operation since 9 April. However, on 7 February 1943, the station announced its discontinuation adding that it had been broadcasting 'almost *two* years'. While 'Army Transmitter North' is now only of historical interest, it is included here because of its unique techniques.

*Audience*

The station claimed to be located in Norway and did broadcast in German to German troops stationed in Norway, but later apparently also to Germany and German audiences in general. It had several speakers. The main speaker obviously had experience in broadcasting and spoke a flawless German. Other voices heard on the programme were those of less well-educated men, perhaps of common soldiers, some of them (particularly the so-called 'Heiner with His Telescope') adept at using slang and deliberately sloppy dialect.

The programme of the station itself was divided into several parts, not all regularly appearing in the same broadcast. It featured: (a) the so-called 'Mirror of the Homeland' (*Heimat-Spiegel*), later called simply 'News from Home'; (b) 'Blows from the *Goulaschkanone*' (Field Kitchen), composed of local news from Norway most of which pertained to the life of soldiers; greetings (some with ironic comments) from relatives back home to individual soldiers whose names and unit numbers were stated; messages from soldiers to soldiers; sports news and music items played on 'request' of soldiers or their families; (c) a special act called 'Heiner (or Heini) with His Telescope', a vaudeville rag who glossed over the personal problems of soldiers with jocosity, their families, army regulations and the like; and (d) a recent addition called 'News from all over the world' which familiarised the listeners with happenings in countries other than Germany (however, in the main Axis countries or those dominated by the Axis). Occasionally, ATN also featured talks and mock front reports on subjects particularly discouraging to German soldiers.

News items and stories were frequently interrupted by music, mostly dance music, which at times merely served an entertainment purpose; however, at other times this formed a part of the station's propaganda technique of indirectness.

*Content*

The content of the broadcasts changed frequently. Certain themes were dropped; new ones were added. In general ATN broadcast short news items rather than talks. Comments in general were either withheld or hidden within the reports, and analyses took the form of evaluative adjectives rather than meaningful interpretations. The news items reported were highly personalised. In order to enhance the gossipy character of the presentation, names of localities and persons involved were often quoted. Generalizations were extremely sparse, almost non-existent, leaving the listener to draw his own conclusions as to the meaning of the incidents reported. Latterly, however, ATN generalised more freely.

Obviously, as a matter of policy, the station kept pace with major and minor political events. News items and feature stories showed a certain degree of front-page topicality. During the summer of 1942 air-raids on Germany received major attention and were depicted primarily with respect to their effects on the life, property and morale of the home population. Other items dealt with new and fancy diseases imported from foreign countries (by foreign workers). Particular attention was given to the corruptive luxury of Party officials and their immoral conduct in public and private life. In general, petty and local officials were assailed, but from time to time the Reich's first cast (Goering, Himmler, Ribbentrop, Baldur von Schirach) appeared in compromising contexts. Such references increased after the defeats in Africa and Russia. Rommel came in for a particularly heavy dose of sarcasm. At first, Hitler himself was never criticised, neither explicitly nor by implication. Later, however, sporadic items appear in which the *Führer* was roundaboutly derogated and ridiculed (for instance, his tone of voice and mode of speech were burlesqued in one of the boisterous, earthy programs in which the station excelled). Towards the end of the year items increased on juvenile delinquency, deteriorating health conditions, black market, food shortages, women in industry and defence work, total mobilisation and the like. In its foreign program ATN dealt with military events (the Russian dilemma, the Libyan retreat), Italian military impotence, Japanese imperialistic greed, trouble in the Balkans, etc.

ATN also revealed from time to time anti-plutocratic tendencies, resentment against instances of social discrimination within the army, peace expectations and peace yearnings.

*Techniques*
ATN shared with the Chief the technique of political travesty, but was more sophisticated in the choice of items and techniques employed. Hiding its true identity and purpose behind the name of official trustworthiness ATN relied on a technique of indirection and subtlety. High treason was cloaked in the guise of noisy patriotism, offended rectitude, and seeming candour.

The denunciations of Nazi leaders (and their wives), third-rate officials, and social elements, were meant to refute indirectly the sanctity and impregnability of the Nazi order.

149

ATN's subversive propaganda was presented carefully and ingeniously. A great number of its items were perfectly innocuous and consisted of official announcements, even such news as was carried on the authentic German radios. In the rest of its items, however, ATN used a number of devices which can be stated in the following maxims: (1) Attribute subversive statements of undesirable facts to respectable authorities. (2) State subversive facts but deny their existence; state them in detail, deny them in general. (3) State subversive opinions but indignantly call them 'rumours', superstitions or the like. (4) Give news which is undesirable (from the point of view of the authorities) and say that the authorities have done (or said) something desirable and praiseworthy in return. (5) Never appeal openly for subversive actions, but describe in detail subversive actions that have come to the attention of the authorities, or (6) war against subversive action which you describe in detail. (7) Attack officially endorsed (orthodox) opinions by first stating them in one item and then phrase the next item in a way to cast doubt on the meaning of the first one, or (8) present uninterruptedly a series of negative items (such as deaths of heroes) without scattering them among more favourable items or comments, and without acknowledging that they were taken almost literally from official German broadcasts. (9) State a negative event in one sentence and have it followed by a positive one which, however, has nothing to do with the first one, or at least does not contradict it or weaken its effect. (10) Magnify undesirable effects through the use of superlative attributes and by citing specific figures. (11) Attack famous opponents by ridiculing their wives. (12) Make use of means of expression (music, inflection of voice) to underscore or reverse the overt meaning of verbal statements.

The above enumeration by no means exhausts the list of devices used by ATN, but it gives the most prominent ones used to demoralise front and homeland by having each worry about the other. ATN's psychological alertness was particularly illustrated by its predilection for rumours likely to create anxieties – 'news' items and talks on repulsive diseases, shocking accidents to women in German factories, assaults by foreign workers on German women, etc.

During the last period of its broadcasts, attacks by ATN became at once more articulate and more general in character. Although no blame was placed at official doorsteps, the progressive deterioration of economic and social conditions was 'admitted' and exemplified by numerous incidents. Yet, such news, however obnoxious, after all may not have differed from the small talk of the average German citizen and, by the same token, may have sounded to him less conspicuous than would have been the case a year ago.

*Identity*

ATN claimed to be sending its broadcasts from Norway and to a very late date tried to maintain this impression. The local colouring was provided by a reportage of events in Norway. It also pretended to be an army station; this was documented by the audience addressed, the type of items used, and by remarks (often relying only on a tone of voice) which betrayed sarcastic contempt for Party upstarts, an attitude always popular with members of the army.

It is quite possible that ATN succeeded in creating and maintaining the fiction with the larger (non-sophisticated) part of its audience. At least up to the last minute ATN itself kept up the appearance of officialness and genuine patriotism. Even the fact and circumstances of its departure were still part of the technique of bluff through indirection. 'Now,' announced ATN, 'in the hour of greatest need, our Comradeship-Service must become silent in favour of other tasks.' None other than the *Reichsrundfunk*, according to ATN, would take over ATN's functions. Due to static and heavy jamming the reception of ATN was irregular.

## THE GERMAN CATHOLIC STATION

This station broadcasts three times daily in German to Germany and uses three different wave-lengths. It was heard by FBIS for the first time on 27 December 1942 and has been monitored since. However, it is not received daily.

### Form of Presentation and Audience

The station features sermon-like talks and prayers by a Catholic priest. The speech is preceded and followed by organ music, and (or) by the chanting of monks. The station signs off with an announcement of its schedule and with the words: 'Hail Christ, the King!' In style, composition and pathos the programmes are thoroughly religious. The subject of the day is always introduced by an appropriate quotation from the Bible and concluded with a prayer. Talk and comments are studded with languages and quotations from the Holy Text. Although criticism is direct and forceful, the speaker prefers to identify persons and circumstances through the use of biblical symbols. There are references to 'Our New Herod', 'Moloch', 'Baal', 'Godless Prophet', 'This man is Christ's Enemy', 'The highest of the Godless', 'Godless Rulers', 'Godless leadership', 'Atheists', 'Heathens', 'The law of the Evil One', 'The New Paganism', etc. Infrequently the *Führer* is mentioned, the 'SS' or a 'perverse nationalism'. But otherwise the effort is made to shroud high personages and political events in the non-political vernacular of the pulpit. Tone and language are similar to those of the former German Freedom Station, the Christian Peace Movement, which broadcast to Britain. This station also reduced the military conflict to an essentially moral choice – between the forces of God and the Devil, peace and war. The Bible was quoted and referred to frequently.

Spoken by the shepherd who is deeply and predominantly concerned with the spiritual welfare of his flock, the words are directed expressly to 'dear Catholics'. Catholic sufferings are reported and the Catholic duties in these times of trial are indicated. But the speaker never refers to the authority of the Church or to German Catholic authorities for endorsement of his statements, messages or appeals. Nor does he even refer to them indirectly. While some of the lines taken are derived from Pastoral Letters, this is never emphasised nor even intimated.

## Content

The station has two main targets: the primary is the Nazi-leadership, specifically Hitler, Nazi ideology and politics, the Nazi State and the Nazi War. The secondary target is the German people who 'for the second time' have let themselves be led astray by false leaders and are, hence, for the second time suffering the punishment of God.

*Attacking the Nazi Regime:* Since the station fights not only for the sanctity of the faith, the integrity of the Church and the sacrament of matrimony, but also for family life, for moral purity, for the right to property and life, German leadership is assailed primarily for trying to destroy just these fundamental values.

Although each broadcast usually deals with one specific subject only, on 12 February, the station, in a skilful review of preceding accusations summarised the most flagrant violations of the regime as a continuous break of the ten commandments, namely idolatry (*Führer* deification), blasphemy, instigation to heresy (keeping the children away from the life of the Church), undermining of family life, organised murder (the feeble, old people, the cripples in gas chambers and the strong and healthy at the front), adultery and promiscuity (demanded by the National Socialistic '*Menschenzüchtungs-Programm*'), commanded theft, hypocrisy, sexual cupidity (appeal to sexuality through pornography) and social greed ('The masters in their palaces ... eat the fruits of their predatory raids.')

Topics of particular concern to the station (some of them handled in more than one broadcast) are:

(1) *Idolatry*
'In our fatherland today we are ruled by Baal worshippers who have made to order for themselves an idol which approves ... their cruelties and murderous lust. They greet each other with the invocation of his name, beseech him for salvation – "Heil".'

(2) Destruction of the true faith through a 'perverse Nationalism' proven by blasphemy such as: 'Jesus of Nazareth was a soldierly person who died on the cross with tightly pressed lips and deeply despising the rest of the human pack' or 'the struggle for life (meaning war) is a law which the Chief of Heaven and Earth imposed upon all his creatures.'

152

(3) *Physical infanticide* committed *against* foreign *children* and the *spiritual infanticide* committed *against German children.*

'They want to take the children away from their parents ... The Godless youth organisations are to take care that Godfearing parents are hated and despised by their own children ... Protect your children from the soul-slaughterers of your children. ... Pull them away from the Hitler Youth. ... And you, Catholic soldiers ... do you want the children of the occupied territories to be exposed to death of starvation or look on as they are slaughtered? Feed them!'

(4) *'Mammalism'*

'The Godless rulers in our fatherland want in the future to get along without parents and without families. ... Man is nothing but a war-loving mammal. ... Children ... to be turned into beings which can be utilised by the state as so-called 'raw material men' (*Rohstoff-Mensch*). ... The human race is no longer the concern of the family, but simply a biological matter under state-control.'

(5) *Racial* and *political imperialism,* called the *arrogance* of *life*:

'To win the whole world – this was the programme of un-Godliness and whoever resisted this programme was persecuted by them ... and with all that the Godless still have the courage to say that this war was forced on us. ... We owe two world wars to this spirit of arrogance. ... No, this war is no defensive war. ... They (the Godless) forced us Germans into this war because they aspire to an extension of their power and to their personal enrichment.'

*Accusing the German People:* The accusations against the German people are grave but condemnation is not final. The German people, too, are guilty of this 'spirit of arrogance', of 'unbelief', of 'hatred', of 'immeasurable injustice' and of their 'reliance on the power of darkness ... and the aid which we have given them in the execution of their criminal plans'. But, says the station, 'they were blinded by Satan'. In fact they were forced into their present plight.

'They began their campaign by first persecuting and depriving of their right to speak their own countrymen in the homeland ... with cunning method they knew how to convince the German people that they were the most wonderful people in the world and that they were called upon to rule over the other so-called inferior races.'

Flattery was followed by folly. If the German people had only recognised the days of their first affliction as days of penance and salvation, the present disorder could have been avoided. Lack of courage and false hope is the people's second sin.

This applies to Catholics as well. 'There were a few optimists among us Catholics who had hoped that the Godless would abandon their hatred for

God's Church, if the whole German people, its Catholic group included, would bear the sacrifices and hardship of the war, and would appear as a German community. ...'

*Strategy and Techniques:* The station distinguishes carefully between the German leadership and the German people. German leadership is indicated and irrevocably condemned. There is no salvation. The end is coming. Synchronized with the Russian defeats are increasing hints of the approaching Apocalypse. It is part of the station's technique to present the various deeds under indictment not so much as evidence of political, social or even moral misconduct, but as offences against the faith – as *sins*. Therefore, the way to redemption is left open, if, as is the case with the German people, the sinner is the victim of seduction, however willing (i.e. weak) he may have been. The German people will have to *atone*, they will be *saved*, particularly if they are ready to *confess*, to *repent*, i.e. to 'extirpate pride and to renounce all the dreams of world conquest and a heaven on earth'.

*Two devices are used to create and deepen the cleavage between leadership and people.* (1) Time and again it is said that *Germany and Nazism are not identical.* In fact Germany is merely the first victim of Nazism: 'There are in our fatherland so many people who are true followers of Christ. Unperturbed by the propaganda of the new pagans and fearless, they live like good Christians in the midst of chaotic moral confusion.'

(2) Those who are willing are called upon to *resist*. The appeal is addressed foremost to Catholics. 'We Catholics must stand together as a solid unit and must not depart from our principles.' Martyrdom is extolled. 'Let us be proud of such witnesses to the faith.' On the other hand, Catholic responsibility is so interpreted as to include duties of definitely *secular* character: 'We are all citizens of a state, and the responsibility for what happens in the State falls on all of us.' Therefore, 'It is our duty to do everything in our power to deprive of their power these moral Godless ones who are at the head of our state.' Harsh words are directed to the lukewarm, who are cultivating the vicarious sins of indolence, indecision, and 'animal egotism'. '*Nobody* in our homeland can escape the moral decision of the present. It is a matter of taking position against the Godless masters of our fatherland and *to fight against* them.'

## Evaluation

In view of the fact that the origin of the broadcasts remains obscure it is difficult to verify the intention and true identity of the sponsors. There is no reason to question the sincerity and seriousness of the approach. The Catholicism of the station is of a very activistic nature. On the other hand, the solemn ceremonial and highly religious form lacks certain symbols and other elements which would help to confirm the identity of the station as Catholic. There are almost no references to events, happenings, or personalities within the Catholic Church, even outside Germany.

As to effectiveness, the question must be raised of the extent to which the devout Catholic in Germany will be found willing to take religious counsel from a medium as thoroughly profane and suspect as the radio is in Germany. In contrast to Anglo-Saxon concepts and habits, there is a strong possibility that at least orthodox parts of the *Catholic audience in Germany*, unaccustomed to services over the air, might resent the delivery of religious preachings through radio channels. On the other hand, *foreign audiences*, particularly Catholics and those not given to 'Vansittartism', may be impressed by the demonstrated cleavage between leadership and people and perhaps be willing to regard the confession of guilt with a partial absolution. Finally, by addressing German Catholics as a solid group within the German orbit with stakes, ideals and motives *separate* from the rest of the German population, religion may prove an effective lever-device to re-awaken and encourage sectarian thinking, perhaps to re-establish traditional sectionalism, at any rate to refute ideologically the unity of purpose and form claimed to be achieved by Nazi Germany.


## THE GERMAN WORKERS' STATION

This station broadcasts to Germany on two different wave-lengths at 00:50, 14:50, 15:50, 16:50, 17:50, 18:50 and 23:50 EWT, always for nine minutes. The language is German, although infrequently special messages to foreign workers are read in French and Italian. The station was heard by the FBIS for the first time on 28 December 1942, and has been received since at irregular intervals.*

*Political Ideology*
The German Workers' Station, although more activistic in its propaganda, closely resembles in political ideology the clandestine station European Revolution which ceased broadcasting in the late summer of 1942.

---

*It is not clear whether this station is identical with the clandestine transmitter which was received on 8 September, as the 'German Peoples' Station'. Although the broadcast then was largely unintelligible, it was undoubtedly a Marxist station.

# 16

# Aspidistra

The 'Most Secret' document printed below, dated 24 November 1941, was signed by 'D. Stephens, Secretary PWE'. He was later Sir David Stephens, Clerk of the Parliaments, House of Lords. According to a brief preliminary 'Note by Secretary' he attached 'for the interest of Ministers a report on the progress of a project that was originated by SO1'. The Ministers in question were Anthony Eden (Foreign Office), Dr Hugh Dalton (Ministry of Economic Warfare) and Brendan Bracken (Ministry of Information), i.e. the three members of the Political Warfare Executive. The document does not disclose that at this stage the BBC was unaware that PWE had acquired an immensely powerful medium-wave broadcasting toy which would *not* be under its control. The project, as described by Stephens, was practicable in theory even if the capabilities of Aspidistra were still untested. Furthermore, the apparatus would certainly not be 'ready for use by April 1942'. According to Mr Stephens:

In the spring of 1941 SO1 worked out a scheme for broadcasting on Enemy and Enemy-controlled wave-lengths at great power and with great variety of attack. The scheme involved the purchase of an existing 500-kW transmitter in America and its adaptation to broadcasting on a number of frequencies and to changing frequency very quickly.

The scheme was put before the Prime Minister, who had been previously interested in broadcasting on Enemy wave-lengths, on 16 May 1941. It received his approval on 17 May.

A brief recapitulation of the project is as follows:

a) The apparatus consists of a 500-kW transmitter adapted to range over the whole of the medium frequency bands and so to attack any Enemy-controlled broadcasting service as conditions demand.

b) It constitutes a radio counter-battery and it has three principal qualities: *surprise, great strength* (it must be louder in the countries to which it is directed than the Enemy-controlled transmitters themselves) and *flexibility*.

c) It was conceived not as a propaganda service, but as a weapon to destroy the Enemy's own propaganda, for use in a critical period of the war. It should be ready for work by about April 1942.

d) Its programme of work will be to ring the changes on Enemy objectives, that is to say, not to transmit at regular times on predictable Enemy programmes, but to choose objectives especially worthy of attack and to open fire on them without warning. These counter-transmissions will be made according to a perfectly definable technique developed in specially chosen speakers by intensive training. Our intervention, which will be anonymous and unannounced, can come at any point in the Enemy's transmissions, because the great power of the transmitter enables us to shout down the transmissions on which we intrude. There would also be advantage in continuing to broadcast on the wave-length of an enemy station for some time after it has shut down, e.g., because of air-raids.

1 The necessary approval of the Wireless Telegraphy Board was obtained in September and a site was found which allowed of sufficient mast height and which complied with Air Ministry and other Service Department requirements. Work has been begun on the site. Part of the transmitter itself is reported now to be on its way from the United States to this country.

2 The original estimate was of an outlay of some £165,000. Of this sum £111,801.4s.10d. has been remitted to his Majesty's Ambassador, Washington, for the cost of the transmitter and some thousands of pounds have been spent on erection and preparation of the site in this country. The total so far paid out is £127,836.6s.9d. Costs have risen since the original estimate and some slight increase over the original figure for initial outlay may be necessary.

3 The scheme is known as 'Aspidistra' (popular song: 'The Biggest Aspidistra in the World') owing to the great strength of the transmitter involved.

4 Hitherto all disbursements have been done by SOE (or previously SO2) in consultation with the Treasury. It is submitted that the balance of commitments should forthwith be transferred to PWE as SOE have no claims whatsoever in the operation of the scheme.[1]

The history of Aspidistra is important in the context of this book because it was Delmer who eventually 'acquired' the transmitter and was able to employ it for purposes which had not been thought of in November 1941.

One result of the German occupation of Europe was that the broadcasting centres of the occupied countries came under the control of the Propaganda Ministry. The numerical preponderance of the transmitters thus obtained could be used for providing local services based upon German directives and at the same time to jam British broadcasts, i.e. to Germany and the Occupied and Satellite Territories. Owing to the number of transmitters at their disposal the Germans controlled a large number of wave-lengths. They did not interfere with the BBC's Home Service. Owing to our lack of transmitter strength we did not jam any German or German-controlled broadcasts.

The possibility of combatting Germany's superiority in the ether was discussed in the Department and Colonel Gambier-Parry was consulted in May 1941. It happened that he had learned of the existence in the USA of a 'giant' 500-kW medium-wave transmitter which had been constructed by RCA for sale to the New Jersey WJ2 commercial station. However, its use had been forbidden by the Federal broadcasting authority because 50 kW was the maximum permissible strength and the apparatus remained unemployed at RCA's factory at Camden, N.J., although the Chinese government had an option to purchase it. Gambier-Parry went to the USA to inspect the instrument and immediately secured an option for HM Government to acquire Aspidistra, named after the music-hall song which the popular Gracie Fields had made famous.

When Gambier-Parry returned to England he prepared a plan for the purchase, erection and use of this transmitter. In a memorandum headed 'A Plea for Counter-Battery Work in Radio Propaganda' he claimed that:

> This apparatus would create a raiding Dreadnought of the Ether, firing broadcasts at unpredictable times at unpredictable objectives of the enemy's radio propaganda machine.
>
> The weapon to perform this counter-battery work must clearly have three principal qualities: it must be a complete surprise; it must be loud – as loud in the countries at which it is directed as the enemy-controlled transmitters themselves; and it must be flexible, to cope with the great variety of propaganda services controlled by the enemy.

When Aspidistra was first being discussed at Woburn, Anthony Eden visited the Abbey and asked Ralph Murray, who was in charge of the Department's recording studios at Wavendon, about the actual broadcasting capabilities of the four $7\frac{1}{2}$-kW short-wave transmitters which were then being employed. Murray explained that their output could hardly be described as strong and told Eden what he knew about Aspidistra. Eden then talked to Dr Dalton, who had ministerial responsibility for all secret broadcasting activities. Dalton drafted a paper which was submitted to the Prime Minister, who immediately sanctioned its purchase. Thus the Department would prospectively be in control of one of the most powerful broadcasting instruments in the world, whether or not it would be able to 'shout down' the enemy on his own wave-lengths.

It is important to note, however, that at that time the Department had no control over the BBC's Foreign Services. Indeed, it was hardly represented inside the BBC, at least by an individual who carried any weight, until Ivone Kirkpatrick, a senior Foreign Office official, was co-opted to Bruce Lockhart's Political Warfare Executive committee in 1941. In its early stages the realisation of the Aspidistra project produced many inter-departmental squabbles in which the BBC, the Ministry of Information, the Air Ministry and the Wireless Telegraphy Board were all involved.

In the meantime Harold Robin who, as a technician, was only inter-ested in Aspidistra's 'guts' was sent to the USA. For this purpose and the transfer of funds to the USA as an employee of the SIS he was temporarily attached to William Stephenson (the subject of William Stevenson's popular biography *A Man Called Intrepid*), who was not only Churchill's personal representative in the USA but Director of British Security Co-ordination in the Western Hemisphere. In other words he was a very senior member of SIS.

Robin spent two months in New York City during the summer of 1941 and travelled daily to RCA's headquarters at Camden, N.J. to immerse himself in Aspidistra's technicalities. He was responsible for approving all the technical specifications and, in fact, arranged for its power to be increased from 500 to 600 kW.

In the meantime a location for Aspidistra was being prepared in Bedfordshire, conveniently close to the Woburn area. When the Air Ministry was consulted about the proposed height of the transmitter's mast in August 1941 serious objections were raised with regard to the site, and SO1 (which was just about to become PWE) was informed that the Wireless Telegraphy Board's approval would in any case be neces-sary. The latter was eventually forthcoming in September 1941 but a new site had to be found. Robin and a colleague, armed with large maps of southern England, attended a meeting at the Air Ministry where one possible place after another was rejected for this or that reason. It was eventually agreed in October 1941 that Aspidistra could be located on a seventy-acre site high up in the Ashdown Forest near Crowborough, Sussex.

By now the BBC was beginning to raise a host of objections to Aspidistra, e.g. its use on enemy wave-lengths would constitute jamming and a Cabinet decision had directed that enemy broadcasts should not be jammed as we did not stand to gain in a radio war. If we jammed the *Reichssender* they would jam the BBC. Furthermore, Italian attempts to butt in with a 'ghost voice' on the BBC had been a failure and Aspidistra might do no better. The BBC revealed that it had been conducting research on an apparatus which could be installed in an RAF bomber and interfere with enemy broadcasts while it was flying over Germany. Brendan Bracken (MoI) complained that there had been no previous consultation with the BBC's engineers about Aspidistra but stated that the BBC would in any case not be able to provide any technical staff.

After endless arguments a compromise was eventually reached in May 1942, namely that Aspidistra would be used to reinforce the BBC's external services when it was not required for PWE's special purposes (which were still undefined!) or by RAF Fighter Command. As late as July 1942 Bracken was still arguing that Aspidistra should be managed by BBC technicians. Bruce Lockhart pointed out that it would have to be operated by the SIS's engineers who would be required to work the station for extremely secret work in connection with the Second Front. Lockhart's arguments prevailed. The BBC would be able to use Aspidistra as an auxiliary transmitter when it was not otherwise employed. However, PWE's plans for its use showed little realisation of either its limitations or possibilities. Indeed, at this time Aspidistra had neither been installed nor tested.

In the meantime, during the spring and summer of 1942 Harold Robin was supervising the digging of a very big hole in the ground near Crowborough. The transmitter, its control panels and its large electric power generator were to be accommodated in a subterranean two-storey building of which the ground floor was to be fifty feet underground with four feet of reinforced concrete on top. The whole excavation area was covered with grass turf and when a number of fast-growing trees had been planted Aspidistra's location was effectively concealed.

Harold Robin's huge pit might have taken an eternity to excavate were it not for the fact that Cecil Williamson, his resourceful colleague, discovered a Canadian Army road-building unit in the neighbourhood. He asked if they were particularly busy; they were not! Waiting for the Second Front was a tedious business and they were positively delighted to bring along six bulldozers and a supply of explosive to loosen the earth and such rocks as were encountered. They completed the 'digging' in about six weeks and according to Robin appeared to exist almost exclusively on a diet of beer, the latter no doubt being paid for from SIS secret funds. The structural steelwork, concreting and all the other building operations were subsequently done by an army of 600 workmen which worked literally around the clock. The site was illuminated at night and the lighting was immediately switched off when a message was received that enemy aircraft were approaching the coast.

Apart from the construction work the installation of Aspidistra required an elaborate telecommunications system, with direct lines to the Air Ministry, the BBC and PWE's new studio at Milton Bryant (MB), close to Woburn Abbey. No broadcasts were made or recorded at Crowborough, which merely generated whatever was received by land line from London or MB. A complex control panel was required to keep in direct contact with the studios and to effect the almost instantaneous change of frequency which, for the British, was to be one of Aspidistra's most important features.

If some features of Aspidistra's interior decor (see the illustration) appear to be strongly reminiscent of the Odeon and other cinema chains of the 1930s, it must be mentioned that Cecil Williamson's pre-war career had been in the film industry.

When Winston Churchill sanctioned the purchase of Aspidistra in May 1941 he was, in a sense, buying a pig in a poke because he cannot have had any very clear idea of how and when it should or could be used. My guess is that Aspidistra appealed to him simply because it was the equivalent of a 'big gun' which the Germans did not possess.

Late in 1941 a series of events ultimately affected, even if at first only indirectly, Aspidistra's ultimate employment. The Japanese attack on Pearl Harbor (7 December 1941) was immediately followed by Germany's and Italy's declaration of war on the US. Then Congress declared war on both, voting the despatch of US forces to any part of the world. Great Britain and the USA were now officially allies, although the British had previously received invaluable help and encouragement from across the Atlantic (cf. the Lease-Lend Bill, approved by the House of Representatives on 11 March 1942).

PWE had already been in touch with certain individuals close to President Roosevelt. Thus Robert Sherwood, a personal friend of the President's and head of the recently established Foreign Information Service, visited Woburn on 10–11 September 1941. The FIS, however, was part of Colonel William G. Donovan's new Office of the Co-Ordinator of Information and the latter soon formed the nucleus of Donovan's Office of Strategic Services (OSS), the forerunner of the postwar Central Intelligence Agency. In 1941 PWE was inclined to regard the OSS as the American equivalent of SOE. According to one source:

Relations between PWE and Colonel Donovan's organisation ... were frequently influenced by British misgivings about the exact status of the American organisations. This uncertainty arose from the very nature of the American organisations which can be described as non-hierarchic and drew their authority directly from the President. To us their credentials appeared often vague and mutually conflicting.

Another passage from the same document, which referred to January 1942, when the US was already an allied combatant, reads:

The question of the status of Colonel Donovan's organisation in relation to the State Department was raised by PWE as it was manifestly unwise for an organisation the policy of which was derived from the British Foreign Office to collaborate fully with an American organisation the policy of which might be repudiated by the State Department. ... The persistent doubts of PWE seemed justified when President Roosevelt transferred control of Colonel Donovan's organisation less the Foreign Information Service to the American Chiefs of Staff. The Foreign Information Service was transferred to the new Office of War Information set up by the President under Mr Elmer Davis. PWE appears to have been apprised of these changes ... before Colonel Donovan, who was in London, had been made aware of them.

The shape and functions of the US propaganda organisations were eventually settled with Donovan's OSS representing a mixture of SIS/ SOE plus PWE's black side, while the OWI resembled a combination of the MoI and PWE's white propaganda department.

By the time of the Allied landings in North Africa on 7–8 November 1942 the political warfare work was largely dominated by the Americans and, furthermore, it was under military rather than civilian control. At this time the British Eighth Army was fighting its way westwards across the Western Desert. 'Torch' was primarily an American operation, but was supported by British troops and the RAF, and the convoy of over 500 vessels was escorted by more than 350 ships of the Royal Navy. Lieutenant-General Eisenhower (US Army) was in overall command. Indeed, on 11 December the Prime Minister announced in the House of Commons that 'Torch' was an American operation and that the US was responsible for political arrangements in North Africa.

On 6 September 1942, when the preparations for 'Torch' were in full swing, the Prime Minister asked for information about Aspidistra, which he realised might play an important role in the forthcoming North African campaign, and demanded a progress report from Robert Bruce Lockhart. On its receipt Churchill minuted: 'First explain what advantages it gives us (8 lines), secondly repeat every three days the day it is expected to be ready to function.' Lockhart did not refer this peremptory enquiry to Reginald Leeper, nor to Colonel Gambier-Parry, but to the BBC's Sir Noel Ashbridge (formerly Controller of Engineering and the Deputy Director General), who reported that:

1 It has a higher power than any station known to be in-use by the enemy.
2 It will strengthen the BBC by making reception possible up to 1100 miles where there is no local jamming.
3 It will overcome jamming in North and Western France unless the Germans take very rapid counter-measures and can therefore be used for operations.
4 If necessary, it could create confusion in enemy broadcasts in Western Europe. This might provoke a jamming war on a large scale in which at present we might come off worst.

It was strange that Lockhart did not consult Leeper, his deputy at Woburn, or Gambier-Parry, but it seems that latterly he had not been able to secure immediate and accurate answers to his questions to Gambier-Parry, probably because the latter was harassed by the final stages of completing Aspidistra's installation.

On 10 September 1942 Lockhart informed the Prime Minister that one missing component was being flown from the USA and that the moment it arrived the instrument would be completed. He mentioned, too, that we had no reserve equipment. The reference to completion was not strictly true because only one of the three 300-ft masts had been erected. On 21 September the Prime Minister minuted, 'When will it work?' On 23 September Lockhart was able to reply that Aspidistra was complete, that the second mast was one third up, and that the third mast was on its way to the site from the docks. Churchill was not satisfied and wanted to know, 'When will it work full blast?'

Lockhart replied that Aspidistra should be able to operate at full strength by 13 October. The Prime Minister realised that the pressure could be relaxed and on 27 September minuted, 'Good. Report any adverse changes only.' Early in October, however, it was necessary to invoke Churchill's assistance to obtain some spare parts. He wrote angrily: 'Have we really built this gigantic machine dependent on valves which are obsolescent with no provision for replacements?' Luckily the problem was solved without too much delay.

While Aspidistra had been purchased under SIS auspices and was to be operated by SIS technical personnel, apart from the BBC and PWE there was one other interested party, namely the Royal Air Force's signals section. Thus Air Commodore Blandy was seconded to PWE with, it seems, a brief to supervise the technical control and security of Aspidistra. Gambier-Parry was able to outmanœuvre Blandy without too much difficulty:

> Air Commodore Blandy was not, however, introduced personally to Colonel Gambier-Parry, neither was he authorised to visit Crowborough. He was to suffer continual difficulties in the following months owing to Air Ministry complaints of Aspidistra transmissions for testing purposes being carried out without notification. Air Commodore Blandy had been appointed to control such transmissions, but was given no evidence of their existence by the Department and received no support in his dealings with Gambier-Parry.[2]

Aspidistra was first employed operationally on 8 November 1942, i.e. immediately after it was known that the American landings were proceeding successfully. It broadcast a pre-recorded speech by President Roosevelt and General Eisenhower's proclamations. Except for two fifteen-minute periods when it transmitted on the Rabat Vichy-controlled wave-length it was used to reinforce the BBC Foreign News Service for a period of forty-eight hours. Following the two 'black' transmissions Vichy radio warned listeners that the so-called official broadcasts from Rabat originated from an unknown clandestine station. One result of the Aspidistra broadcasts on the Rabat wave-length was that the Admiralty briefly supposed that Rabat had already been captured by the Americans. This was an early example of counterfeit operations carried out without first informing all on our side who might be misled by them.

Aspidistra remained with the BBC's European Service for the time being, providing forty per cent extra power and greatly increasing its effective range. Indeed, the BBC was able to overcome the jamming of its French broadcasts during a highly critical moment in the formation of French opinion. Aspidistra had done all that it had been allowed to do with triumphant success at its first trial. Gambier-Parry was promoted to Brigadier early in 1943.

1   FO 898/11

2   F & CO document

# 17

# Anglo-American Relations: Propaganda in North Africa 1942–3

While we were greatly relieved to see the Americans enter the war as active Allies they did not always understand our language nor we theirs, especially during the early stages of the partnership. Misunderstanding had greatly diminished by late in 1943 when General Eisenhower insisted upon complete integration at senior staff level. Except for the successful employment of Aspidistra in November 1942 PWE's involvement in the 'Torch' Campaign appears to have been a minor one. Soon after the war it was recorded that, 'There was some difficulty in tracing the exact development of PWE preparations for the landings in North Africa. PWE was ordered to render all possible assistance to this American operation but arrangements with the Americans were largely verbal and there are no formal requests in the PWE files.'

According to the same source, 'A "black" publication of American (OSS) origin was shown to PWE. This was a Yellow Book, purporting to be produced by anti-German elements in the Vichy Administration. It was entitled *Les violations de l'armistice franco-allemand*. PWE made the practical suggestion that the format given to it by OSS would reveal its [American] origin. An edition was therefore printed in a more plausible Vichy format and produced by about 15 October (1942) for OSS.' According to the document my unit did the work and also designed and printed five leaflets for OSS but I have no recollections of those events.

However, I do remember being invited to visit an OSS office in Curzon Street where I was received by three or four crew-cut young gentlemen – typical products of Harvard, Yale and Princeton – who told me that they had heard that I had access to what they described as 'some very interesting printing types', adding that they would greatly appreciate the opportunity to use them. Aghast at the prospect of these enthusiastic amateurs invading the Fanfare Press I said that my private plant had so much work in hand that I could not offer any facilities and quickly made my escape.

During the summer of 1942 Colonel Donovan's OSS had a representative with access to PWE's inner circles. This was Mr Percy Winner, an American journalist who, during the mid-1930s, had been the Havas news agency's chief correspondent in North Africa and had also been manager of the International News Service's Rome office. On 8 June 1942 he wrote a six-page closely typed 'Memorandum for Colonel Donovan: Notes on personalities and problems in London'. When I read it many years later I was fascinated by his assessments of PWE's Brigadier Dallas Brooks, the SIS's Brigadier Stewart Menzies and two of the leading personalities in SOE.

> Brooks, an officer of the Royal Marines, is a member of the PWE Advisory Committee, who maintains liaison with the Chiefs of Staff. He is a formal, rather stuffy, not overbright individual who is immensely vain and susceptible to flattery. He carries out his tasks with a good deal of efficiency but completely lacks imagination or an awareness of the problems of political warfare.

Robert Walmsley, who knew Brooks far better than I ever did, described him to me as 'an immensely able political soldier' and disagreed with Mr Winner who may have failed to tune in on a British wave-length. PWE owed a lot to his gifts as a diplomat and to his access to the highest levels of the British Chiefs of Staff and the Joint Intelligence Committee.

Brigadier [later Major-General Sir] Stewart Menzies, 'C' in the SIS, 'has his doubts about us and although he will play ball on each specific matter brought up with him, he has not up to the present taken any initiative in co-operation'. Winner thought that 'C' had 'not much confidence in our American type of organisation as opposed to the British [one]'. He continued: 'It is important to impress upon him (a) our real authority in this field, (b) the "professional" attitude and skill of our operatives, (c) the rapid and steady growth of our organisation, (d) the absolute dependability of our "security" arrangements.'

It is improbable that OSS possessed any of these desirable qualities in 1942. The SIS may have been far from perfect – for instance, before its outpost at Bletchley Park began to solve the 'Enigma' problems it was nothing like as omniscient as Herr Hitler and many others supposed it to be – but in the intelligence field we had far more experience than the newly created OSS.

As for SOE:

> At Baker Street . . . the key man is now Sir Charles Hambro of the banking and business family (head of the Great Western Railway). He is an

extremely aggressive person with boundless energy. Because of his family connections he is especially interested in Scandinavia but his particular interest at the moment is Latin America where he feels the United States is doing a very poor job. Baker Street is a hive of intrigue ...

Winner had a higher opinion of SOE's Brigadier Colin Gubbins, who was then Hambro's second in command: '. . . a tough, really able fighting man who takes care of the training of SOE field operatives'.

The remainder of Winner's extraordinary document contains a lot of ill-informed and often malicious chatter about other contemporary British personalities, e.g. Dr Hugh Dalton, Brendan Bracken, Robert Bruce Lockhart, Reginald Leeper, David Bowes-Lyon and certain senior people at the Ministry of Information, and their alleged mutual intrigues.[1]

Winner turned up in Algiers where he was the 'Senior Supervisor' of General Eisenhower's Psychological Warfare Section, although the latter was soon to become the Psychological Warfare Branch of Allied Force Headquarters under the command of Colonel Charles B. Hazeltine, 'whose appointment reflected the primitive regard for propaganda activities in the early days of the war, for Hazeltine was a cavalry officer [US Army] who knew nothing at all about his intended tasks'. According to another source, 'The exact status of such civilians as Mr Winner ... at different times is rather obscure and in some cases Americans have acted in dual capacities as members of the Office of War Information and officers of PWB.'

The Psychological Warfare Branch was a branch of the US War Department and functioned as part of military intelligence under the US Chiefs of Staff to whom its executive staff was directly responsible. Its work was based on the assumption that Psychological Warfare was an integral part of the Armed Services and not a new Service in itself. Many of the American civilians, of whom Winner was but one, found it difficult to follow the commands of their uniformed superiors and, probably late in 1942, Brigadier General Walter Bedell Smith, Eisenhower's Chief of Staff, complained that 'Europe and Africa together are too small to hold Winner and the United States Army.' It must be admitted, however, that the political situation in North Africa was at that time horribly confused and it is hardly surprising that Winner and others found it difficult either to sympathise with or follow the directives which emanated from very senior local military sources.

Theoretically PWB was supposed to be an Anglo-British affair but its British component only amounted to about sixty individuals and was greatly outnumbered by no less than 360 Americans of whom few had any practical experience of political warfare. In the meantime in London PWE's chiefs were becoming increasingly worried about the situation in Algiers and arranged to attach Thomas Barman, an experienced member of the Department, to the staff of Harold Macmillan, who had been appointed as Minister Resident on 30 December 1942. Sylvain Mangeot, a leading member of PWE's French Section, also went to Algiers and wrote a 'Most Secret and Personal' letter to his friend and colleague the late Hraci Arsan Paniguian, also of the French Section. (Pan, no one knew him as anything else, was one of PWE's most famous characters; ostensibly an Armenian he was a citizen of the world and eventually of Great Britain.) Colonel Hazeltine, according to Mangeot, was:

> ... not only an ignoramus but was quite prepared and, in fact, determined to carry on all propaganda in the name of his Commander-in-Chief from Algeria to Tunis and thence to Italy, France, Germany and Scandinavia ... The more I see of things here, the more imperative I feel is the need for policy to be framed and enforced from London. If we repeat the tragic mistake of letting things slide and awaiting events, there is no telling what ghastly muddles we shall not be involved in – wading across Europe in tow of incredible American ignorance, and even more incredible American personalities. All the good work that PWE has done from London will be wasted and we shall appear as first-class hypocrites or plain fools, or both.[2]

Mangeot's letter was read by senior members of PWE and, reinforced by Barman's report, did much to bring about the decision that Richard Crossman should go to Algiers. He was accompanied by Robert Walmsley, who wrote in 1946:

> The period May to August 1943 is a blank so far as I am concerned since, together with Crossman, I had been sent to Algiers to 'clean up' in PWB ... it is amusing to remember that the 'appointment' of Crossman and myself had never been made at all as PWE fondly imagined it had, that both of us were on the point of returning at once to England, but remained in more or less subordinate positions to see what could be done, and that I myself – supposed to construct the whole PWB intelligence – had no executive power whatever. In spite of all this, however, I think we did more or less what we were supposed to do by PWE, and Crossman did rather more by staying abroad (or outside PWE) for ever. PWE had either been misled or misled itself into assuming that the appointments of Crossman and myself (as well as of an American director, C. D. Jackson, of the whole affair) had been agreed.

It is unlikely that Crossman regretted his ultimate transfer from PWE to 'the Americans'. His superiors in London had always disliked and mistrusted his tendency to 'make policy' rather than implement those formulated by others. In this white propaganda area he could easily be controlled by Ivone Kirkpatrick, the Department's senior executive in the BBC, not to mention by Hugh Carleton Greene, who ran the BBC's German section. Furthermore, on the black side Delmer had achieved an independence which made it impossible for Crossman to 'control' him.

Before and after the 'Torch' period at Woburn Dr Leslie Beck was successfully dealing with a succession of political problems connected with the French RUs. These were not black but, rather, 'co-operational' stations which were to have increasingly important links with the internal French resistance organisation. Dr Beck's important role in PWE – he had close links with de Gaulle's people in London and was respected by the Americans – requires further investigation.

Early in 1943 Delmer learned that PWB Algiers was proposing to conduct black radio operations and wrote a closely reasoned paper in which he outlined the objections. He pointed out that the would-be black propagandists had neither the experience, the specially trained scriptwriters, the 'voices', nor the necessarily large volume of accurate and specialised intelligence material. His final conclusion was that, 'There appears to be nothing to be gained and much to be lost by PWB starting black operations. Every effort should therefore be made to dissuade them from embarking on such projects.' The effort was presumably made because nothing more was heard about black from Algiers.

1   I am indebted to Dr Charles Cruickshank for a copy of Mr Winner's preposterous document, which is in the US National Archives.

2   F & CO document

# 18

# The Italian Surrender

When *Radio Italia* ceased to broadcast on 15 May 1942 PWE was without an Italian RU for nine months until *Radio Risorgi* began to operate on 16 February 1943. Apart from the fact that very few people in Italy possessed radios capable of receiving short-wave transmissions – hence there was no easily identifiable audience – at Woburn there were undoubtedly staffing problems. Harold Robin told me about 'the Sicilian sea captain who always spoke without a script holding a bottle of whisky in one hand and refused outright to swallow the PWE line. One day he stamped out of the studio, spat on the front doorstep and returned unaided [to internment] to the Isle of Man, from whence he came.'

*Radio Risorgi* began to operate in February 1943 when plans for the Sicily landings were being made, although they did not take place until July.

The RU purported to be the mouthpiece of a group of well-informed anti-Fascists with the entrée into diplomatic circles in neutral countries. The policy advocated was the return to power of the House of Savoy and the placing of Badoglio [Chief of the Italian General Staff] in power. Contact with Badoglio and the Court was implied. The object was to discourage dissatisfaction with the Fascist regime and urge action against it.

The transmitter purported to be in the north of Italy. The broadcasts were 80 per cent fact and 20 per cent fiction. Rumours were created by distorting facts and giving diverse significance to actual events as well as by completely fictitious stories. The speakers were chosen from anti-Fascist prisoners of war who had volunteered to do propaganda work. They were not good speakers, and became depressed owing to the security restrictions on their liberty. The employment of prisoners of war was ill advised. Security restrictions also limited the supply of intelligence and made it impossible to give the impression sought.[1]

Delmer was to fare far better with German prisoners of war at a later stage, probably because they formed part of a large and very lively team

170

which included all his expert black artisans from RAG and some interesting new recruits. Although Delmer's PoWs sometimes chafed at the security restrictions it is clear that they were happier than the Italians who can have seldom gone far from the house at which they lived in isolation except to record at 'Simpson's'. In any event *Radio Risorgi* was closed down on 15 September 1943, a week after Italy unconditionally surrendered.

The next Italian RU to go into action was *Radio Livorno*, which first broadcast on 25 July 1943, the day Mussolini was arrested and Marshal Badoglio became Prime Minister of Italy. It was under the direct control of the Naval Intelligence Division's 17z section which had been specially formed somewhat earlier to work with Delmer's new *Kurzwellensender Atlantik* station, which began to transmit live from new studios at Milton Bryant on 22 March 1943. *Radio Livorno* also operated from MB, rather than 'Simpson's'.

> The station purported to be run by an Italian naval officer and a naval wireless operator situated somewhere in the Leghorn area. The officer posed as the spokesman of a secret and patriotic association within the Italian navy. Some difficulty was experienced with the personnel. The first speaker, an Italian ex-naval officer, refused to continue after the first transmission and had to be replaced; his substitute proved to be extremely touchy.
>
> *Radio Livorno*'s aim was to build up solidarity in the Italian navy, to convey the impression that the Germans were the real enemy and to suggest that attempts to scuttle would be made only in accordance with German wishes. At the same time white propaganda was encouraged to speak sympathetically of the difficulties under which the Italian navy laboured and to hint that the British naval authorities were not really hostile to it. ... The Naval Intelligence Division had sometimes restrained the BBC [which knew nothing about *Radio Livorno*] from making capital out of the inefficiency of the Italian navy.
>
> Finally a signal was drafted for promulgation by the Commander-in-Chief of the Mediterranean Fleet inviting the Italian navy to surrender and indicating how it might do so.[2]

On 9 September 1943, the day after Italy's unconditional surrender was announced by General Eisenhower, also by Marshal Badoglio on Rome radio, the Italian battle fleet left Spezia and Genoa for Malta and the greater part of it arrived there safely.

On 14 September the Commander-in-Chief of the Mediterranean fleet sent the following signal to the Admiralty:

The Admiral (Da Zara) stated that he and his men had been much influenced by Admiral Cunningham's appeal issued immediately after the Armistice. They *assumed* [author's italics] that the Merchant Marine would be used to supply Italy and that after a reasonable interval Italian warships might be allowed to escort their own convoys. He said that for four years the Italian sailors had been taught by every means that 'green was red' and that it would take time to teach them that 'green really was green . . .'

In a memorandum to Robert Bruce Lockhart, Ritchie Calder, PWE's Director of Plans, stated that, 'It should be noted that the "assumption" which was so effective was entirely created by us,' i.e. PWE and *Radio Livorno*, working according to the instructions of NID and the Admiralty.[3]

However, the armistice terms required the surrender of the Italian fleet and air force and it is evident that *Radio Livorno*'s efforts must be equated with no more than a preliminary psychological softening–up process. It would be interesting to read the NID's own contemporary account of *Radio Livorno*'s contribution. If Lieutenant-Commander Donald McLachan ever wrote one, a copy of his report does not appear to have reached PWE.

Mr (or Lieutenant-Commander RNVR as he was in 1943) Martelli must be allowed the last word. In a letter to *The Times* published on 18 June 1973 he wrote:

> I was one of the first British officers to go on board the flagship when the Italian fleet was lying off Malta, and one of the first questions I asked the Italian admiral was what he thought of our propaganda. The answer was that except for the BBC he had never heard of it [i.e. *Radio Livorno*]. Nor had his Chief of Staff, my old friend Conte Ferrante Capponi (formerly naval attaché in London), who had missed the sailing from Taranto, but whom I met and questioned later.
>
> The truth is that the Italian Navy was intensely loyal to King Victor Emmanuel, who after dismissing Mussolini resumed the title of Commander-in-Chief of the Armed Forces, and that when he ordered them to surrender to the British in accordance with the terms of the armistice of 2 September 1943, they obeyed unhesitatingly.

Thus I am inclined to believe that no one of any consequence in Italy ever listened to *Radio Livorno*, hence that Ritchie Calder's 'assumption' of its success and Delmer's very positive account of the operation in *Black Boomerang* must both be discounted.

1   F & CO document
2   F & CO document
3   Ritchie–Calder to Robert Bruce Lockhart, 21 September 1943 (FO 898/65).

# 19

# Kurzwellensender Atlantik/
# Soldatensender Calais

*Kurzwellensender* means short wave station. The *Soldatensender* (soldiers' station, originally *Calais* but renamed *West* when the Allied armies swept past the Channel ports on their way to Belgium and the German frontier) was directly based upon Delmer's *Atlantik* formula and, indeed, eight months' experience of operating the *Kurzwellensender*. The latter first broadcast on 22 March 1943. *Calais* followed on 18 November and now the giant 600-kW Aspidistra *medium-wave* transmitter at Crowborough was used. Delmer had succeeded in partly 'capturing' Aspidistra from the BBC's European Service – much to the BBC's chagrin – and this opened a new chapter in his extraordinary career in PWE.

Whereas *Gustav Siegfried Eins* was a black station and purported to be operating inside Germany, *Atlantik* and *Calais* were 'grey', meaning that they did not even begin to pretend that they were within the borders of the Reich, or even somewhere in the Occupied Territories. It was left to the listener's gullibility or commonsense to decide whether or not the preliminary announcement, 'Here is the *Kurzwellensender Atlantik*' (or later, 'Here is the *Soldatensender Calais* linked with the *Kurzwellensender Atlantik*'), together with details of wave-lengths and broadcasting times, prefaced a transmission by a *Feindsender* (enemy station). A 'grey' station depended upon the attractiveness of its programme to obtain an audience – this concept was undoubtedly Delmer's – and the cover merely provided the audience with a psychological excuse, or an alibi, and at the same time ensured that the programme was presented in a manner which did not offend its prejudices.

Before attempting a brief description of the origins of the *Kurzwellensender Atlantik* I must refer to a tribute to the later *Soldatensender Calais*, which was in many respects the *Atlantiksender* but with the benefit of some months of experiment and expansion behind it. It was written by a member of the US Office of War Information staff at the American

174

Embassy in London to a woman friend in New York City. His letter was intercepted by the British Postal Censorship and a copy reached PWE. The present generation of readers will probably never have heard of Ted Lewis or the nostalgic 'blues' song, 'Me and My Shadow', nor may they be aware that the Propaganda Ministry would not allow anything remotely resembling American jazz to be broadcast in Germany. However, the U-boat crews and countless young Germans serving in the *Wehrmacht* in France and elsewhere in Europe greatly enjoyed it, and such was the excellence of Delmer's 'German domestic news service', with its intimate details of 'life in the Reich', that when discovered in the act of listening to a *Feindsender*, the culprits could always declare, with a look of innocence on their faces, 'But surely it was a German station?' Later it was discovered that the German intellectuals who listened to *Calais*, which they could hear on medium-wave, would have preferred rather more Bruckner and less Irving Berlin. As for OWI's Mr Jan Houbolt's tribute:

> ... there is a German station on the air, comes through as strong as the BBC and calls itself *Calais*. It is the best piece of propaganda I have ever listened to – the station pretends to be a Nazi station speaking about the Allies as the enemy, giving lots of personal messages to German soldiers and sailors outside Germany ... It gives reports of the bombings of German cities by the enemy and goes into detail about the addresses, naming numbers and streets in the places bombed.
>
> It tells as if it is straight news that (for instance) gas and water in such and such a section of Berlin have not yet been repaired after such and such a night. Then it mentions soldiers by name and rank, bringing to one the greetings of his wife in Hamburg, to the following a reminder not to forget his fifth wedding anniversary next Thursday, to another the admonition not to share his package of delicatessen from home with the officers as 'they have enough'.
>
> And the music ... ah, there again you have the master touch. It is American jazz with a German flavour ... even the music sounds authentic German. You have never heard Ted Lewis's 'Me and My Shadow' with a German singing in German in the Lewis manner. The American music changes with pure German music; German choirs and soldiers' songs sung by what sounds like mass-singing by a large number of people.
>
> In the same sentence which gives a back-handed slap to the Nazis, you will hear how many enemy (meaning Allied) ships were sunk, giving the names of the captains of the subs and who got wounded in the sub in the encounter. The thing is so cleverly done that friend and foe have just got to listen to it. It is as refreshing, commanding and appealing as anything I have listened to.

As I have already mentioned, the *Soldatensender*'s production techniques merely represented an extension or refinement of those developed for the *Atlantik* station. The latter was originally 'sired' by the Admiralty's Naval Intelligence Division. Indeed, it is unlikely that PWE's chiefs would ever have had the courage or imagination to give Delmer the necessary technical facilities or support in the absence of the NID's active intervention. What clinched the matter was the invitation to place PWE's services, and above all Delmer's, at the disposal of a vitally important operational command, because the Battle of the Atlantic was certainly not being won in 1942. So far the RAF had been inclined to regard PWE more as a nuisance than an asset, while the military had been inclined to ignore it.

In his unpublished *Naval Memoirs*, which were used by Mr Patrick Beesly for his *Very Special Admiral: The Life of Admiral J. H. Godfrey, CB*, published nine years after Godfrey's death (*aet.* 80) in 1971, the former Director of Naval Intelligence described the origins of the *Kurzwellensender Atlantik*. He had already recruited Donald McLachan, who was to play an important role in by far the most important period in Delmer's wartime career, by the simple process of extracting him from the Intelligence Corps where, according to Beesly, he 'was employed on some not very demanding duty ... and got him into naval uniform before the Army realised the magnitude of their loss. After three or four months in the German Section [Commander Ian] Fleming reported that he was "ripe" and Godfrey revealed to him his new job.'

It was, [Godfrey wrote] by means of insidious propaganda, to undermine and destroy the morale of officers and men in the German (and for a time, the Italian) Navy. This was achieved by the use of overt and covert wireless broadcasts, by the distribution of leaflets from the air, by the spreading of rumours and other subversive means.

Sefton Delmer, the arch operator of this technique, worked in the Political Warfare Executive (PWE). I had many talks with Tom Delmer and Donald McLachan and after pondering over the matter for two or three months and familiarising myself with the workings of PWE I came to the conclusion that a small component of PWE, working as an undercover section in NID, was an activity that had war-winning attributes, provided it was realistic, ruthless and was provided with an adequate sting.

The chief difficulty in starting a new section to operate an entirely new process is to find the right sort of staff. The qualifications for the job were a deep knowledge of German mentality, a capacity to see things from the German point of view and to know what would hurt them most, combined with an instinctive flair for high-grade journalism and 'putting things across' in a way that would influence public opinion. In this case public opinion was that of the German Navy personnel, their wives and families, and particularly the U-boat fleet.

McLachan possessed these qualities to a marked degree. He had been on the editorial staff of *The Times*, *Times* correspondent in Berlin, a schoolmaster at Winchester and Editor of *The Times Educational Supplement* before he came to NID. He was a terrifically hard worker with very strong nerves. He was ready for the job and also ready to take great responsibilities. I think Donald was genuinely pleased when I asked him after dinner at 36 Curzon Street if he would like the post. He accepted and I then asked him and Ian Fleming [Godfrey's Personal Assistant and later the author of the famous 'James Bond' thrillers] to put the machinery in motion for creating a Naval Section (17z) in collaboration with PWE. I was greatly relieved and confident that there would be no lack of sting with him, Ian Fleming and Sefton Delmer in charge.

As Section 17z developed I formed the personal view that an element of perfidy, verging on the unscrupulous, was one of the ingredients essential to its success, and that this was being adequately looked after. My principal function was to protect it from internal political interference, from depredations of people who said this 'isn't quite playing the game', and to preserve the anonymity of the men and women who actually did the work. We set up a high-powered cover committee (which never met) to whom was responsible a working group consisting of Captain Charles Lambe (a later and very distinguished First Sea Lord but at that time Deputy Director of Plans Division), Ian Fleming (who represented me as DNI), Donald, and when necessary a representative of Operations and Press Divisions.

Evidence regarding the effectiveness of the campaign is conflicting. It often provoked the German propaganda machine into ill-considered and unfortunate counter-action but German naval morale never broke as it had done in 1918. On the other hand there is no doubt that German sailors' relatives did listen to the clandestine broadcasts and it may have been a factor in persuading prisoners of war that their British captors knew all about them, even details of their personal lives, and therefore disposed them to talk more freely than they otherwise would have done. It is in any case an illuminating example of how Godfrey's mind worked (Beesly concluded), his views on his own role and the methods he employed in setting up a new section.

## According to Patrick Beesly:

McLachan had access to all Britain's most secret sources of information and was given a very free rein by his chief. Difficulties soon arose with the BBC who monitored the script of the German naval programme containing much unpublishable material, but these were overcome and McLachan began to get involved in the release of special items of naval interest to the

BBC in which all the necessary propaganda points were made but from which all material not available to the Press was excluded. This proved so successful that not only he but representatives from the other two Services became more and more involved in PWE's and the BBC's propaganda work.

The reference above to Britain's 'most secret sources of information' indicates that McLachan was able to supply no doubt heavily 'scrambled' versions of German naval and other intelligence material decrypted at Bletchley. This would have been comparatively low-grade 'Sigint' (Signals Intelligence) material and the security of 'Ultra' would certainly never have been compromised.

In *Black Boomerang* Delmer mentioned that he first heard of the actual imminence of the *Atlantiksender* operation when he lunched with Donald McLachan just before or after Christmas 1942. It was also briefly mentioned at a high-level PWE/Foreign Office meeting on 23 December when Reginald Leeper reported that, 'A new station [will] shortly come into operation to demoralise U-boat crews.'

For the *Atlantiksender* there was no question of using the old system whereby all the RU programmes were pre-recorded at 'Simpson's' and the discs then taken by road transport to the transmitting stations at Gawcott and Potsgrove. While live transmissions were feasible in cases of emergency from Wavendon Tower, the new Delmer operation was going to require far more space, time and facilities than could be provided there. Luckily the two-storey building which had been specially built for the Woburn end of the high-powered medium-wave Aspidistra transmissions at the time of the North African landings in November 1942 was empty and available at Milton Bryant, and Delmer moved in with his still small staff, probably on 5 February 1943. In the meantime Harold Robin was installing the first short-wave transmitters at the Aspidistra site miles away at Crowborough, where he would eventually be operating two 100-kW transmitters – infinitely more powerful than any that had been available to PWE in the past – with the addition of four $7\frac{1}{2}$-kW transmitters and what he described as 'some small outlets'.

According to Delmer in *Black Boomerang*, the broadcasting centre known as 'MB' was situated in five acres of grassland with tarred footpaths and surrounded by a high wire fence. It was guarded day and night by armed, uniformed warders who were accompanied by police dogs when they patrolled the area during the hours of darkness. Otto John described his own arrival at MB late one afternoon in December 1944: 'Finally the car stopped before an iron grille behind which there was a door leading to a guard-room. Through the half-open door I could see men in uniform and sub-machine-guns with their barrels glistening against the wall.'[1]

Once the MB organisation got into its stride it resembled a combination of the BBC (but on a far smaller scale), a secret intelligence centre and a press agency. The time was to come when it had its own aerial photographic interpretation section, radio monitoring service, a direct telephone line to the Combined Services Detailed Interrogation Centre, and even the editorial staff which produced a small daily newspaper for delivery by air to the German troops in France. It is possible, however, that Delmer's most cherished 'toy' was the *Hellschreiber* (radio-operated teleprinter machine) which brought the DNB (official German news agency) press releases and routine Propaganda Ministry directives at the same time as they were received by newspaper editorial staffs in Germany. At MB they were liable to stimulate action before their recipients in Germany had even read the material because the *Atlantiksender*'s news bulletins were broadcast at frequent intervals and could quickly be brought up to date. Furthermore, a straightforward item of German news could be as quickly 'twisted' to give it a meaning which the DNB certainly never intended. Delmer's policy was to offer his audience an adequate proportion of genuine material into which the 'disinformation' was skilfully inserted. Particular attention was paid to the music – 'the American jazz with the German flavour' – and many currently popular German recordings reached Woburn from Stockholm. It was the music, after all, which helped to secure and retain an appreciative following although the time was to come when listeners in Germany and elsewhere in Europe discovered that they could learn more about what was 'really happening' from the *Atlantiksender* and *Calais* than from any of the stations controlled by Dr Goebbels.

Delmer began the *Atlantiksender* operation with the assistance of his old hands from RAG, although additional staff soon began to arrive: at first a handful of German refugees some of whom had probably previously worked for the BBC but had never been allowed to broadcast, also a number of German prisoners of war who had been very carefully screened and were delighted to be able to make their own contribution to the downfall of the Third Reich. Frank Lynder could recall at least ten petty officers from the U-boat branch of the *Kriegsmarine*. It was they who knew all the latest U-boat jargon and could provide detailed descriptions of the local topography of the U-boat bases and the names and physical attributes of the waitresses who worked in establishments patronised by the crews – all useful background material. German PoWs who didn't prove useful were returned to the camps while others were retained and used as 'voices', meaning that they actually broadcast, some of them with increasing skill and confidence. Individuals from the *Luftwaffe* and *Wehrmacht* also eventually found their way to MB. Harold Robin told me that 'the full complement of personnel working on the programme was around a hundred', but this must have been at a much later stage.

Delmer's most valuable early recruit was undoubtedly Clifton Child, then aged thirty and formerly Corporal Child in the Royal Corps of Signals. He had been transferred to the W.T. Reserve in 1941 when he joined the Political Intelligence Department of the Foreign Office. With a first-class academic background as a historian he had studied at universities in England, Germany and the USA and, most important for his career at MB, had an excellent knowledge of the German language.

Professor John Hawgood, also a member of the PID staff which was in any case just about to be dissolved at Woburn, sent Delmer a brief note about Child on 2 February 1943: 'I should like your permission to show the Gustav Siegfried stuff to my assistant Mr Child,' he wrote. 'I should also like to request that you might have him put on the [Security Officer's] RAG visiting list . . .' Delmer met Child and forthwith invited him to take charge of his Intelligence Section. Child's incredible flair for drawing logical and entirely correct conclusions from apparently obscure evidence sometimes brought Delmer into conflict with the highest echelons of the Secret Intelligence Service who suspected that he must have had unauthorised access to the excessively secret 'Ultra' material, i.e. decrypts of the German 'Enigma' cyphers.

At much the same time Leonard Ingrams generously supplied C. E. Stevens from the Ministry of Economic Warfare. Stevens was an Ancient History don from Magdalen College, Oxford, who was not only endowed with a photographic memory but could remember everything that he had ever read, which was a great deal. Furthermore, he had an intimate knowledge of the MEW files and was trusted there. Thus he was able to obtain any available information without long-winded explanations. The combination of Child and Stevens was nothing less than formidable. Indeed, they may well have contributed to some Germans' irrational belief that the *Atlantiksender* must have its agents everywhere in Europe, including the *Führer*'s headquarters.

Delmer also persuaded the War Office to release Major Karl Robson

16  Faked currency for use in German armed forces canteens. On the reverse side there was a vulgar verse quatrain to the effect that it could be employed equally well for wiping Hitler's arse. The text appeared to have been typewritten. The illustration is about half the original size.

17  Bogus commemorative stamp for General von Witzleben who was hanged on 8 August 1944, i.e. after the failure of the von Stauffenberg plot to assassinate Hitler at the latter's headquarters. There is no evidence that it was ever used in Germany.

18  I am uncertain whether we forged the Moroccan fr. 1 air mail stamp with the *Deutsche Reichpost in Marokko* overprint or merely added the overprint to looted supplies of the genuine article.

19

19 The dissemination of a bogus German postage stamp showing Himmler's head in place of Hitler's was one of Delmer's more inspired ideas. The plan was to stimulate a flow of rumours that the insensately ambitious Heinrich Himmler was planning to supplant the *Führer*. The operation failed because recipients of mail bearing the new Himmler stamp – they included journalists in Sweden and Switzerland – simply failed to notice the presence of this surprising philatelic novelty.

20

20 Forgeries of German armed forces air mail stamps. They were probably manufactured for use by SOE. The fakes were of such good quality that they were never noticed and I never saw any 'come backs' which referred to them.

„ Wenn wir nicht den größten
Feldherrn aller Zeiten hätten,
dann hätten wir jetzt
den Frieden..."

Generaloberst Franz Halder
22. Juni 1943

Parole der Woche Nr 20/1943/Zentralverlag der NSDAP., München      0155

21

21 Another *Parole der Woche* ('Saying of the Week') sticker. The text was attributed to Colonel-General Franz Halder, one of the many senior German generals whom the *Führer* (who believed in his own military omniscience), had sacked. According to Halder's apochryphal remark: 'If we did not have the greatest Commander-in-Chief of all times, then we would now have peace . . .'

22–25  Forged French postage and administrative stamps

26  Forged German postage stamps showing Hitler's head

# Merkblatt

# Deutsche Nachrichtenhelferin!

## Merkblatt zur Verhütung von Geschlechtskrankheiten.

### Deutsche Nachrichtenhelferin!

Hüte dich vor geschlechtlichen Ausschweifungen! Sie setzen deine Leistungsfähigkeit herab und sind deiner Gesundheit nicht zuträglich.

Eine geschlechtskranke Helferin kann keinen Dienst leisten; selbstverschuldete Dienstunfähigkeit aber ist einer deutschen Wehrmachthelferin unwürdig. Von dir erwartet das Vaterland nicht nur volle dienstliche Leistung, es will auch, daß du einst Mutter gesunder Kinder wirst.

Meide den Alkoholgenuß, er lähmt die Willenskraft und führt oft auf Abwege!

Meide den Umgang mit Zufallsbekanntschaften, besonders im besetzten Gebiet! Sie sind fast immer geschlechtskrank!

Hast du in einer leichtfertigen Stunde dich zum außerehelichen Geschlechtsverkehr verleiten lassen, so entziehe dich nicht in unverantwortlicher Weise den Sanierungsvorschriften!

Die Sanierung möglichst bald nach dem Geschlechtsverkehr vorgenommen, schützt vor einer Geschlechtskrankheit.

Sie ist wertlos, wenn sie zu spät ausgeführt wird.

Höre auf deine Vorgesetzten und folge den Befehlen, die sie zur Verhütung von Geschlechtskrankheiten gegeben haben. Beherzige die Gesundheitsbelehrungen und Mahnungen deines Truppenarztes!

Verheimliche niemals dein Leiden und versuche unter keinen Umständen, dich selbst zu behandeln! Höre nicht auf die Zuflüsterungen und Ratschläge unverantwortlicher Laien! Jede Laienbehandlung von Geschlechtskrankheiten ist gesetzlich verboten. Unzweckmäßige oder ungenügende Behandlung rächt sich oft schwer durch nicht wiedergutzumachende Folgen für dich und deine künftige Familie.

Nimmst du an deinem Körper Anzeichen wahr, die dir verdächtig und krankhaft erscheinen, so melde dich umgehend bei deinem Truppenarzt.

Jede Geschlechtskrankheit ist heilbar, wenn sie rechtzeitig und sachgemäß behandelt wird. Darum verzweifle nicht, wenn du erkrankt bist, sondern vertraue dich deinem Truppenarzt an; er wird dafür sorgen, daß du wieder gesund wirst.

---

Herausgegeben vom Oberkommando der Wehrmacht.

1 000 000. OKW. 10. 42.

27  Bogus *Wehrmacht* leaflet warning German girls in army signals units against venereal disease

# Ausweis für Fliegergeschädigte Nr. 86052
## (gültig als Abreisebescheinigung).

### Der Inhaber dieses Ausweises

| (Name) | (Vorname) | (Beruf) |

geb. am ........................................ in ........................................

sowie Ehefrau ........................................ , geborene ........................................

und .......... Kinder, davon .......... unter 18 Jahren,

sowie .......... sonstige Angehörige,

bisherige Wohnung ........................................

sind fliegergeschädigt.

(Ort, Straße)

Alle Parteidienststellen und Behörden werden um weitgehende Unterstützung gebeten.

(L. S.)

........................................ den ........................................ 194....

**Der (Ober)-Bürgermeister**
Obdachlosensammelstelle Nr. ...........

---

**(Hier vom Einwohnermeldeamt abtrennen und s o f o r t an obige Dienststelle zurücksenden.)**

| (Name) | (Vorname) | (Beruf) |

geb. am ........................................ , ........................................

(bisherige Wohnung)

und .......... Kinder (Vornamen) ........................................

........................................ und sonstige Angehörige ........................................

........................................

........................................ gelangten heute hier für

........................................ zur polizeilichen Anmeldung.

(Straße und Hausnummer)

........................................ , den ........................................ 194....

**Der (Ober)-Bürgermeister**
Einwohnermeldeamt

(L. S.)

Nr. 1826. Formularverlag Emil Sommer, Grünstadt.                    **Wenden!**

---

28   Forged identity certificate for air-raid victims, useful also for deserters in civilian clothes

29    A de luxe Edition of 'Nostradamus Predicts the Course of the War'.

'Fräulein Elizabeth' welcomed a change from her daily 'faking and forging' tasks and the opportunity arrived when the text of *Nostradamus prophezeit den Kriegsverlauf* arrived. We decided to give it a miniature de luxe format. The author, who may have been the egregious 'Captain' de Wohl (although it might have been the gifted René Halkett) made a selection of about a hundred typical Nostradamus quatrains.

Elizabeth hand-lettered the genuine French texts in a typical sixteenth-century French script and a German translation followed each of the quatrains. The commentaries (also in German) were printed on the right-hand pages in a roman type and are not illustrated here.

Publication was ascribed to the Regulus Verlag at Görlitz, which specialised in occult books, and the authorship to Dr Bruno Winkler, of Weimar, who in his Introduction thanked Dr Heinrich Lesse, curator of the ducal library at Ratisbon, for the loan of a unique (but non-existent) Nostradamus MS. Dr Winkler was alive in 1940 (see W. A. Boelcke, *Kriegspropaganda 1939–41*, p. 304), but we probably invented Dr Lesse.

We gave due credit to a fictitious Herr Paul Georg who, according to the colophon (dated 15 March 1943) was responsible for the design work. The booklet was printed on the thinnest available Bible paper and its 124 pages weighed less than an ounce.

According to the quatrain illustrated here: 'Hister [i.e. Hitler] who carried off more victories (prizes) in his warlike fight than was good for him; six [men] will murder him in the night. Naked, taken unawares without his armour, he succumbs.'

There was no evidence of reception in Germany.

# Steckbrief

Gesucht wird der Obergefreite <u>Hans Möller</u> (nachst. Lichtbild) wegen Mordes und Plünderung, sowie Uniform= und Ordens=anmaßung.

Der Gesuchte wurde in der Nacht vom 4. zum 5. Februar 1945 während des Terrorangriffs auf Osnabrück beobachtet, als er Wertgegenstände aus einem brennenden Haus in der Spichernstraße in Osnabrück entwendete. Als er vom Oberwachtmeister der Schutzpolizei Schulopp zur Rede gestellt wurde, gab er auf ihn mehrere Schüsse aus seiner Dienstpistole ab. Oberwachtmeister Schulopp wurde auf der Stelle getötet. Möller wurde von anderen Beamten des Wachdienstes sowie von mehreren Einwohnern verfolgt, entkam jedoch. Auf der Flucht gab er noch 4 Schüsse ab, die aber niemanden trafen.

Der Gesuchte wurde am Nachmittag des 9. Februar an einem Tisch im Restaurant Felsenkeller in Minden erkannt. Er trug diesmal die Uniform eines SS=Obersturmführers und das EK I. Es gelang jedoch nicht, ihn festzunehmen. Haftbefehl ist erlassen worden.

Der Gesuchte ist ein gemeingefährlicher Verbrecher, der nicht zögert, jeden niederzuschießen, der ihn erkennt. <u>Bei Identifizierung ist sofort von der Waffe Gebrauch zu machen.</u>

Ferner wurde festgestellt, daß der Gesuchte schon früher öfters widerrechtlich Uniformen von Führern der Waffen=SS mit dem EK I getragen hat. Er besitzt außerdem gefälschte Ausweispapiere auf die Namen höherer SS=Führer. Da er über die Fachkenntnisse und das Auftreten eines SS=Führers verfügt, gelingt es ihm meistens, für einen solchen gehalten zu werden.

Die Bevölkerung wird hiermit aufgefordert, an der Unschädlichmachung des Gesuchten tätig mitzuhelfen. Er hält sich vorwiegend in den Gauen Westfalen Nord und Süd, Südhannover=Braunschweig und Osthannover auf. Es besteht jedoch Grund zur Annahme, daß er sich in den Donau= und Alpengauen herum=treibt.

Zweckdienliche Mitteilungen sind an die unterzeichnete Dienststelle zu den Akten J IV 183/45 zu machen. Nach erfolgter Festnahme des Gesuchten ist die Dienststelle Feldpostnummer 25 431 zu St. L. 56/45 zu benachrichtigen.

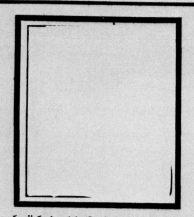

**Personalbeschreibung:**

Geboren 24.10.1920 in Roest b. Kappeln (Flensburg).
Zuletzt wohnhaft in Bielefeld.
Kennzeichen: Größe 1,76 m. Gestalt mittel. Augenfarbe blau. Haare dunkel. Narbe am Hals.
Trägt vorwiegend Uniformen der Waffen=SS, möglicherweise auch der Luftwaffe oder d. Heeres mit Offiziersrangabzeichen.

Osnabrück, d. 11. Febr. 1945
Kriminaldienststelle, Korsika=Siedlung 6.

Der Polizeipräsident
i.A. Bach,
Kriminalrat
u. SS=Sturmbannführer.

30 'WANTED! SHOOT AT SIGHT!' – namely Lance-Corporal Hans Möller for murder, looting, using forged SS officers' papers and even wearing an unearned Iron Cross (First Class!). We fabricated many similar posters, either to keep the Gestapo busy chasing fictitious 'criminals' or to bemuse German soldiers.

# Steckbrief

# 10 000 Mark Belohnung!

Gesucht wird wegen Fahnenflucht in Verbindung mit Unterschlagung und Vermögensflucht der nachstehend abgebildete

## ⚡⚡ Standartenführer Karl Bollmeyer

**Personalien :**
Geboren: 25. Juni 1887.
Geburtsort: Nienburg a.d. Weser.

Zuletzt wohnhaft: Bremen, Altenwall 24.
Beruf: Kaufmann.
Besondere Kennzeichen: keine.

---

⚡⚡ Standartenführer Karl Bollmeyer wird seit dem 10. Dezember 1944 vermißt. Nachforschungen, die in Verbindung mit seinem Verschwinden durch das Fahndungskommando des Finanzamts Bremen angestellt wurden, ergaben schwere Verfehlungen gegen die Steuer= und Vermögensfluchtgesetze. Der Gesuchte mißbrauchte sein Amt als Mitglied der Gauwirtschaftskammer Weser=Ems, um im Rahmen von Transaktionen seiner Firma A. Held, Bremen, schwere Beruntreuungen an staatlichen Vermögenswerten zu begehen. Es besteht Verdacht, daß der Gesuchte, der den Rang eines ⚡⚡ Standartenführers bekleidete und seit dem 10. Dezember verschwunden ist, ins neutrale Ausland, vermutlich über die schweizer Grenze, zu entkommen versucht. Sämtliche Parteidienststellen sind angewiesen, den Bollmeyer dingfest zu machen. Haftbefehl ist ergangen. Die Bevölkerung wird gebeten, an der Auffindung und Festsetzung des Gesuchten mitzuhelfen.

Zweckdienliche Mitteilungen sind zu den Akten J III 824/44 an die unterzeichnete Behörde zu machen.

Für Angaben, die zur Verhaftung des Gesuchten führen, ist die obenstehende Belohnung ausgesetzt.

Der Polizeipräsident
Schroers,
Generalmajor d. Polizei.

Bremen, den 20. Dez. 1944
Kriminalpolizei, Am Wall 1.

---

31  A Bremen criminal police poster offering 10,000 Marks reward for the arrest of Karl Bollmeyer, a probably non-existent SS officer who had allegedly deserted and embezzled army funds

to act as his deputy at MB. Robson had been a newspaper correspondent in Berlin before the war, was bilingual in German and English and, most important, could edit the material written for news bulletins and other purposes by individuals (such as German PoWs) with no previous journalistic experience. Furthermore, as Delmer himself admitted in *Black Boomerang*, Robson was quite capable of bringing him down to earth when he was flying too high or his projects, in Robson's sober estimation, seemed too ambitious.

Delmer was never satisfied with any particular current achievement or signs of success, but was eternally planning the next move ahead. When the *Atlantiksender* team was rehearsing for its first broadcast on 22 March 1943 Reginald Leeper had just left Woburn and returned to the Foreign Office and Tom was very much the ruler in his own private kingdom at MB. It never occurred to PWE's chiefs to install anyone at Woburn to 'control' him because he had now emerged as a major personality in that extraordinary Department. He was endowed with a compound of charm and diplomatic skill which persuaded influential 'outsiders' to collaborate with him. One of his great merits was his capacity to delegate; he could never be bothered with the minutiae of administration, preferring to leave the pettifogging details to others who were only too happy to oblige him in this respect. Frank Lynder (the Sergeant) was devoted to him, although I know that René Halkett was more critical. In reply to my question, 'What did you really think of Delmer?' Lynder simply replied: 'He was my god!'

Early in 1943 Lynder was already beginning to establish himself as Delmer's specialist in German *Kriegsmarine* matters and was developing a good all-round knowledge of life and work in a U-boat. He had served a sort of apprenticeship by helping with the *Wehrmachtsender Nord* broadcasts, in which there was at least a naval element, but now he was given far greater responsibilities and, incidentally, the opportunity to work for sixteen hours at a stretch. He himself broadcast very seldom, although on one occasion he did deliver a tear-jerking and completely improvised account of the sinking of the *Scharnhorst* alleged to be from the lips of a German sailor who had been among the few rescued by the British. Lynder told me that there was no element of cynicism in this performance and he almost felt as if he had been fished out of the cold sea himself.

The psychological warfare campaign against the U-boat crews was based upon a very considerable and constantly growing knowledge of every aspect of their life at sea and more relaxed periods at their bases on the French Atlantic coast. Much of the evidence, particularly that of a technical nature, was derived from the increasingly skilled interrogation of captured U-boat men. When they realised how much we already knew about their still uncaptured colleagues, and the officers in particular, and U-boat equipment and operational techniques, the German naval PoWs were liable to talk with helpful loquacity. But there was always something we did not know and the new pieces had to be fitted in to a never-ending jigsaw puzzle.

If I include a condensed version of Lynder's long, recorded account of his relationship with Eddie Mander it is because it demonstrates how and why a previously loyal supporter of the *Führer*, although never a Party member, eventually decided to 'help the enemy'. It is true that *Flotillenoberfunkmeister* (Flotilla Chief Petty Officer Telegraphist, in itself a high and very responsible non-commissioned rank) Eddie Mander had a few personal grievances, but to these were added gradually a hatred of Hitler and the Nazi Party and complete contempt for the officers under whom he had been recently serving. Lynder mentioned that he was temperamentally a 'loner'. He had seen service in the German merchant navy before the war and even before 1939 held his *Debag* certificate – the British equivalent would have been a document issued by the Marconi people to the effect that the holder had first-class technical qualifications. However, when he was transferred to the *Kriegsmarine* he was 'sent back to school' in the company of absolute beginners. This was certainly a blow to his professional pride. Eventually he found himself in No. 7 U-boat flotilla where he was quite soon promoted to the rank of *Flotillenoberfunkmeister*.

Soon after his return from his ninth operational cruise – to emerge unscathed from that number of expeditions was quite an achievement – he was caught selling a couple of bags of raw coffee beans to a French black market operator. He was then given a choice between transfer to a penal battalion on the Russian front or three more operational cruises. Lynder commented, 'There is clearly something wrong with a navy which prescribes those alternatives as a punishment!' Mander went to sea again under a young and inexperienced commander. According to his version all the junior officers were what the crew contemptuously called 'Hitler Youths' and only the Chief Engineer and himself had any experience. When the boat was attacked by a British cruiser off Freetown (Sierra Leone), the commander was the first to jump overboard yelling, 'Sink her!' The British rescued the complete crew and soon transferred them to the battleship *Nelson*. On the following Sunday the captain of the *Nelson* invited the Germans to attend a thanksgiving service for their rescue. The 'Hitler Youth' officers all refused but Mander persuaded the others to go.

Mander gave his interrogating officer so much useful information that he was soon sent to Delmer. 'I never again had anyone as good and useful as Mander,' Lynder remarked. 'The problem was that any U-boat wireless operator's information could soon be obsolete. We used to show them captured documents or other technical material as far as possible, but it was never easy to keep up with all the latest developments.'

Mander's career at MB lasted for rather less than a year. There were complaints from fellow German PoWs about homosexual advances and Eddie Mander was forthwith returned to a PoW camp.

At the time when the *Atlantiksender* team was rehearsing prior to their first broadcast on 22 March 1943 the war had reached a critical stage and was just beginning to turn in favour of the Allies. The remaining Germans had capitulated at Stalingrad on 2 February; Winston Churchill arrived in Tripoli the following day and addressed the British troops there; a fortnight later the Eighth Army was fighting Rommel's forces in Tunisia, and the Battle of the Atlantic was about to reach its climax. The U-boats were having to pay a heavy price for their successes and no fewer than ninety-six were sunk between January and May 1943. We were not to know that towards the end of May Grand Admiral Doenitz would throw in the sponge and withdraw from the North Atlantic convoy route. As Patrick Beesly remarked, 'It is true that he attempted a comeback in the autumn and that even after this he never, right up to the last day of the war, abandoned the struggle in one form or another, but the two sides were never again so equally matched nor the battle so ferocious as in those five months and above all in March.'

While the *Atlantiksender* supplied plenty of 'American jazz with a German flavour', it was also employed for operational purposes. Thus on 6 April 1943 Delmer received the following note from McLachan:

> Arrangements have been made for G9 (*Atlantiksender*) to carry out the following operation in consultation with the Director of Mining operations. On days following mining operations by the RAF and RN G9 will carry a report of mining operations carried out the previous night. This report will normally include 25–40 per cent true locations, 20 per cent half true and the remainder entirely false.
>
> It is thought that this operation may cause the enemy in the long run considerable embarrassment. For two reasons: firstly, because even with modern detection apparatus, the enemy can never be absolutely sure that they have plotted all mining operations by aircraft; secondly, because

knowledge of where these operations have actually been carried out will normally be confined to German naval group and area HQs. The average minesweeper and merchant seaman listener will find it impossible to distinguish between truth and falsehood in our reports.

In an undated document, which was probably given limited circulation in May 1943, Delmer reported that the black broadcasting activities of the 'Enemy and Satellite' RUs were at last being co-ordinated.

1 The heads and servicing staffs of all the Enemy and Satellite RUs have now moved into the MB Compound and this concentration has already begun to yield good results in closer collaboration.

2 The new German RU station *Deutscher Kurzwellensender Atlantik*, with its fifteen different 30-minute news and music transmissions a day, is acting as a kind of news and rumour clearing-house for the whole E & S black unit, and has already had success in backing up in German some of the rumour campaigns of the Italian, Hungarian, Romanian and Bulgarian units. A good deal of DKA material is finding its way into the press of the contiguous neutral countries.

3 *Collaboration between the German units and the Italian has been particularly close:* such subjects as the activities of the alleged Italian peace party and its negotiations, looting by Germans in Sicily, unrest and mutiny in the Italian navy, German intentions to seize the Italian navy and many more have been carried by both the Italian and the German units, essentially the same picture being conveyed, though the comment varies from station to station.

4 For instance the Italian *Italia Risorgi* unit (clandestine mouthpiece of Italian pro-Savoy, anti-Fascist, anti-German army circles) reports with satisfaction the receipt of encouraging messages concerning an agreement on peace terms in the event of the overthrow of German rule in Italy, while the German *Chef* (mouthpiece of German anti-Bolshevik, anti-Jewish, anti-Nazi, anti-British, anti-American officers' organisation) denounces Italian treachery and gives specific details concerning the movements of Italian agents and their negotiations.

5 Germany's clandestine Catholic priest reports with satisfaction the success of the Pope's efforts to mediate and bring peace to at least 'one great South European Catholic victim of our godless warmongers' and points out that the Pope is helping enlightened men of that country to abolish the present rule of injustice and restore in its place the rule of social order, law and religion, in which 'state and citizen will equally respect the law'.

6 The Hungarian, Romanian and Bulgarian RUs also have helped to spread rumours concerning Italy – particularly with regard to peace moves. Of course care is taken that the broadcasts do not all coincide on one day but are properly timed.

7 *Collaboration with the Occupied Territories Directorate* is also improving thanks to a weekly meeting with them. The French, for instance, are very usefully helping in the German anti-U-Boat rumour campaign and the 'Latin Block' end of the Italian peace party story, while the French, Dutch and Norwegians are taking up the German campaign to undermine occupying German services' morale, e.g. the desertion line: 'for every German bumped off, five can desert. The Gestapo does not know who is missing because he's been bumped off or who is missing because he has deserted.' 'Sweden is the German soldier's heaven – it is full of "dead" Germans.'

The first reactions to the *Atlantiksender* were available in time for the April 1943 'Evidence of Reception Report'. According to a pro-British Swedish newspaper published on 22 April, 'The word "Tunisgrad" is often found scrawled on the walls [of houses] in German towns.' The station had suggested this mocking allusion to the Germans' defeat at Stalingrad on 15 April. There were a great many references to the *Atlantiksender* (and after 14 November 1943 to the medium-wave '*Soldatensender Calais* linked with the short-wave transmitter *Atlantik*') in the Swedish press and to a much lesser extent in Swiss newspapers. The Swiss were chary of annoying the Germans and their censorship prevented very much publicity being given to the *Atlantik–Calais* broadcasts. However, the fact that in December 1943 there were fourteen references to *Atlantik–Calais* material in the Swedish press indicates that the broadcasts were stimulating a great deal of interest, perhaps because they were so different from anything put out by the BBC. Quotations from the Swedish press soon found their way into newspapers in the free world, including Great Britain. According to the December report, 'The value of the Swedish press come-backs is indicated from a reliable report that there is a large demand in Germany for foreign news. Although Swedes are not allowed to take their newspapers ashore in Germany, they are left lying around in ships and German port officials take them when they leave.'

According to the June 1943 'Evidence of Reception' document:

The Berlin correspondent of the *Basler Nationale Zeitung* reported that as a result of the breaching of the Möhne dam [by the RAF on 16–17 May] many farmers in the Ruhr district were slaughtering cattle illegally on the black market, as the authorities could not discriminate between those drowned in the floods and those slaughtered illegally. *Atlantik* put out this story on 2 June.

The first report of German troops listening to *Atlantik* has been received from Tunis. The PoW who realised it was an enemy station pronounced

185

it 'good stuff'. He used to tune in to it and the Spanish stations to get an all-round view of the news.

*Aftonbladet* [Swedish] reported from Berlin that recent photographs in the German papers showed soldiers of the Moslem SS division in Croatia wearing a fez instead of the usual uniform cap. 'Now it is obvious that the Grand Mufti of Jerusalem stands behind this SS division as during his journey through Croatia he summoned Moslems to combat the British and the partisans.' This looks like an elaboration of *Atlantik*'s fantastic story that the Grand Mufti had been so impressed by the SS that he had decided to form a corps of his own.

*Atlantik*'s technique is probably referred to in an editorial in the *Westfälische Neueste Nachrichten* (19 June) when it says: 'It is difficult to distinguish between three genuine news items and a falsified fourth one.'

With the increase in the number of Germans captured in North Africa more and more information became available to British interrogators. Thus in August 1943 it was reported that:

Two German Air Force officers, both captured in Tunis in May, had heard GS1 in Russia. One of them, a liaison officer, repeated in detail a story put out by the *Chef* on 27 October 1941, thus showing that he must have repeated the anecdote frequently otherwise he could not have remembered it for so long. The other, a communications officer, had last heard it [GS1] in February. He had come across some comrades [presumably officers] who were listening to the *Chef*. The signal was remarkably loud. He repeated one of GS's indictments of the Italians, with which he heartily agreed. He said it was unknown where the broadcasts came from.

Interrogation of some 200 PoWs in North Africa shows that *Atlantik* has established itself very strongly among the troops. Quite a number had listened in groups with their comrades, and one man said that it was regularly switched on in the tent quarters near Trapani [Sicily]. Another described it as the '*meist gehörte Sender*' [the most listened-to station], having a larger public than the German official stations.

*Atlantik*'s initial appeal is its music; no other station caters so successfully for the musical tastes of the average German soldier. An attraction is that it is 'safe'. If an officer enters a room during an *Atlantik* news bulletin he may easily mistake it for an official German station; if, however, he recognises it, the listener can plead that he sincerely believed it to be a genuine German station. The news bulletins are considered informative and interesting. A number of anti-Nazis expressed admiration for the cleverness of its camouflage.

In September a German officer who had left Germany in May said that, 'GS1 was much the best of all the clandestine stations; obviously it had real contacts and real inside information. It was operating in Poland. It was close to the Katowice wave-length and was well heard.'

Documents captured after the defeat of Germany show that by August 1943 the Gestapo was so impressed by the accuracy of *Atlantiksender* reports that they were being investigated individually. It was suggested that the station *must* have close contact with the German Armed Forces. The officer who initiated the enquiries believed that the station was located in Switzerland.

It was at this time that Delmer was writing papers suggesting that Aspidistra should be used to transmit the *Atlantiksender* programme on medium wave, and with the imminence of 'Overlord' (the forthcoming invasion plan), to expand it in order to attract an audience among the German armed forces in the west. After endless acrimonious arguments with the BBC, who were using Aspidistra to reinforce their European Service programmes, as from 14 November 1943 Delmer was allowed to employ Aspidistra between the hours of 8pm and 11pm for the '*Soldatensender West* linked with the short-wave *Atlantiksender*'. Three months later the *Soldatensender* was given an additional hour and was on the air daily until midnight. The time was to come, although I am unsure of the date – it could have been before June 1944 when the landings in France began – when the *Soldatensender* was broadcasting literally round the clock, with the 'day's work' at MB commencing at 6pm.

From the end of 1943 Aspidistra was also being used by the RAF for 'Operation Dartboard' which successfully interfered with the German ground control's instructions to the *Luftwaffe*'s nightfighters when the RAF was on bombing missions over Germany. For some time Harold Robin's technical experts at MB had been convinced that certain German medium-wave musical transmissions concealed a code of instructions. Since Aspidistra could alter its wave-length with the minimum of delay and at the same time was more powerful than the *Luftwaffe*'s ground control transmitters, the German nightfighter pilots were obliged to listen to the *Soldatensender*. Various other 'tricks' were employed to confuse them, e.g. recording the *Luftwaffe*'s ground control instructions on, say, a Monday and re-broadcasting them the following day and hence sending the nightfighter pilots in the wrong direction.

By the end of 1943 encouraging reports were being received from German PoWs:

Of several U-boat men who had listened to *Calais*, one believed it to be a French station for German soldiers. Another stated that he knows of two commanding officers in the U-boat service who keep careful notes of what *Calais* says about officers under their command.

In this context it must be stated that the intelligence specialists at MB knew a great deal about the U-boat officers and the *Calais–Atlantik* programmes frequently revealed a surprising amount of interesting personal information.

In December 1943 the Argentine Embassy at Washington denied reports that its government was releasing German seamen to enable them to take part in U-boat warfare. This was undoubtedly a 'come-back' to Grand Admiral Doenitz's invitation, issued via *Atlantik*, to the fifty-three *Graf Spee* internees to return to Germany for U-boat duties. The internees were at the time concentrated in groups under the surveillance of local military or naval commanders.

By January 1944 there was a growing body of evidence of listening by the German armed forces.

An Able Seaman from the *Scharnhost* [sunk off the North Cape on 26 December 1943] has stated that he listened in every evening. The captain of a blockade runner sunk in the Bay of Biscay declared himself an enthusiastic *Calais* fan. He thought our information marvellous. He had been particularly impressed by the account (19 December) of the attack on another blockade runner. As he had come from Japan he must have listened regularly at sea.

It is now evident that listening among German Air Force units in the west is not only widespread but persistent. The squadron leader of a unit at Cognac said that he and his brother officers listened regularly. They were obliged to stop other ranks from listening but he knew that they did so. Although the jamming was severe he was always able to get the station either on short- or medium-waves. He remarked on the cleverness and listener-interest of the show, and on the technical information, quoting actual examples. Sometimes he listened in with naval officers whom he met at Bordeaux.

In February 1944 the 'Evidence of Reception Report' included an item from 'secret American sources at Berne'.

Despite the death penalty [for illegal listening], broadcasts by the USA, Britain and the Soviets are listened to in Germany. The *Atlantiksender* is the most popular. Many Germans think it is somewhere in Europe, two suggestions being near Paris or in a German ship in the English Channel. The promoters of these suggestions claim that the station has the protection of high-ranking German army and naval officers and is in co-operation with the British.

Secret sources report good reception of *Atlantik*, both on medium- and short-wave, at Danzig in November last. The same source [probably the SIS] declares that the transmissions are regularly heard at Brest.

188

The impression gained from recent PoWs interrogated in this country is that listening at their bases to *Atlantik* broadcasts is now the rule for naval personnel rather than the exception. Included among the stories quoted, which U-boat crews say they have heard on *Atlantik*, are several which were never put out, showing that our information service is being credited with universal knowledge, much in the same way as Lord Haw-Haw was here at the beginning of the war. One regular U-boat listener was much impressed by our denunciation of GSR (radio location detector). A campaign to sow distrust in this device has been carried on for some time. The operational effectiveness of *Calais* is also exemplified by a report from a *Luftwaffe* captain who was sent under conditions of the utmost secrecy to interview blockade-runner captains waiting in the Gironde and was then amazed to hear us address a message to the hush-hush ships concerning their forthcoming operations.

Delmer recalled the last story in *Black Boomerang*. The *Luftwaffe* captain returned to his quarters and to his delight heard the *Atlantiksender* play a programme of Japanese music and then repeat verbatim the instructions he had just delivered to the captains of the blockade runners. 'I laughed and laughed until the tears ran down my cheeks,' he said. 'But how did you manage it? Did your agents smuggle microphones on board?' The answer was simple: naval intelligence knew that armed blockade runners were preparing to sail to Japan and by a fortunate coincidence the broadcast was made at exactly the right time.

According to the March 1944 report:

Evidence of listening by civilians in Germany is still scanty but a February report states that *Calais* is considered absolutely first-rate and amazingly up-to-date with its information. The informant is inclined to believe that although it may be operated from England or Allied territory, it may be a genuine secret station in view of the accuracy and speed of its information, for example on the subject of air-raid damage.

In April a 'most interesting report' was received from Ankara:

It gives an accurate and detailed account of the programme make-up of *Calais-Atlantik*, and says it is regularly listened to by officials of the German Embassy, as well as by anti-Nazi Germans. Some of the German officials are said to believe that *Atlantik* is a genuine German station, though most think that it is British, and a few that it is Russian. Surprise is expressed that it is so much better-informed than the BBC; not only is it more interesting, but its foreign news is more accurate.

The following interesting reaction comes from a censorship intercept.

On 29 October *Atlantik* reported that personal belongings left behind at U-boat bases were being stolen when the owner had been posted as missing or killed and gave the names of some victims of these thefts, amongst them that of Ulrich Jahn. Jahn was captured and his mother wrote to him on 6 December and told him that the disappearance of his personal belongings which he left behind at his base has still not been cleared up. She goes on to say that she had heard from local friends 'that the whole affair had been broadcast over the radio'. This provides good evidence of listening by civilians in Mecklenburg.

By D-Day (6 June 1944) the *Soldatensender Calais* evidently had a widespread following among the *Wehrmacht* troops in France, and its short-wave version (*Atlantik*) was being heard all over Europe and far beyond.

I only found one *Atlantik* script at the Public Record Office. Rather to my surprise it was in English, whereas I supposed that they were all written in German. However, it demonstrates the kind of 'insider's gossip' which was broadcast night after night with apparent success. Sohler, mentioned in the first paragraph, was the officer commanding the 7th U-boat flotilla at La Baule. It was probably transmitted in *c*. May 1944.

Sohler has redoubled his security measures, partly because of fear of invasion and partly because of the current wave of sabotage at Lorient. During the clean-up a beautiful girl, a blonde called Rita Doris, has been shot as a spy. She came from Saarbrücken . . . She was previously a bar girl. She was known to scores of U-boatmen and had frequently been on U-boats. At one time she was engaged to Engineer Petty Officer Junghardt, who was on —'s [name illegible] boat, now sunk.

At the beginning of January 1944 a German officer arrived from home, dressed himself in dockworker's kit, typed himself a pass authorising him to board all U-boats, stamped it with an inked 5-Mark piece and boarded in all ten U-boats, going into the wireless telegraphy rooms, etc. In one U-boat he removed the torpedo-setting key, put it in his pocket and walked ashore. He was not challenged by any of the sentries. On his report being presented security was tightened-up, and now double passes are issued. This happened at St Nazaire.

The *Kompaniechef* at Endrasslager, St Nazaire, is Kapitän-Leutnant Lipin. He is very jittery because of invasion rumours. Naval personnel are required to do a lot of infantry drill, and the latest rumour is that U-boat personnel are not to be transported inland on invasion, but are to stay put. This is directly contrary to all previous information on this subject.

Sohler has recently purchased a huge eight-cylinder sports car; the rumour is that it is for invasion purposes so that he can make a quick getaway into the interior.

Sohler's *Schnelltruppe* (defaulters) are now called 'Sohler's galloping troops'. They are being given even heavier and dirtier work to do because most of them have been arrested for defeatism. They have sworn that Sohler will be the first invasion victim, because they are going to do him in.

Sohler has decided to scrap the villa housing scheme at La Baule, and quarter all the 7th Flotilla U-boatmen at the Endrasslager under much closer restrictions. The same thing is to be done with the 6th Flotilla. The crews are to be accommodated at the Burckhardt Lager, which is now nearing completion after delays due to bomb damage. The 6th Flotilla officers will still be housed in the Hotel Majestic.

Kapitän-Leutnant Lipin, the new commander of the 7th Flotilla, made an introductory speech to the assembled crews. He said: 'I am sorry I shall be forced to give you severe punishments from time to time; you must understand it is on higher orders.' Whereupon a senior rating in the rear rank shouted 'Boo!' and was promptly given seven days' arrest.

One can be tolerably sure that Rita Doris, the beautiful blonde bar girl, had actually existed, also that the topographical information was completely correct. Sohler's new sports car may well have had twelve cylinders by the time the local rumour-mongers had got to work on it.

German naval personnel were often astonished at the accuracy of our local knowledge. When interrogated, Leutnant Joachim Hünefeldt, Second Watch Officer of a U-boat, said that he thought that the British must have many agents spying among them because the Calais broadcasts invariably indicated that the speaker was exceedingly well informed about small details. He recollected an occasion when a small send-off ceremony had taken place at his base. Within a few hours all the details, including the names of the departing officers, were reported by the apparently omniscient Calais station.

1   Otto John, *Twice through the Lines*, 1972, p. 172

# 20

# 'Mr Howe's Unit'

The unit first began to function on a small scale late in 1941 but I did not know of Delmer's existence, let alone of that of *Gustav Siegfried Eins* and the small team at RAG, until about March 1942. By that time GS1 was well established and the *Wehrmachtsender Nord* was being planned. It was as well that I did not become involved in Delmer's work any earlier because I needed a little time in which to get my own 'production organisation' under way. When I began to work for Delmer in the early spring of 1942 I was only just ready to deal with anything he might happen to despatch in my direction, and he was soon sending a great deal.

The fact that the next chapter is fairly well illustrated will tend to exaggerate my unit's importance in PWE's black set-up. However, it must be remembered that whereas a representative collection of PWE's black printed matter can be found at the Imperial War Museum, very few broadcasting scripts are available and in the context of 'sound' only the recordings of the last two days of the *Wehrmachtsender West* (which have now been converted to magnetic tapes) are at the same location. The printed matter simply provides a partial record, perhaps little more than an echo, of current black broadcasting which in any case eventually reached a far wider audience than the relatively small readership which, mostly more by accident than design, happened to discover my unit's products.

The brief details of work in progress for Delmer during the week ending 7 January 1943 (described in the next chapter) indicate that eighteen items were currently in hand for him, but nothing is said about productions in hand for the other PWE regions and various Allied intelligence services. The latter occasionally employed me, but not for black propaganda operations. The collaboration between Delmer and myself was never 'scientifically planned' nor, for that matter, even discussed at any length between us. It simply happened. Nor did I ever see much of him. When he was in London he was far too busy to have time to visit my office. I used to spend an occasional weekend at RAG in 1942 but hardly set eyes on him from 1943 onwards when he became increasingly busy with the *Kurzwellensender Atlantik* and later the *Soldatensender Calais* (later *West*). Indeed, of all the people who were more or less closely associated with him in those days I probably saw least of him.

I joined the Department during the first week of November 1941, soon after it became the Political Warfare Executive and about four months after Woburn Abbey (but not the Riding School) was vacated and practically everyone not concerned with secret broadcasting or white leaflet production returned to London to work at Bush House and other premises close to the Aldwych. Many years later Harold Keble, who ran the white production unit, told me about a lunchtime conversation with Leonard Ingrams soon after the latter received my 'Political Warfare and the Printed Word' memorandum from MI5. It seems that Ingrams was so impressed by this document that he stated his determination to secure my immediate employment, adding that if the War Office raised any objections he would organise intervention at ministerial level. However, I am sure that nothing as dramatic was ever necessary. Thus I reported to Ingrams early in the afternoon on the day I returned to civilian life and he escorted me to PWE's London offices at 2 Fitzmaurice Place just across the road from the Ministry of Economic Warfare's building in Berkeley Square. I was informed that I would share an office with 'young David Alexander' whom, he said, I might be able to help in various ways. As we walked across the square he remarked, 'You can come and go as you please; you are an artist!', a remark which endeared him to me. Alexander was absent so Ingrams left me there, saying that we would meet again soon.

When Alexander arrived he turned out to be a lieutenant in the Intelligence Corps and was running some kind of postal operation for Ingrams. He said that he had a team of elderly French ladies who addressed envelopes in the kind of distinctive French handwriting known as '*Sacré Coeur*' (as taught in the best Parisian convent schools). He told me, too, that they used typically French violet-coloured ink which was purchased by a trustworthy intermediary because his work and identity were secret. I cannot remember what was enclosed in the envelopes but doubt whether it was anything particularly nefarious. I was informed that batches of envelopes were sent to Lisbon, whence they were smuggled into France for mailing there.

Ingrams must have told Alexander that I was some kind of printing specialist because he wanted to know if I could forge the current French postage stamp design, Pétain's head, as it would be more economic to

193

print them in England than buy them in France. Completely ignorant about how the Department tackled such problems, all I could say was that a philatelic forgery operation was theoretically possible. His next enquiry was whether I would be prepared to help him *steal* the Savoy Hotel's complete set of French 'Bottin' directories as the management was unwilling to release them. Not wanting to be returned to the army after a police court appearance I gave him an evasive answer. His next requirement was easier to satisfy: he was running short of envelopes which 'looked French' and could I help him to procure, say, five thousand? I said that I knew a small manufacturer in the Bishopsgate district in the City of London. 'Then let's go and see him *now*,' David said.

When I arrived at HQ Anti-Aircraft Command that morning it never occurred to me that only a few hours later I would begin my new career – well, whatever it might be, because I certainly hadn't a clue – by accompanying an Intelligence Corps lieutenant on a modest shopping expedition for something as innocent as a few envelopes. On our way to Bishopsgate Alexander told me what little he knew about the Department – it cannot have been very much and he probably knew nothing about its clandestine broadcasting activities. But I learned of the existence of a very secret place called 'The Country' (i.e. Woburn Abbey) and of another equally secret institution known as 'Baker Street', meaning the headquarters of SOE which, he said, specialised in sabotage and sent agents to France. He also told me that his parents lived at Geneva, that he had been largely educated in Switzerland and could pass as a Frenchman.

At the envelope manufacturer's place the manager recognised me and was inclined to be helpful. I allowed Alexander to conduct the negotiations and he produced a specimen envelope ('made in France') and said that he wanted a few thousand made up from assorted shades of cheap tinted glazed manillas. I had previously told my new friend what to ask for. The manager measured the specimen and said, 'This one isn't English!' Neither of us reacted. 'Is your firm going to give me an official order?' the manager asked, evidently supposing that I was still with the Shands at Hertford. 'No, you will simply send your invoice to your old customer Mr Ellic Howe, c/o Box 100, Western District Post Office, and he'll know how to arrange for payment,' Alexander replied. 'In the meantime can I personally collect the envelopes the day after tomorrow?'

'Ah, Secret Service?' the manager said with a knowing smile.

'Something like that,' Alexander replied, 'but keep quiet!'

On our way back to Fitzmaurice Place I asked Alexander about the mechanism for the payment of accounts.

'Simply send the bill to Mr Walter Stewart-Roberts, our Director of

Finance, with a brief note to the effect that they were ordered for Mr Ingrams,' he said. During the next three and a half years I was to forward hundreds of invoices, some of them for very large sums, to W.S.-R. who never queried a single one of them. On the financial side, at least, life was to be singularly uncomplicated.

When Alexander collected the envelopes I suggested that we should overprint them to make them look as if they originated from French banks and insurance companies and was able to produce some appropriate specimens from my collection of miscellaneous French jobbing printing. This plan delighted Alexander but I had no idea where to get the printing done, at least not under circumstances which the Department would consider as 'secure'. So I consulted Leonard Ingrams who told me to contact a certain Mr Crutchley (this was not his name), who dealt with secret printing, and gave me his telephone number. Mr Crutchley occupied ground-floor premises in Queen Victoria Street, close to the headquarters of the Secret Intelligence Service, and appeared to be operating a small dye-line (blue print) plant for reproducing engineering drawings although this may have been merely a cover. In his back room I noticed specimens of the labels used to route goods wagons in French and Belgian railway marshalling yards and inferred that willing helpers in enemy-occupied Europe were happily diverting consignments intended for Germany to other destinations. Mr Crutchley offered to help me with my work but was disinclined to reveal where and by whom the work would be executed.

A few days later Ingrams summoned me and said, 'We ought to try to *do* something, but what?' implying a black operation involving printing which would at least set the Rhine on fire. In the absence of any better idea I suggested that the Swedish Master Printers Association might be delighted to send a suitably subversive New Year's greeting card to several hundred individual printing firms in the Reich. My assumption that SOE had an office in Stockholm and would be able to provide a mailing list and attend to the posting was at least correct. The plan appealed to Ingrams who quickly proposed an Old Testament text: 'Cursed be he who removeth his neighbour's landmark,' (Deuteronomy 27, xviii). 'After all, that's what the Germans have been doing all over Europe,' he said, 'and it will infuriate the Gestapo!' My plan was not particularly black, but at least it provided a starting point. So I went to the London Library in St James's Square, checked the quotation in *Cruden's Concordance*, and copied the text from a Lutheran Bible.

The conversation with Ingrams can be dated: it happened a couple of days before Berthold Wolpe (later a Royal Designer for Industry) married on 11 November 1941. I had met him soon after he arrived in England in *c*. 1937 and was aware that he had been a pupil of Rudolph Koch, a renowned German type designer and graphic artist, hence completely qualified to provide the kind of German 'Gothic' lettering that would be appropriate. So Berthold was summoned to a local Mayfair hotel – I had no idea if it would be in order for me to see him at my presumably secret office – and was coerced into undertaking the work without delay. He protested that his approaching nuptials made any particularly urgent commission most inconvenient but agreed to collaborate when I explained that the successful prosecution of the war depended upon his immediate consent. So in due course Berthold delivered the artwork to me at the hotel and departed to get himself married. And I, in my turn, took the artwork and the instructions for a couple of lines of very simple typesetting to Mr Crutchley.

A week or ten days passed by and there was no news from the secret printing department. In the meantime Ingrams was impatiently asking for a progress report which I was unable to supply. Finally I visited Mr Crutchley and was told that the task of making the printing blocks for David Alexander's envelopes and a set of two-colour line blocks for the New Year cards required enormous skill and therefore time, although I knew that a 'short morning' would be quite sufficient. I insisted upon being told where the blocks were being made and who would be entrusted with the printing. Mr Crutchley thereupon very unwillingly supplied the information.

The next morning I arrived at Mr Crutchley's pet process engraving establishment at 8am, found David Stephens, the workshop manager, and peremptorily informed him that I expected to take delivery of *all* the blocks, including the Wolpe two-colour line set (which I required to be proofed in colour and in register) by 2pm. He cheerfully agreed to this outrageous proposition and the blocks were ready when I returned. I was still in touch with him many years later when he was process manager at the *Evening News*. My next visit that day was to Mr Crutchley's printers where the managing director was visibly upset when I told him that I intended to collect Alexander's overprinted envelopes and the Swedish Master Printers' cards exactly forty-eight hours later and did not propose to take no for an answer. Much later I discovered that this printing firm had worked for Section D in the old days.

So David Alexander received his envelopes and Leonard Ingrams despatched the seditious New Year's cards to Stockholm. A few months later he showed me a page from a popular Swedish illustrated photogravure weekly periodical. It contained a large reproduction of Berthold

Wolpe's magnificent lettering and I gathered that as a result of German protests the Swedish government had offered a reward for the identification of whoever had been responsible for producing the cards. Unfortunately in those days office copying machines did not exist or I would have made a few copies.

When I had been at Fitzmaurice Place for about a fortnight Ingrams told me to prepare myself for an overnight visit to 'The Country' and said that a car would be waiting outside the building at 2pm. The only other passenger in a very large Buick six-seater saloon was a Mr Gannon, the black-bearded specialist in Spanish affairs whom Delmer had encountered under the same circumstances when he first visited Woburn a few months earlier. He sat in front with the driver and remained silent. The road northwards out of London was familiar because the first ten miles led to Stanmore and HQ Anti-Aircraft Command. At the Mill Hill traffic lights we halted alongside an AA Command staff car which contained three officers who knew me at least by sight. One of them recognised me and he and his companions stared at me with unconcealed disbelief. The powerful Buick then accelerated ahead of them and I wondered what they might conceivably be saying. I learned the answer a few days later when Major Francis, my camp commandant friend, telephoned me at Fitzmaurice Place. I had given him a number which could be reached via the War Office switchboard. He wanted to know if and when it would be convenient to deliver to him various items for which I presumably had no further use, namely two battle-dress uniforms, an overcoat, two pairs of boots and sundry other objects which were the property of HM Government. Thus I was invited to drink a cup of tea with him the following Saturday afternoon.

'Some really wonderful rumours are circulating about you in the officers' mess,' he told me. 'You have been seen smoking a large cigar in a luxurious limousine with a chauffeur and a black-bearded bodyguard in front. The story is that you *must* be a very senior member of the Secret Intelligence Service!'

The reason for my visit to Woburn was to meet David Bowes-Lyon, who was now Leeper's local deputy in succession to Valentine Williams. Bowes-Lyon told me that I would encounter various individuals who might have a use for my services, but I did not see anyone who appeared to be at all interested in what I might be able to offer and I was glad to return to Fitzmaurice Place. When I arrived there the following morning David Alexander told me that Leonard Ingrams wanted to see me.

'I have something here which will really test your skill,' he said, and showed me a copy of the German *Kennkarte* (identity card), a small four-page document which was printed on a dark green bookcloth with the addition of a simple light brown tint-plate on the centre spread. 'The SIS people are having a lot of trouble with it,' he continued, 'and I stuck my neck out and suggested that you should be allowed to tackle it.'

I recognised the *Fraktur* typeface, which was one in very common use in Germany, and was tolerably sure that the Monotype Corporation could either supply or make the necessary matrices. I could also hazard a guess to explain why the SIS forgers could not produce a satisfactory result. They were trying to retouch (clean up) enlarged photographs or negatives of the *Fraktur* type and eliminate traces of ink-spread. However, the SIS retouchers, whoever they might be, were not sufficiently familiar with the nuances of *Fraktur* designs and were simply botching the work. Furthermore, they cannot have known that the identical typeface was almost certainly available in England and that all their laborious retouching was completely unnecessary. Theoretically no particular skill would be required to forge the *Kennkarte*, merely a little legwork and the freedom to use my own connections in the printing industry without having to ask for a series of permissions to do this or that. The appropriate moment had come for me to make a determined effort to eliminate Mr Crutchley.

When I explained my difficulties to Ingrams I inferred that Mr Crutchley was simply 'farming' the work to various long-established connections. All I wanted was the freedom to use my own technical 'network' which, I suggested, should be able to produce anything that was required a great deal more quickly than Mr Crutchley and Co.

'Well, then, go ahead,' Ingrams said, 'but impress upon your friends that the work is very secret. You can tell me what you are doing but otherwise keep quiet. Nobody in the Department knows much about you, which will be a help, and I'll tell Bowes-Lyon and Walter Stewart-Roberts [Director of Finance] that I am allowing you to make your own arrangements.'

The fact is that neither Ingrams nor anyone else had given any thought as to *how* I would operate and I suspect that he was relieved rather than disconcerted when I proposed my own solution. At that time I did not even know of the existence of Colonel Chambers, PWE's elderly security officer and liaison with MI5, although he was later to be a good friend and useful confidant. Indeed, already aware that the break with Mr Crutchley must come sooner or later, I had recently had a private discussion with Ernest Ingham, managing director of The Fanfare Press, whose small plant was in St Martin's Lane, halfway between Fitzmaurice Place and Bush House. At the time I knew nothing about the impending move to the Aldwych.

Fanfare's name and work were probably hardly known outside the small group of firms which specialised in advertisement typesetting for the London advertising agencies. Most of them were subsidiaries of process-engraving establishments whereas Fanfare were not 'block-makers' and had no stereotyping or electrotyping equipment. Unlike the other typesetting firms they operated a small but efficient letterpress printing plant in the basement below the composing department. Before the war the latter had employed at least twenty hand compositors on day and night shifts. When I arrived on the scene only half a dozen compositors remained, of whom two worked at night.

The specialist advertisement typesetters emerged during the 1920s. A new generation of agency typographers – these people did not exist before the 1914–18 war – demanded the latest typographical novelties, most of which were imported from one or other of half a dozen German 'hot metal' type foundries who were then very active in commissioning and marketing new designs. The London newspaper proprietors and periodical printers were unwilling to buy these types but quite prepared to receive complete plates (stereos or electros) from advertisers who were prepared to pay for outside typesetting. Nor did the London newspaper and periodical compositors have any objections because they were paid at high piecework rates for setting the complete publication. Thus in order to attract advertising agency customers the specialist typesetting firms were increasingly prepared to hold adequate founts of most of the latest German types which had been designed for advertising and jobbing printing rather than bookwork.

The Fanfare Press was a subsidiary of the London Press Exchange, an important advertising agency which found it convenient to operate its own typesetting and printing departments. My impression is that Fanfare did very little work for outside customers although they produced most of the Gollancz book jackets which, invariably printed in black and magenta on a vivid yellow paper, were always conspicuous in bookshops and on railway station bookstalls. Stanley Morison had been responsible for the original design concept in which book jackets were considered as eye-catching 'posters' rather than works of art. Ernest Ingham, who was an old friend of Morison's and an accomplished typographical designer, was responsible for practically all the later Gollancz jackets. At the same time he was a skilled letterpress printer and the Fanfare Press imprint could be found in a number of distinguished limited editions.

Even before I talked to Ingham I realised that Fanfare could provide an excellent base for my still rather vague purposes. Apart from their excellent repertory of display types from the German foundries they had printing facilities: they operated a double-demy Miehle two-revolution cylinder press for bookwork and larger formats and a battery of three or four Vertical Miehles for jobbing. None of these letterpress machines are manufactured today and have been superseded by far more productive offset presses. Fanfare did not have its own Monotype plant (keyboards and casters) for mechanical composition but sent much of the work which required hot metal setting across the road to Harrison and Sons Ltd's London factory.

When I appeared upon the scene Fanfare was short of work for even its greatly reduced staff because newsprint and paper rationing had severely reduced the demand for both advertisement typesetting and jobbing printing. I was unable to commit PWE to anything very specific, because I had little or no idea of what the Department would need. Ingham, however, was quite prepared to give my work top priority and provide Francis Doherty as my local production manager. By this time Ingham was running the London Press Exchange with a skeleton staff and rarely appeared at the Fanfare Press. Doherty had been rejected for military service on medical grounds and so, too, had his assistant John Drage. With the 'recruitment' of these two men, both of whom had been accustomed to the pre-war 'mad rush' associated with much of the firm's work, I was potentially in a very strong position. Whereas Mr Crutchley cannot have known much about printing and was in any case a 'slow mover', Doherty and Drage were very expert and, as time would show, completely capable of handling as many as thirty jobs in various stages of production without complaining that they were being overworked.

I must now return to the *Kennkarte* forgery which Leonard Ingrams entrusted to me one December morning in 1941. Two telephone calls were necessary: one to Doherty to the effect that if all went well our collaboration would begin a few hours later, the other to William Burch, the Monotype Corporation's managing director, to ask if he could see me at noon. The answer was yes. The Department allowed me to use my own small car and supplied the necessary petrol coupons so I arrived at the Corporation's works at Horley, twenty-five miles south of London, without much delay. Owing to petrol-rationing there was very little traffic on the roads in those days and even in London one could cover a lot of ground very fast indeed.

When I saw Burch there was no need for me to use the 'it's so secret that I can't tell you anything' gambit. I simply said, 'I want to forge this and the *Fraktur* series number is so and so,' at the same time showing him the *Kennkarte*. 'Furthermore, I will probably have to tackle somewhat similar items and the types will mostly be *Frakturs* although I may occasionally need something that you originally cut for the French market,' I added.

'Am I allowed to enquire for whom you are working?' Burch asked. 'The Political Intelligence Department of the Foreign Office,' I replied. He then said that he would be glad to *lend* me anything I required: matrices, keybars, etc. All I had to do was to telephone a Mr Quixley who would immediately put the equipment on the next van to London or if necessary use a special messenger. I now had access to the products of the punch store which I had visited with John Tarr some months earlier. Ten minutes later Mr Quixley arrived with a small cardboard box containing the matrices for the *Kennkarte*. After expressing my grateful thanks to the benevolent Mr Burch I hurried back to London and the Fanfare Press. Francis Doherty took possession of the matrices and immediately went across the road to Harrison's Monotype department to order a small fount to be cast for hand-composition, furthermore for delivery within an hour. In the meantime I had cut a small sample of the bookcloth used for the *Kennkarte* and drove to a bookbinders' cloth merchant in the Blackfriars district and was able to buy a couple of yards of material which matched the shade and quality of the German original fairly closely, in fact quite adequately for proofing purposes.

I then called upon Lancelot Spicer, the chairman of Spicer's Ltd, an important firm of paper merchants in the same district. He was an old friend who, like Mr Burch, did not ask many questions. Yes, he would be glad to place an order with the Winterbottom Bookcloth Company at Manchester for a 'minimum making' and an exact match for quality and shade – all 'Very Urgent!' Later Spicer told me that Winterbottom's managing director had telephoned him and guardedly mentioned that the pattern was probably of German origin. 'Well, why not?' Spicer replied. 'We've always had a thriving export department!'

In the course of a brief conversation I casually mentioned that I would probably need special makings of paper with forged watermarks, expeditious 'matchings' and the services of the firm's paper laboratory. R. B. Fishenden, another old friend, was in charge of the latter. Spicer summoned his Mr Skinner who, he said, would look after all my requirements. A few weeks later, when Leonard Ingrams wanted an expeditious forgery of the *Reichsbank* letterheading and we were having trouble matching the paper – there was apparently no time for a special

201

'making' – it was Mr Skinner who quickly discovered that the paper used for the bottle labels of a well-known brand of beer would provide a sufficiently close match.

When I returned to Fanfare two compositors were busy setting an actual facsimile of the *Kennkarte* and Mr Dawkins, the machine room overseer, was adjusting the brown shade of ink required for the background tint plate. At this stage the tint pattern could not be matched exactly but Doherty said that the problem could be solved inside forty-eight hours. Mr Dawkins stayed late to overprint the black type image over the brown tint and when I arrived at St Martin's Lane at 8am the next morning the first proofs of the *Kennkarte* forgery were dry enough to handle. The forgery itself was, say, 90 per cent perfect, and for 100 per cent perfection we simply needed the cloth from Manchester and a better tint plate.

When I showed the proofs to Leonard Ingrams soon after 9am he could not conceal his surprise at the speed with which what I described as provisional proofs had been produced and expressed the view that they so closely resembled the genuine article that they were unlikely to arouse any suspicions if actually used in Germany. 'But *how* did you get so close to the original specimen in under twenty-four hours?' he wanted to know. I said that just as stage magicians are never willing to explain how their tricks are contrived, I was not prepared to tell him anything about mine and he did not press the point.

Perhaps the only memorable feature of the *Kennkarte* episode was that once Leonard Ingrams allowed me to follow my own devices the unit's manufacturing base was settled within a few hours: Fanfare for most of the printing, Spicer's for paper, and the Monotype Corporation for a long succession of loans of matrices which were otherwise unavailable in England. Although I eventually employed almost a score of firms for various purposes, very few of them were aware of my connection with the so-called Political Intelligence Department of the Foreign Office. Lancelot Spicer opened most of the doors for me and all my suppliers needed to know was that the work was secret, invariably very urgent and that their invoices were to be sent to me personally at a post office box number. By 1943 I even had my own private process engraving plant, with David Stephens in charge, in an alley off Chancery Lane.

During a period of about two months after the *Kennkarte* operation Ingrams kept me fairly busy with miscellaneous forgeries for SOE: letterheadings, travel documents, etc. The work was not very interesting because it did not present any particular challenge. Towards the end of February 1942 David Alexander and I moved to an office in a remote corner on the sixth floor of Bush House when the majority of the Woburn people were brought back to London. The room was at the end of a cul-de-sac and could only be approached by a winding corridor. It had probably been allotted to us on the basis that it was thought advisable to locate the 'fakes and forgeries' department in a secluded position where there was no passing traffic.

The first of a series of French philatelic forgeries was put in hand for David Alexander at this time. Like all the later German ones they were executed by Waterlow and Sons Ltd, who had been printing genuine postage stamps since at least the 1890s and were expert security printers. However, Alexander soon departed in the direction of Baker Street and SOE and I never saw or heard of him again. David Bowes-Lyon went to Washington and my periodical visits to see him at Woburn Abbey ceased. In the meantime Ingrams had arranged for me to meet Sefton Delmer for the first time. Delmer was not interested in forgeries but, rather, in the production of bogus German printed matter, the precondition being that if he could not supply a model I would have to design something that 'looked German'. A couple of weeks later the text for *Europa in Gefahr* ('Europe in Danger') (see page 209) arrived on my desk and my long and increasingly active association with Delmer began.

Soon after Easter 1942 Ingrams told me that he would no longer be associated with my work but did not explain why. With hindsight I realise that Dr Dalton's departure to the Board of Trade loosened the hitherto close connection between the Ministry of Economic Warfare and PWE because Lord Selbourne, Dalton's successor at MEW, very sensibly kept clear of PWE. As I liked and respected Ingrams I regretted his departure from my own small scene. He was another whom I never saw again. By the summer of 1942 I had no identifiable 'chief'. Furthermore, nobody appeared to want to grab my minuscule 'empire' which, if anyone gave it a moment's thought, would have been regarded as incredibly arcane. However, I kept in touch with Walter Stewart-Roberts because he paid all the bills and with Colonel Chambers, because if anything went wrong on the security side only he could come to the rescue. Apart from that he was an enthusiastic philatelist and the delighted recipient of unperforated proofs and all the other philatelic minutiae I could supply. In the Colonel's eyes I could do no wrong.

The volume of black printing increased quite suddenly during the summer of 1942. Most of the projects came from Delmer but Dr Beck, representing the French section, also arrived on the scene. Thus on 25 July 1942 Reginald Leeper informed the Secretary of State for Foreign Affairs (Anthony Eden) that:

A special black leaflet, copy attached, has been prepared for distribution inside Vichy France. 2000 copies, ready for posting, in forged envelopes and with forged stamps, will be smuggled across the Pyrenees through the existing chain of couriers. Addresses are largely taken from advertisements in the Vichy press and from censored letters. This apparently pro-Pétain leaflet deserves closer inspection.

During that summer I was literally run off my feet coping with the unexpected succession of orders for black printing. Although I was now helped by a young secretary, apart from having to do all the design work I was constantly on the move between Fanfare, Spicer's and the blockmakers. The situation was transformed when 'Fräulein Elizabeth' arrived late in August. I cannot now remember how I found her although it is likely that Francis Meynell, the founder of the Nonesuch Press, who had no connection with the Department, mentioned that a first-class German graphic artist was working in an advertising agency with which he had some kind of contact. When I met her it emerged that she had been trained by E. R. Weiss, himself a well-known type designer, in Berlin and had designed the 'Elizabeth' typeface for the Bauer type foundry at Frankfurt am Main. When she left Germany she worked for the important Mondadori printing and publishing firm in Milan and then came to London. When she eventually arrived at Bush House after the inevitable security vetting she immediately took charge of all the design work and my own workload was greatly lightened. She was then a demure spinster in her late thirties.

Elizabeth's German 'Gothic' lettering was superb and she quickly learned how to forge the countless rubber stamps used by the Nazi Party and *Wehrmacht*. In the absence of a genuine model she could invent something that was completely convincing. Most of the typescripts received from Delmer were untidy so she attended to the copy preparation and finally the proof-reading. I was delighted when certain regular 'customers' simply gave me a perfunctory greeting when they arrived and went immediately to Elizabeth's corner of the office. She made a major contribution to the unit's performance.

My secretary died at about the time Elizabeth arrived and was succeeded by young Audrey Archer who ran the routine office work – and there was a lot of it – with great efficiency. The next and last recruit was Diana Courtney, a junoesque young woman who looked very smart in her khaki Women's Transport Corps uniform. She was my personal despatch rider and used to dash round London on a motorcycle until she had a minor crash and the Department decided that she would be safer in a small car.

By November 1942, a year after I joined PWE, 'Mr Howe's Unit' was firmly established and taken for granted, at least by the comparatively few who knew it existed, as an integral part of the Department's organisation. Nobody except myself had any very clear idea of how we operated or about our external technical ramifications. By this time we were also occasionally working for the Free French and the Belgian, Dutch and Norwegian governments-in-exile who had somehow discovered us. Colonel Chambers knew about these contacts but no one else.

Owing to illness I was away for two months early in 1944. Elizabeth and Audrey Archer at Bush House and Francis Doherty and John Drage at Fanfare knew all the routines so well that my absence was hardly noticed. The volume of work decreased after the liberation of France and Belgium and we enjoyed a relatively peaceful existence until the end of the war. According to an F & CO document we dealt with about 2000 'orders' during a period of three and a half years although these must have included several hundred reprints. We could supply almost anything from a few forged letterheadings to several million forged German ration cards. Forty years later I do not look back upon that period with any particular nostalgia.

# 21

# Black Printed Matter

In this chapter it is impossible to describe and illustrate more than a typical selection of the multifarious items which my unit manufactured for Sefton Delmer between the early spring of 1942 and the end of the war. In an undated memorandum written late in 1943 Delmer mentioned that,

> The same two-way co-ordination has been maintained between *Atlantik* and the German [black] leaflets. Reports first put out by *Atlantik* have been given further circulation as leaflets and leaflets issued first have been referred to and quoted as soon as their circulation inside Germany has been established. The station and the leaflet department have worked particularly closely together in furthering both the Malingering and Desertion campaigns.

I was unaware of the 'two-way co-ordination' between black broadcasting and printing because I never knew about the *Atlantiksender* until it was merged with the *Soldatensender Calais* late in 1943 and even then seldom listened to either.

The brief details (printed below) of the eighteen items currently in hand for Delmer during the week ending 7 January 1943 indicate the diversity of German black printed matter that was being produced at that time, i.e. about a year after Leonard Ingrams allowed me to make my own manufacturing arrangements. However, before discussing what was happening in January 1943 I must quickly deal with a few previous developments.

Delmer had realised that black printed matter, ranging from simple gummed stickers to far more complicated projects, could reinforce his broadcasting activities providing that they could be delivered to the German armed forces anywhere in Europe, from the U-boat bases in France to Norway, or even to the civilian population inside Germany itself. It was not until long after the war that I realised how widely my material had been distributed – never in impressively large quantities, it is true, but sufficient to disturb the German security authorities.

Delmer's first personal contact with Major Thurston (probably a pseudonym), who was head of SOE's German section, was around June 1942 when we took him out to lunch. I was already working very happily with his colleague Captain Colin Wintle who acted as SOE's liaison officer for all the PWE/SOE regions as far as black printed matter was concerned. Except for the forged German ration cards which the RAF dropped in very large quantities, SOE were our exclusive delivery agents for Germany and the Occupied Territories. A simple routine was quickly established: final proofs were sent in duplicate to Wintle and Delmer and it was Wintle who specified the quantity to be printed and in many cases later ordered reprints of what might be described as 'popular lines'. The so-called 'Malingering Booklet' was a case in point. While a standard text was eventually established over a period of about eighteen months about twenty 'editions', each with a different camouflaged cover, were printed and reprinted in consignments of about 10,000 copies. Some of the stickers, typically the one with the single word *Scheisse* (shit) in large black letters and applied to German official posters all over Europe, was in regular demand.

Small gummed stickers with the word *Scheisse* (shit) were affixed to German official notices all over Europe. The specimen illustrated shows the SS *Runen* symbol.

Delmer's first black printed operation, the famous 'Mölders Letter', belongs to the December 1941–January 1942 period.[1] In *Black Boomerang* he said that I had been involved in its production but I knew nothing about it at the time nor, indeed, until I read his book many years later. No contemporary documents relating to the letter exist in the PWE files nor, for that matter, does a specimen of the *original* letter, meaning the one that was extensively copied in Germany, survive there. Nevertheless, the operation appears to have been outstandingly successful.

Colonel Werner Mölders (1913–41) was a famous German fighter pilot and after his 101st victory in aerial combat in July 1941 he was awarded the Iron Cross with crossed swords and brilliants and then promoted to Inspector of Fighter Pilots. He was a national hero. When in the Crimea on 21 November 1941 he was summoned to Berlin to attend the state funeral of Colonel-General Ernst Udet, one of the most renowned of the

1914–18 generation of fighter pilots, who had committed suicide on 17 November after being blamed by Hitler and Goering for the *Luftwaffe's* failure to defeat the RAF in the Battle of Britain. Mölders never reached Berlin because his aircraft crashed when attempting to land *en route* at Breslau. Mölders' death was of interest to the RAF intelligence people and a recently captured *Luftwaffe* officer PoW was questioned about him. One particularly interesting item of information emerged, namely that Mölders himself had been a devout Roman Catholic. While he undoubtedly met his death in a genuine accident Delmer's *Gustav Siegfried Eins* station was soon proclaiming that his aircraft had been shot down by 'Himmler's Bolshevik scum' in accordance with the Party's prevailing anti-religious campaign. For good measure they also suggested that the Party authorities had commandeered the convent near Münster where Mölders' sister, who may not even have existed, was a nun.

The next step was to persuade the RAF to drop a presumably small quantity of specially-prepared leaflets in the neighbourhood of German nightfighter stations in the Münster area when the *Luftwaffe* aircraft stationed there were aloft looking for RAF bombers. Frank Lynder thought that one or two low-flying and very fast 'Mosquitos' were used for this purpose. The text was typewritten and, furthermore, printed on facsimiles of standard *Luftwaffe* signals message forms. The letter was preceded by a few introductory remarks which were alleged to have been added by an anonymous *Luftwaffe* fighter pilot, himself also presumably a Roman Catholic. The plan was to make it appear as if the leaflets had been disseminated by an anti-Nazi German pilot. Indeed, it seems that the Gestapo were completely deceived because there is no evidence to suggest that they ever suspected that the leaflets had been printed in England.

The text of Mölders' letter, alleged to have been written to a non-existent Roman Catholic dignitary ('Probst Johst') at Stettin, could not have been more anodyne. Mölders informed his friend and spiritual adviser that the *Luftwaffe* fighter pilots were no longer mocking the Church but, rather, returning to it and that he himself faced the prospect of death, 'strengthened by the Sacraments of the Church', with equanimity. What infuriated the authorities was that Mölders, of all people, should be subtly drawing attention to the Party's anti-religious attitude which was in any case causing increasing resentment in Roman Catholic circles.[2] What was surprising – Delmer would have been delighted if he had known about it at the time – was the speed with which copies of the letter were made and circulated in Germany. The Gestapo cross-examined Mölders' mother who denounced the letter as a forgery, also

Probst Daniel at Stettin, who actually existed. The text was read in many pulpits, a number of typewriters and duplicating machines were confiscated, and a few clerics were arrested. In April 1942 the Nuremberg-Fürth police reported that in their area no fewer than eleven Roman Catholic and seven Evangelical clergymen had read the letter from their pulpits and copies were circulating as far from Münster as Upper Bavaria.

The earliest known related document is the letter dated 15 January 1942 which a certain Herr Albrecht of Cassel wrote to his friend Frau Götz von Olenhusen, who lived not far from Göttingen. It read: 'I enclose a letter from Mölders to his priest which I received from a Corps brother. The contents speaks for itself and one cannot read without a sense of sarcasm that such a man was enjoined to "Now abide in Valhalla",' namely the final resting place of the ancient Nordic gods.[3]

The first black project I produced for Delmer was a little twelve-page booklet with the title *Europa in Gefahr*. According to a brief prefatory note it purported to have been printed by 'a group of patriotic men who considered it their duty, in spite of the serious political situation, to bring this document, which came into our possession by chance, to the notice of the public'. The document in question was a report alleged to have been written at Shanghai on 27 February 1942 by Lieutenant-Colonel von Seckendorff-Sümmern for Party Comrade Puttfarken, the Party's representative at Shanghai. The writer said that he felt it to be his duty as a veteran National Socialist to acquaint Herr Puttfarken with certain facts so that he could forward the information to the appropriate office in Berlin. He vividly described the bestial atrocities supposed to have been perpetrated by the Japanese against the British and even some Germans in Hong Kong. The really important revelation was that the Japanese would gladly allow the white races to fight one another to the point of mutual destruction and then dominate the world.

In August 1942 Leeper received a brief report to the effect that, 'the "Yellow Peril" [i.e. *Europa in Gefahr*] seems to be going particularly well and the booklets of Catholic sermons [written by Delmer's Father Andreas] are also circulating in N.W. Germany. The Yellow Peril was given to an SOE man by an entirely independent source who brought it out of Germany.' My own impression is that the 'independent source' represented one of the war's more extraordinary coincidences.

What Delmer described as the 'SS brochure' was another early production. On 13 July 1942 he wrote to Colin Wintle:

We regard the *Drückeberger an die Front* ('Shirkers to the Front') leaflet and the SS brochure as priority A in our recent output and we should be most grateful if you could give them priority in dissemination.

*Drückeberger an die Front* fits in with our campaign to exploit the women's call-up in Germany in depressing the morale of the troops. It contains the operational rumour that women volunteering for the social services are liable to be sent to the factories, hence to discourage them from volunteering for the social services. It stimulates hostility and contempt for the civil service and the Party administration, all of them in reality very essential for the sound functioning of the German war machine.

The propaganda objective of the SS brochure is to give evidence of a split between the Party and SS and the army and to back up the identification of the SS with the forces of Bolshevik nihilism; also to make the SS appear to be the main internal enemy of Germany and an army of civil war and revolution.

The brochure's title was *Leitfaden für SS-Anwärter* ('Manual for candidates for the SS'). It contained a good deal of fascinating and largely fictitious information about the particular privileges alleged to be enjoyed by the SS, also certain details which would undoubtedly have horrified any respectable German mother who happened to read the pamphlet. Here I refer to 'The Ilse Hagemann Case' which, illustrated with reproductions of faked documents, vividly described how Fräulein Ilse met her untimely death at Witebsk in March 1942 at the hands of drunken SS rapists who 'filled her genitals with caviare and pieces of ice'.

On 12 September 1943 Leeper was informed by Delmer that 'We have completed for distribution an elaborate scientific treatise on the new wholemeal and barley bread in Germany and that we are on the right lines has been shown by a remarkable article in the *Danziger Vorposten* recently received. This might have been written by a committee of Mr Delmer, Mr Rayner and Dr McCurdy.'

The ostensible author of the scientific treatise, however, was Herr Dr H. Thaler, director of the German Research Office for Food and Agriculture at Munich, who carefully explained to Secretary of State Dr Herbert Backe at the Reich Ministry of Food and Agriculture that the current wartime methods of milling bread grains were liable to induce various kinds of abdominal cancer. This information was accompanied by references to respectable medical journals and I vaguely recall that a typed summary of the booklet's contents was also prepared.

By the end of 1942 SOE was actually able to mail black printed matter *inside* Germany. There was no question of its agents having to buy the necessary postage stamps because they had already been forged in London. Thus on 22 December 1942 Wintle wrote to Delmer:

You will be pleased to learn that we have had reports about the tricky posting operation of the bread booklets. You will recall that the posting

210

Deutsche Forschungsanstalt      München, Karlstraße 29.
für Lebensmittelchemie.      Oktober 1942.

Herrn
    Staatssekretär Dr. Herbert Backe,

Reichsministerium für Ernährung und Landwirtschaft,
       Berlin W. 8, Wilhelmstraße 72.


     Herr Staatssekretär!

Ich erlaube mir, die folgenden Ausführungen Ihrer geneigten Aufmerksamkeit zu unterbreiten. Als deutscher Mann und Wissenschaftler kann ich nicht länger die **volksmörderische Brotpolitik** des Reiches schweigend mitansehen.

Aus medizinischen und volkswirtschaftlichen Gründen, im Interesse des Sieges und der Volksgesundheit muß das jetzige Vollkornbrot, sprich Voll sch m u tz brot, schleunigst aus der Volksernährung verschwinden. Die jetzige, 100%ige Ausmahlung des Brotgetreides muß eingestellt, und das Volksbrot, wie früher, aus höchstens 80%ig ausgemahlenem Mehl hergestellt werden. Die dadurch wieder freiwerdende Kleie würde dann der Vieh= und Geflügelfütterung zugute kommen und die Fleisch=, Fett=, Milch= und Eierzuteilungen würden damit wieder auf eine annehmbare Höhe gebracht.

**Neuzeitliche Forschung hat klar und deutlich aufgezeigt, daß jede Ausmahlung des Brotgetreides über 80% schwere, gesundheitliche Schäden zur Folge hat. Die gegenwärtige 100%ige Ausmahlung kann nur volksmörderisch genannt werden.**

The first page of a booklet produced to spread the idea that current methods of milling the German flour were liable to cause serious damage to health, including male impotence had to be carried out in two particular towns. We now hear that the majority of the total consignment has been successfully posted in two towns and that the remainder has already gone over the border in the right direction, but no reports of it actually having been posted have yet been received.

It is probable that I sent Delmer a weekly production report from at least the summer of 1942 until the end of the war. I was only able to find one of these reports, dated 7 January 1943, at the Public Record Office. It contains brief details of the eighteen items currently in hand for Delmer and nothing about work for the other PWE regions. However, it indicates the diversity of the printed projects then in hand. The titles were invented in my office in order to provide an easy means of identification when telephoning the Fanfare Press or any other printer concerned, e.g. for the forged German ration cards where as many as four large offset firms collaborated owing to the very large quantities required for dissemination by the RAF.

H 277    *Brandt-Rasputin Leaflet.* I understand that Delmer will give me the typescript soon.

H 279    *Himmler Postage Stamp.* This was submitted to SOE for quantity order on 19 December. They seem to be taking rather long to make up their minds.

H 283    *German 'Leave' Ration Card.* Printing starts this weekend.

H 292    *Winterhilfsbriefmarken* [bogus charity postage stamps]. Delivery today and tomorrow, 10,000 books.

H 298    *Naples Letters.* Seven have been sent to SOE this week.

H 299    *Passive Resistance Stickers.* A reprint of 15,000 of each design will be delivered to SOE at the end of this week.

H 306    *Plague Booklet.* 5000 were delivered to SOE on 7 January.

H 308    *Frank Stamp.* A design should be ready pretty soon.

H 311    *'Die Front will Frieden' Sticker.* See note on H329 below. [An error because H 329 had no connection with this item.]

H 312    *Malingering Booklet (ballistics edition).* Advance copies should be ready in a day or two.

H 315    *Zenit IV.* 500 delivered to SOE on 5 January.

H 317    *'Die Soldatenfrau' Leaflet.* Submitted to SOE for quantity order.

H 319    *Reprint of H134 (a)* [Not identified].

H 327    *Health Chart.* Ready for submission to SOE but awaiting Delmer's approval.

H 329    *'Efka' Cigarette Paper Pack.* Financial sanction for this project has been received and a preliminary order for 5000 will be ready in a month's time.

H 330    *Zenit V.* Advance copies willl be ready today.

H 331    *Hot Hitler Sticker.* Proofs will be ready today.

H 332   *Reprint of H237. (Schlag auf Schlag sticker)*. SOE have ordered a further 10,000. These will be ready this week.

*H 277   Brandt-Rasputin Booklet*. The manufacture of this miniature 24-page publication involved the production of a fairly adequate forgery of a letter in the handwriting of Karl Ernst Krafft, whom various British intelligence services briefly supposed during the summer of 1940 to be Hitler's personal astrologer, and the collaboration of 'Captain' Louis de Wohl (i.e. Ludwig von Wohl), whom Robert Bruce Lockhart accurately described in the second volume of his *Diaries* (1981) as 'the German astrologer and exhibitionist'. Since I have told the Krafft-de Wohl story in adequate detail in *Urania's Children: The Strange World of the Astrologers*, the reader is referred to this book. The gentleman who provided the forgery of Krafft's handwriting was then serving a prison sentence and made no charge for his work. Thanks to the good offices of Colonel Chambers, Scotland Yard arranged for his services and I never met him.

It is absolutely certain that Hitler did not believe in astrology and had no use for astrologers, although Herr Krafft, who was a Swiss citizen, would dearly have liked to work for the *Führer*. In any case, in November 1942, the date of the forged letter, he was a virtual prisoner in a Propaganda Ministry building in the Lützowstrasse in Berlin where he was supposed to cast the horoscopes of Allied leaders and generals so that his 'predictions' could be tinkered with by Dr Goebbels's people for political warfare purposes. However, by that time the *Führerastrologe* was suffering from a nervous breakdown and refusing to do any work.

In the meantime de Wohl was living in fair comfort in an apartment at Athenaeum Court in Piccadilly and was in receipt of a weekly income remitted to him in cash by MI5, although he was also paid by PWE for the work he did for Delmer. If the reader is puzzled by the fact that I refer to the late Herr von Wohl as 'Captain', I must explain the circumstances of his 'commission'. SOE had sent him to the USA on an 'astrological mission' in May 1941 and he returned to London in February 1942. One of his tasks in the USA was to disseminate predictions disadvantageous to the Germans, i.e. via the popular astrological press and lectures. He supposed that he would be rewarded for his services by being commissioned in the British army and it is likely that someone in SOE had rashly promised to arrange it for him. Years later a friend who served in MI5 told me what actually happened. 'De Wohl was desperately anxious to be an officer in the British army,' he said, 'and pushed the Colonel in charge of my section to the point of extreme exasperation. To keep him quiet the Colonel said, "I've arranged it for you. You *are* a Captain in the British army. Of course I cannot give you anything in writing as it's much too secret and of course you cannot use the rank." De Wohl was overjoyed and promised total secrecy. However, unknown to us he bought himself a smart military uniform and was soon spotted walking down Piccadilly looking just like an unmade bed.' Here I must interpolate that the 'Captain' was both tall and running to fat. I encountered him on several occasions in a room at Bush House which was reserved for 'private and secret' meetings and he was always in uniform. When I happened to mention to Colonel Chambers that I was seeing de Wohl at Bush House he issued immediate instructions to prevent the 'Captain' from getting past the security guards at the sixth-floor entrance to PWE's offices so I had to visit him at Athenaeum Court instead.

The text of the forged handwritten letter reads:

Berlin-Halensee
14 Nebelung [i.e. November] 1942

My dear —
You now have the promised copy of my letter to the *Führer*. I know that it is safe in your hands. May all benevolent forces help so that the evil may be averted. Fiat voluntas ...
Always your K. E. Krafft

Berlin-Halensee
am 14. des Nebelung 1942

Mein Lieber!

Hier haben Sie den versprochenen Durchschlag meines Briefes an den Führer. Ich weiss, er ist sicher in Ihren Händen. Mögen alle guten Mächte helfen, dass das Übel abgewendet werden kann. Fiat voluntas...

Stets Ihr

K. E. Krafft.

Dr. Krafft's letzter Brief, — mit dem er uns das hier abgedruckte Schreiben übersandte.

In den ersten Novembertagen des Jahres 1942 entschloß sich de bekannte Astro-Biologe Dr. K. E. Krafft nach reiflicher Überlegung un Besprechung mit seinen Freunden, einen Brief an den Führer zu schreiben

Dieser Brief, geschrieben auf Grund tiefgründiger astrologische Forschungen und einer eingehenden, persönlichen Kenntnis der Verhält nisse im FHQ, enthielt eine Warnung.

Der Schreiber hatte begründete Hoffnung, das Ohr des Führers z gewinnen. Er war schon in der Kampfzeit regelmäßig von Adolf Hitle zur Ausarbeitung von Horoskopen zugezogen worden, und wurde nach de Machtergreifung zu dessen ständigem astrologischen Berater. Seit 194 hatte er sich ganz der vom Führer angeregten Neuherausgabe der Werk von Michel Nostradamus gewidmet, und sich mehr und mehr vom FH zurückgezogen.

Jetzt aber wurde ihm klar, daß es seine Pflicht sei, den Führer v gewissen Umtrieben im Hauptquartier zu warnen. Er suchte um ein Audienz nach, stieß jedoch auf verhüllten Widerstand. So blieb da Schreiben die letzte Hoffnung, den Führer in letzter Stunde auf di drohende Katastrophe aufmerksam zu machen.

Am 8. Dezember 1942 wurde Dr. Krafft, der sich vorübergehend i Berlin-Halensee, Joachim-Friedrichstraße 54, aufhielt, in seiner Wohnun von einem Offizier des Führerbegleitbataillons aufgesucht. Dr. Kraf packte in Eile einen Koffer und verabschiedete sich von einem anwesende Freund mit den Worten : „Gott sei Dank, daß der Führer auf mich gehö hat. Wir standen dicht vor der Katastrophe".

3

This was followed by a brief account of Krafft's decision to write to the *Führer*, his work for Hitler over a period of many years, and his own recent increasingly frequent absence from the *Führer*'s headquarters as he was working on a new edition of the prophecies of Nostradamus. Then, on 8 December 1942, according to the printed text, 'Herr Doktor' Krafft was fetched from his home by an officer of Hitler's personal bodyguard and never seen again. This was followed by twenty-one pages of glorious nonsense which included a lengthy reference to Dr Karl Brandt, one of Hitler's personal physicians. Brandt was said to have been treating Hitler for prostate problems with a cocaine-based drug called Cycloform and massive doses of ovarial hormones. There were close-up photographs of the eyes of Brandt and Rasputin and it was suggested that Brandt would be Rasputin's equivalent in a German context. It was also indicated that Brandt's evil influence on Hitler had not only led to the dismissal of Colonel-General von Brauchitz but also to Hitler's decision to assume personal command in Russia. The names of nineteen other dismissed German generals were also listed.

The purpose of this rather complicated publication was to spread rumours about the deterioration of Hitler's physical and mental health. No 'come-backs' are recorded.

*H 279   Himmler Postage Stamp.* According to an undated memorandum written by Delmer, but undoubtedly in May–June 1943:

> To back up a rumour campaign that Himmler has prepared everything for his succession to Hitler we have prepared a special edition of the German 6 Pfg. postage stamps with Himmler's head instead of Hitler's. These, with the necessary paraphernalia for cancelling the stamps, have been sent to a neutral country [actually Stockholm] where they have been put in the letterboxes of a small number of people, including newspaper editors, with the intention that the recipients should discover and report the new stamp. German denials of the issue would then be accompanied by rumours that these stamps were part of an issue secretly prepared by Himmler, a few sheets of which had been given premature distribution, either accidentally or maliciously. Hitherto the addressees have been too unobservant, but SOE will go on trying until one of them reacts.

I can remember procuring the 'necessary paraphernalia' for cancelling the stamps, also providing a supply of business postcards which were exact copies of those used by the Fränck'sche Verlagshandlung (booksellers and publishers) at Stuttgart. These postcards, adorned with the Himmler stamp and properly postmarked, were dropped into a number of letterboxes in Stockholm, including those of philatelic dealers. Delmer recalled in *Black Boomerang* that the operation was a complete failure because nobody noticed the stamp. SOE's Polish collaborators did their best to disseminate letters in Germany and SOE's people in Switzerland delivered German newspapers with the stamp on the wrapper, but all to no avail. After the war the Fränk'sche Verlagshandlung were shown one of their cards with the stamp and were greatly surprised.

After the unsuccessful attempt to assassinate Hitler on 20 July 1944 there was little or no news of the *Führer* who was lying low at his closely guarded headquarters in East Prussia. Delmer exploited Hitler's apparent disappearance by launching an intensive rumour campaign. Once again Himmler was intending to supplant the *Führer*.

*H 283   German 'Leave' Ration Card.* According to Delmer in *Black Boomerang* he saw some forged German ration cards on my desk and I told him that they had been made for use by SOE's agents. This may have been the case but I have no recollection of producing anything of this kind for SOE's exclusive use. However, it was Delmer who conceived the plan of forging very large quantities of the perforated sheets of ration stamps which were available for members of the general public who were on holiday or temporarily absent from home. The originals were printed on a pale blue specially watermarked paper. When the Germans changed the watermark as a security precaution so did we. SOE was able to procure advance copies of new issues and by getting the paper made with the minimum of delay and using four or five offset printers we were

H 283: Forged ration card for use by German civilians temporarily away from home invariably able to give the RAF several million cards for almost immediate delivery to Germany.

The specimen illustrated here was valid for two days and could be used in restaurants. It entitled the holder to a small quantity of bread, meat or meat products (e.g. sausage) and butter. A similar but larger card, valid for six days, provided the user with the same comestibles, also margarine, sugar, coffee–substitute and cheese. Typical specimens can be seen at the Imperial War Museum.

According to a confidential report issued by the Regensburg Criminal Police on 25 March 1943 on the basis of information received from Himmler's *Reichssicherheitshauptamt* (State Security Office), enemy aircraft had recently dropped cards valid for two, six and seven days and the forgeries were deceptively efficient and could not be easily recognised as such. Members of the general public, however, were informed that the British fakes could easily be identified and that users would be sentenced to long prison sentences or even the death penalty. However, the evidence available indicates that if used with discretion our ration cards could provide German citizens with acceptable additional nourishment.

Delmer did not greatly mind whether or not the illegal use of the forgeries was discovered in Germany. If they were employed successfully the German rationing system would be sabotaged. People who were prosecuted and sent to prison simply added to the number of those with a grudge against the Nazi regime. The 'evidence of reception' reports are too numerous to quote and a typical one will suffice. Towards the end of 1944 a prisoner of war captured at Namur in September said that when the forgeries were dropped over Berlin in the autumn of 1943 the workers quickly collected them and succeeded in exchanging them for meat and butter. This happened in the Neukölln district.

*H 292   Winterhilfsbriefmarken* i.e. bogus war charity postage stamps. These were contained in a forgery of the standard German stamp books. There is no evidence that they ever circulated in Germany but they were certainly used for internal mail in Poland where Polish postal workers no doubt franked them with malicious pleasure.

*H 298   Naples Letters.* On 15 November 1942 Delmer wrote to Major Thurston at SOE:

> Yet another posting operation which I propose is this: we have a number of intercepted telegrams from the Naples military hospital informing

H 292: *Winterhilfsbriefmarken*

relatives or the *Ortsgruppenleiter* [local Nazi Party officials] of certain soldiers in the Naples hospital. In this case I suggest sending a letter to the relatives from the *Kriegslazarett* [military hospital] Naples saying that the golden trinkets which were in the possession of the deceased have been sent to the *Ortsgruppenleiter* in . . . where they can be collected, Heil Hitler! This should cause a lot of bad blood.

My impression is that the letter-heading of the *Reserve-Lazarett II* at Naples was faked rather than forged. According to Frank Lynder's recollections there was an epidemic of jaundice in Rommel's *Afrika Korps* at this time and the intercepted telegrams were sent by the German military authorities at Naples to the appropriate *Wehrkreiskommando* (military district HQ) in Germany. The latter was instructed to request the *Ortsgruppenleiter*'s office to send someone to visit the deceased soldier's relatives and inform them that he had died from the effects of jaundice. Delmer supposed that an official visit might make a good impression but, on the other hand, if there were many deaths to be reported in a given district the sad news might only be announced gradually in order to prevent talk.

Frank Lynder told me that there were two versions of the 'Naples Letter' and he could remember the gist of their texts. The first was supposed to have been written by a nurse:

Dear Frau Müller,

Actually we nurses are forbidden to correspond with relatives but your Heinz was such a nice boy. He died in my arms at 11.30 pm on. . . . His last thoughts were for you. Before he died he gave me the native jewellery which he bought for you in Benghazi, a ring and a trinket. You can fetch them from the *Ortsgruppenleiter*'s office together with his watch. If I come to Dresden-Loschwitz perhaps I can see you.

With all good wishes,<br>Irene Gärtner.

If the bereaved wife or mother followed Sister Irene's instructions she would be told that nothing was known about the ring and trinket. The hoped-for reaction would be that the Nazi Party thieves had stolen them.

The alternative text read:

Dear Frau Müller,

They have certainly told you that your Heinz died from jaundice. That was not the case. We were in the same Company and he was a fine chap. They had to amputate his leg and afterwards gave him a [lethal] injection. This often happens to war cripples. I'll visit you after the war. [No signature!]

Frank Lynder told me that rumours eventually circulated in Germany that severely crippled soldiers were 'liquidated'. He said, too, that he and Albright (i.e. Adam) probably wrote about thirty of the letters at RAG and that the balance were handwritten by trustworthy German refugees who had no idea for whom they were working.

*H 306* *Plague Booklet*. This purported to be an offprint from an official German Ministry of Health publication. Its purpose was to suggest that contact with the Russian territory and troops threatened to bring an outbreak of Plague within the Reich borders, or alternatively that infected Russian rats (who travelled west on leave or other trains?) could be the source. 'Naturally no statistical information about the present incidence of cases of Plague in the Reich territory can be published and statistical details can only be supplied to doctors working in the public health service.'

The purpose of this publication was undoubtedly to reinforce rumours already launched by *Gustav Siegfried Eins*, and its author or editor can only have been Dr John McCurdy.

*H 308* *Frank Stamp*. Hans Frank was thirty-nine when Hitler appointed him Governor General of the *Generalgouvernement*, namely those

SONDERABDRUCKE AUS DEM REICHS-GESUNDHEITSBLATT

HERAUSGEGEBEN VOM REICHSGESUNDHEITSAMT

No. 9

# PEST

Verlag: Reichsverlagsamt

H 306: The front cover of the Plague Booklet, a facsimile of an existing German publication issued by the German Ministry of Health

regions of Poland which had not been incorporated into the Reich or absorbed into Soviet Russia. His corrupt and brutal rule in Poland stimulated a lively and secret Polish underground movement known as 'Operation N[iemcy, i.e. Germany]'. These people had access to printing presses and produced a lot of black 'literature' in German in the best Delmer style. Polish postal workers fixed small gummed stamps with the slogan 'Deutschland kaput' to letters from the Russian front which passed through their hands on their way to the Reich, and railway workers inserted locally produced black printed matter into crates containing munitions, etc. on their way to Russia.

Simon Wiesenthal, the famous scourge and identifier of German war criminals, who had excellent sources of information, told me that he thought about 250 sheets each containing twenty copies of the Frank stamp reached Poland during March 1943. Herbert A. Friedmann, the American analyst of propaganda forgeries, who examined all the surviving envelopes that he could trace, considered it likely that all the Frank

H 308: The bogus Frank Stamp which was successfully mailed from Poland together with the authentic Hitler Stamp to an address at Dresden in Germany

stamps were mailed from five different places in Poland between 11–19 June 1943 to addresses in the Reich. The illustration shows part of an envelope which actually reached Dresden. The Frank stamp was used in conjunction with the regular Hitler's head issue, the object of the operation being to spread rumours that Frank was proposing to play a *Führer*-role in Poland.

*H 312   Malingering Booklet (Ballistics edition).* This may have been the first small-format edition of a little handbook on simulating illness and thereby avoiding military or any other wartime duties. It was originally published as H 270 *Sportsvorschriften für die Kriegsmarine* ('Instructions for Sport in the German Navy'). *1000 Worte Französisch* ('1000 French Words') was published a little later.

There were at least twenty other 'editions', each with its own deceptively innocent cover design: miniature hymn books for Roman Catholic

One of about twenty different camouflaged covers used for the 'Malingering' Booklet. The author's name in English means 'Dr Do-Good' and the title means 'Illness Saves'

and Protestant soldiers, Belgian railway timetables, pocket guides to Oslo, short stories by well-known authors and so on. The text was trans-

Ende des Krieges verhältnismäßig gemütlich bei leichtem
..st in der Garnison abwarten. Ein schwerer Fall dieser Krank-
macht es völlig unmöglich, daß der Betroffene schwere Arbeit
Mit ein bischen Glück kannst du schließlich erreichen, daß du
dem Wehrdienst entlassen wirst.

**..eilweise Lähmung.**

hier angegebenen Maßnahmen haben eine gewisse Ähnlichkeit
den unter 1 angeführten. Du mußt aber verstehen, daß zwischen
..en ein grundsätzlicher Unterschied besteht. Die Nuß, von der wir
..t gesprochen haben, war nur ein mechanisches Hilfsmittel, um dir
richtige Art, dich zu bewegen, beizubringen. Auch im Folgenden
..es sich um kleine, runde Gegenstände handeln, die an verschiedenen
..len des Körpers durch Binden in der richtigen Lage gehalten
..den müssen. Der Zweck hierbei aber ist, eine tatsächliche Krank-
..serscheinung hervorzurufen, nicht nur ihre Nachahmung zu
..nen.
..mung eines Armes oder Beins ist natürlich eine Beschwerde, auf
..hin kein Arzt vermeiden kann, den betreffenden Mann krank zu
..iben, und zwar mindestens so lange, wie die Lähmung andauert.
..e Lähmung zu simulieren, ist so gut wie unmöglich. Jeder Doktor
..e einen Mann, der behauptet, gelähmt zu sein, ohne daß er es
..lich ist, schnell hereinlegen.
..ist nicht schwer, eine wirkliche Lähmung hervorzurufen, von der
..Arzt nicht feststellen kann, woher sie kommt, und die er als eine
..hafte Krankheit anerkennen muß. Diese Beschwerde hat den
..en Vorteil, daß sie keinerlei schauspielerisches Talent erfordert.
..betreffende Mann hat weiter nichts zu tun, als die hier gegebenen
..chläge zu befolgen, und dann zum Arzt zu gehen und ihm die
..rheit zu sagen. (Er darf natürlich bloß nie herauskommen lassen,
..er getan hat, um die Beschwerde hervorzurufen. Aber so idiotisch
..o ja wohl niemand sein.)
..mungen dieser Art können an verschiedenen Stellen hervorgerufen
..den. Das Prinzip ist immer dasselbe: Wenn man für einige
..einen dauernden Druck auf einen Nerv ausübt, dann beginnt
..einer Weile der Nerv auf kürzere oder längere Zeit zu streifen.

Die Nerven sind gewissermaßen die Telephonleitungen, über die das
Gehirn seine Befehle an die Muskeln durchgibt. Wenn die Leitung
unterbrochen ist, können die betreffenden Muskeln, die „angeschlossen"
sind, eben keine Bewegungen machen. In Wirklichkeit können solche
„Unterbrechungen der Leitung" aus allen möglichen Gründen hervorgerufen werden. Das braucht dich nicht zu kümmern. Laß ruhig
den Doktor sich darüber den Kopf zerbrechen, was in deinem Fall der
Grund sein könnte. Du weißt es selber natürlich auch nicht, und
kannst ihm „leider" nicht helfen. An der Tatsache, daß das betreffende
Glied gelähmt ist, kann keiner zweifeln, aus dem einfachen Grunde,
weil es wirklich gelähmt sein wird.
**Wo die Nerven liegen, auf die der Druck ausgeübt werden muß,**
siehst du aus den Abbildungen 8, 9 und 10. An diesen Stellen wirst

Abbildung 8.

A) Der Nerv am „Musikantenknochen", angezeigt durch den Kreis
am Ende der gestrichelten Linie.
(Rechter Arm.)

B) Derselbe Nerv, am linken Arm
mit angedeuteter Bandage.

du mit einigem Suchen den Nerv fühlen können. Er fühlt sich an
wie ein dünner Strick und ist natürlich auf Druck empfindlich.
Das bekannteste Beispiel ist der Nerv, der über den sogenannten
„Musikantenknochen" läuft. (Abbildung 8.) Der Nerv liegt hier dicht
unter der Haut an der inneren Seite der Ellbogenspitze. Bekanntlich ruft
schon ein leichter Stoß an dieser Stelle das bekannte Schmerzgefühl

..1                                                                        35

A double-page spread from the booklet *Krankheit Rettet*, describing methods of temporarily paralysing one's arm

lated into French, Flemish, Italian and Norwegian. It was also printed
as single sheets on very thin Bible paper which were inserted into 'Efka'
and other cigarette paper packets and in a different and larger format
for insertion into a forgery of the envelope for the official Reich
lottery tickets. From the late summer of 1942 onwards the 'Malingerer'
reached members of the German armed forces all over Europe and
occasioned countless denunciations on the part of the military and
civilian authorities.

The 'Malingerer' concept was originated by Dr John McCurdy,
Delmer's psychological adviser, although much of the text appears to
have been written by René Halkett, who had at one time briefly studied
medicine. He tested many of his 'prescriptions' for simulating illness on
long-suffering local guinea-pigs, of whom Frank Lynder was one. The
text was gradually expanded from 64 to 104 pages and eventually included useful information for foreign workers, such as advice on how to
buy drugs at pharmacies without attracting attention, how to alter

doctors' prescriptions and how to forge their rubber stamps (by the simple process of transferring the impression as soon as possible by using a raw potato cut in half), also how to distil herbs for producing strange symptoms and so on.

The reader was informed that:

Daily *Volksgenossen* [comrades] – in the armed forces or civilians – who feel unwell are dismissed by doctors and certified fit for duty. The reason is clear. Under the circumstances of total war medical men have been instructed not to release manpower for a single day if it can be possibly avoided ... The physician can only intervene and help on the basis of information *you* supply. It is essential that you should be able to describe symptoms in the proper manner ... the first mistake is to provide information which is too accurate; the second is to show the doctor how ill you are, so that he sees that you are unfit for duty. The correct procedure is to give him the impression that, 'Here is a conscientious soldier or worker who has the misfortune to be ill *against his will*.'

Next the reader was advised not to specify the malady from which he claimed to be suffering or to use medical terms: 'The malingerer never fails because he has said too little, but often because he has said too much. Thus in this booklet you will not find the names of the illnesses which are described. It is safer if you don't know them. If the doctor wants to, he will tell you from what you are suffering himself ... You must clearly say that you don't want to be ill, and make it easy for him to believe that you are sick.' It was then explained that there is a choice of illnesses, 'so simply choose your symptoms and stick to your story. Leave the rest to the doctor. You don't select the malady; the doctor identifies it himself.' Advice was given on how to simulate such ailments as pains in the back, jaundice, major digestive problems, partial paralysis (e.g. of an arm), amnesia and tuberculosis. Later editions which, it was hoped, would be studied by industrial workers and in particular those employed in chemical plants, included the appropriate ailments.

The German authorities greatly disliked the 'Malingering' Booklets and paid us the compliment of translating them back into English for the benefit of the British or Allied troops. There were also a great many 'come-backs' indicating that various editions were circulating in Germany and the Occupied Territories, not to mention warnings against them in a succession of *Wehrmacht* confidential leaflets.

If Delmer had still been alive he would have been delighted at the rumpus caused in the Federal Republic in 1980 by the circulation of a somewhat similar publication with the title *Wege zu Wissen und*

*Wohlstand oder: Lieber krankfeiern als gesund schuften ('Paths to knowledge and wellbeing: better to enjoy ill health than be fit and work')*, allegedly written by Dr A. Narcho, Dr Marie Huana and *Privatdozent* (university lecturer) Dr Kiff-Turner. Its purpose was to enable purchasers to make false claims for financial support from the German equivalent of the Department of Health and Social Security. A first edition of 3000 copies was quickly sold and the reprint (at least 6000 copies) was distributed by about a hundred left-wing bookshops. The authors did not claim copyright and recommended individual readers to reprint it in large editions and sell it cheaply. If our 'Malingerer' was black, its successor was even blacker!

*H 315 Zenit IV. Der Zenit* was a bogus astrological magazine of which half a dozen issues were produced at regular intervals in 1942-3. It can be assumed that the texts were largely written by Louis de Wohl with occasional subversive interpolations added by various astrological 'experts' at RAG. The first issue, dated October 1942 and described as 'No. 8', consisted of eight pages reproduced from Fräulein Elizabeth's typing. It contains little of interest but No. 9 included a reference to Hitler's physician Dr Brandt. It was asked why the care of the *Führer*'s health was entrusted to a man whose Neptune was in square aspect to Hitler's sixth 'House', i.e. the sector of Hitler's horoscope which referred to the latter's health.

The early typewritten issues of *Der Zenit* were not particularly black and whatever subversive material was added tended to be buried in the usual vague astrological terminology. The standard improved with Vol. II, No. 1, dated March 1943, which was printed and had an attractive cover in red and black designed by Fräulein Elizabeth. Furthermore, the periodical was printed and included advertisements. The 'editor' was now Dr Hubert Korsch, who had been well known in German astrological circles before the war. However, nobody at RAG was aware that he had been in a concentration camp since May 1941 when scores of German astrologers were arrested soon after Hess's flight to Scotland since it was supposed that one or other of them had advised him about a suitable date for his departure.

By now SOE was disseminating copies for the edification of the U-boat crews in the French Atlantic ports and it was noted that Admiral Dönitz was paying attention to the advice previously given that U-boats should not be allowed to depart on 'unfavourable days'. Readers were asked to consider the sad case of U-335. This vessel had a good horoscope when launched but that of its commander, Kapitän-Leutnant H. Pelkner,

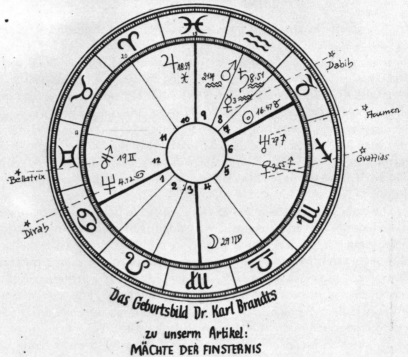

# DER ☆ ZENIT

✠ MONATSZEITSCHRIFT FÜR DAS DENKENDE DEUTSCHLAND ☆

NOVEMBER 1942 ✠ ERSTER JAHRGANG ✠ NUMMER 9

*Das Geburtsbild Dr. Karl Brandts*

zu unserm Artikel:

MÄCHTE DER FINSTERNIS

✠ IM VERLAG: DAS GEISTIGE DEUTSCHLAND ✠ ERFURT ☆

H 315: The first version of the cover design for *Der Zenit*, a bogus astrological magazine mainly intended to discourage the U-boat crews from going to sea. The text was typewritten

H 330: A later, more sophisticated version of *Der Zenit* with a two–colour cover and the text printed letterpress

A miniature airmail edition of *Der Zenit* with advertisements printed on the back cover

was 'bad', and this explained why U-335 was sunk after four days at sea on 3 August 1942. Not surprising, perhaps, considering that the transiting moon was in square aspect to the sun and Pluto in his horoscope. A table showing favourable and unfavourable days for U-boat operations was also included. Needless to say, not many days in March 1943 were considered auspicious and 25 March was described as 'distinctly unfavourable'. It is conceivable that a U-boat was sunk on that day because the March issue was probably not printed until a couple of months later by which time the Naval Intelligence Division had already confirmed that the 'prophecy' had come true.

Long after the war I met Herr Wilhelm Wulff, the Hamburg astrologer who had worked for Himmler's famous masseur Felix Kersten and, during the last weeks of the war, even for Himmler himself. Herr Wulff told me that he had been summoned by Artur Nebe, the head of the Criminal Police, who showed him a copy of our *Der Zenit* and asked him to assess it. The issue in question had arrived at Stettin together with a consignment of machine tools from Sweden. According to Wulff, our 'Captain' Louis de Wohl's work was technically correct. I was unsure how to react, whether to feel reassured or to laugh.

*H 317* *'Die Soldatenfrau' Leaflet* was a bogus *Wehrmacht* leaflet printed for the benefit of soldiers who had not been on home leave for a year. It explained that if their wives reported that they were pregnant but denied even a hint of infidelity with German civilians or even foreign workers there was no cause for alarm. The cause was probably psychological, induced by over-exertion in the war industries or the abdominal swelling and flatulence caused by the German bread. It was mentioned, too, that overwork was liable to induce infertility and premature ageing. The purpose of the leaflet was to induce feelings of anxiety about conditions on the home front.

*H 327* *Health Chart* was a fake of an official medical leaflet and soldiers were instructed to keep it in their pay book. It described the symptoms for a number of serious infectious diseases and was therefore an extension of the Malingerer's Booklet. The publication might be described as a stimulus to hypochondria.

*H 329* *'Efka' Cigarette Paper Pack*. These were used to contain the Malingerer texts printed on very thin Bible paper. SOE's agents used to leave them in cafés frequented by German soldiers.

H 329: An 'Efka' Cigarette Paper Pack

*H 331   Hot Hitler Sticker.* The pithy German text means: 'Hitler warm, room cold; Hitler cold, [i.e. dead] room warm.' The Polish underground also printed and used this slogan.

H 331: 'Make Hitler cold – then the room will become warm again.'

'Whoever eats helps the enemy.'

Subversive imitations of current Propaganda Ministry 'Saying of the Week' posters

*H 332* '*Schlag auf Schlag*' *Sticker.* This was a greatly reduced version of a typical Propaganda Ministry 'Saying of the Week' poster and we must have used the Promi model for at least half a dozen suitably subversive gummed stickers. The latter had the advantage of being easy to carry and could be applied quickly in any convenient place during the black-out. H 332 provided greatly exaggerated details of German losses in Russia.

**Schlag auf Schlag**

Jhrt die deutsche Wehrmacht gegen unsere Feinde, zu Lande, zu Wasser und in der Luft! Seit Beginn der Frühjahrskämpfe, der Schlacht auf der Halbinsel Kertsch bis zur Beendigung der Schlacht von Stalingrad, fielen im Osten 960.000 deutsche Soldaten. Seit Beginn des Russland-Feldzuges am 22. Juni 1941 haben die deutschen Truppen insgesamt 4.600.000 an Toten, Schwerverwundeten und Vermissten verloren.

Der Friedhof, den unsere Truppen 1942 bisher in Sowjetrussland neu eroberten, ist grösser als die britische Insel.

An der Heimatfront haben Übermüdung, Unterernährung und Antreiberei rund 65.000 Männer und Frauen in Betriebsunfällen getötet. Weitere 115.000 verloren ihr Leben durch Luftangriffe. Voll Stolz blickt der Führer auf diese geschichtlich einmaligen Erfolge und ist bereit, uns alle erdenklichen weiteren Opfer aufzuerlegen,

**bis das deutsche Volk verblutet am Boden liegt**

H 332: 'Blow by blow until the German people lies bleeding on the ground' — A bogus version of a Propaganda Ministry poster exaggerating the number of German dead in Russia and graphically demonstrating that the 'cemetery' conquered by the German troops in Soviet territory was bigger than the British Isles

This concludes my account of the work in hand for Delmer on 7 January 1943. A month later there would have been many new items.

The unit produced many leaflets which encouraged German soldiers

# DEUTSCHER SOLDAT!

**D**IE schimpfliche Zunahme der Fälle, in denen Mannschaften und sogar Offiziere der mir unterstellten Einheiten und Dienststellen sich ihrer Wehrverpflichtung durch Übertritt auf schwedisches Gebiet entzogen haben, gibt mir Veranlassung, auf Folgendes hinzuweisen :

1.) Wenn auch die Strafbestimmungen für das ehrlose Verbrechen der Fahnenflucht (§ 6 KSStV) Tod oder Zuchthaus vorsehen, so ist doch in der Praxis die Strafe immer Tod.

2.) Fahnenflucht ist nicht nur ein ehrloses Verbrechen, sondern auch ein fast aussichtsloses Unterfangen. Entgegen gewissen, vom Feind verbreiteten Gerüchten, besteht in Schweden kein Asylrecht für deutsche Wehrmachtangehörige, die innerhalb 24 Stunden nach Überschreiten der Grenze oder in Uniform von der schwedischen Polizei auf schwedischem Boden aufgegriffen werden. Solche Fahnenflüchtige werden unverzüglich an die nächste deutsche Dienststelle ausgeliefert.

Nach den geltenden Bestimmungen wird Asylrecht nur solchen Personen gewährt, die Zivilkleider tragen oder deren Kleidung nicht als die international anerkannte Uniform eines deutschen Wehrmachtteils identifiziert werden kann, und die sich länger als 24 Stunden in Schweden aufgehalten haben.

3.) Allen Wehrmachtangehörigen wird zur Pflicht gemacht, mit allen Kräften daran mitzuarbeiten, daß das wachsende Übel der Fahnenflucht ausgerottet wird. In diesem kritischen Augenblick höchster Bereitschaft und höchster Gefahr kommt es auf jeden Einzelnen an.

Der Militärbefehlshaber
für die besetzten norwegischen Gebiete
(gez.) von Falkenhorst
Generaloberst.

Oslo, 18. 2. 1943

Bogus poster above the name of General von Falkenhorst commanding the German troops in Norway, which states that German deserters into Sweden could remain there if they were in civilian clothing and had been in Sweden for more than 24 hours to desert by crossing the nearest border, if practical, into neutral territory. According to an 'official' printed notice dated 18 February 1942 above the name of Colonel-General von Falkenhorst, commander of the German troops in Norway, the Swedish authorities would give asylum only to individuals who wore civilian clothes and had been in Sweden for at least twenty-four hours. This could be construed as an encouragement to procure a civilian outfit and depart. Then on 3 July a similar poster announced that the Swedish government would now grant asylum to German deserters in uniform.

A typed leaflet (undated) stated that the intending deserter need not have any fear that the Gestapo would take reprisals against his family at home 'because the *Feldgendarmerie* [Field Security Police] have no idea who has been "bumped off by the Norwegians or simply done a bunk". If you come over to us you'll be surprised at the number of "living corpses" who are now happily living in the internment camp. Comrades who have already finished with it [the war] await you in beautiful Sweden and make you welcome.'

In other typewritten leaflets intending deserters were told how to cross the border into Switzerland and Spain respectively. In the case of Switzerland they were instructed to report immediately to the nearest police or army post and produce their German papers. The instructions for Spain were more detailed: '1. Wear old and shabby clothing (easily obtainable in France); 2. Don't report at the frontier but get as far into Spain as you can; 3. If you are stopped by the police or *Guardia Civil* say that you are from Alsace-Lorraine and can only speak broken French; 4. Do not carry any identification papers or arms; 5. You can be in possession of French or any other currency *but not Spanish money*; 6. Refuse to see any German consul or official. State very clearly that you are a refugee from Alsace-Lorraine who doesn't intend to sacrifice himself for Hitler.'

An 'official' printed leaflet dated 3 April 1943, allegedly for distribution to company commanders in the German army, stated that German prisoners of war in Canada and the USA were being offered opportunities to take over vacant farming land and make themselves self-sufficient. They would, furthermore, be granted Canadian, American or even Brazilian nationality at the end of the war. This idyllic prospect was denounced (by us, of course) as a shameful attempt to deprive the Fatherland of its best blood.

1 See H. Witetschek, '*Der gefälschte und der echte Mölders-Brief*' in *Vierteljahresheft für Zeitgeschichte*, Vol. 16, 1968, pp. 60–65.

2 For the anger recently caused by the confiscation of church bells, except for those of historical or artistic interest, for melting down for the armaments industry, see H. Boberach, *Meldungen aus dem Reich*, 1965, pp. 232–3. For Mölders in this book see p. 233.

3 Herr Albrecht's letter is in the possession of the recipient's son, Herr A. Götz von Olenhusen, of Freiburg i. Br.

# 22

# The Final Period

In the absence of a War Diary carefully maintained at MB from 14 November 1943, when the *Soldatensender Calais* 'linked with the short-wave station *Atlantik*' first broadcast, until the end of the war, I find it difficult, if not impossible, to provide an orderly account of what actually happened. When Delmer wrote *Black Boomerang* he provided very few dates because he could not remember them, while the documents at the Public Record Office contain many obscurities. However, it is extraordinary how much Delmer had achieved since 23 May 1941 when *Gustav Siegfried Eins* first broadcast and the Corporal was his only assistant. Three years later, according to an annotated list of RU houses dated 14 March 1944, he led a team of about a hundred collaborators including about forty German PoWs. The remainder consisted of a miscellaneous collection of Poles, Czechs, Slovaks, Bulgarians and Romanians. My suggestion that there were about forty German prisoners of war is only a guess. The fact that sixteen individuals were accommodated at a house known as 'The Holt' at Aspley Guise and a dozen at 'Dawn Edge' in the same village appears to suggest PoWs who slept in the equivalent of dormitories.

The considerable increase in the number of individuals who worked at MB was closely connected with Delmer's ultimately successful attempt to grab the 600-kW Aspidistra transmitter from the BBC, who were naturally reluctant to part with it. On 21 July 1943 Delmer wrote a paper in which he suggested that,

> Germany has reached a state of deterioration which makes the application of more offensive methods of political warfare advisable . . . BBC broadcasts to Germany rightly confine themselves to straight news, meaning of military and strategic developments, and to comment thereon. They refrain from revolutionary agitation against the regime as such agitation, coming from the mouth of the openly enemy BBC, would be ineffective. The main burden of revolutionary action against German subjects, and from the internal German point of view, is carried by PWE's black propaganda, which purports to address Germany from inside and speaks to Germany

from the German rather than the enemy point of view. 'Black' says 'we' where the BBC says 'you'.

He went on to explain that whereas the BBC was able to employ one long-, three medium- and twenty-five short-wave transmitters, using as many as eighteen simultaneously, PWE's black broadcasts to Germany, which mainly emanated from the *Kurzwellensender Atlantik*, were limited to the use of four $7\frac{1}{2}$-kW short-wave transmitters of which only two were available for simultaneous broadcasting. The results, he suggested, had so far not been too discouraging. In a recent Combined Services Detailed Interrogation Centre survey among German prisoners of war it had been established that eighty-eight per cent of those questioned had listened to the BBC and twenty-one per cent to clandestine stations. However, whereas only one per cent had heard what the BBC had said *quoted in conversation*, seventeen per cent had heard black stations *quoted and commented upon*. The inference, therefore, was that black techniques would be likely to stimulate more effective 'listener reaction' than the BBC. Furthermore, Delmer's plan was to reach the German civilian population which, for the most part, was unable to receive the short-wave *Atlantik* broadcasts. For this purpose it was essential for him to have access to the 600-kW Aspidistra transmitter.

We have evolved in the past year (he continued) a new form of black which in terms of colour shades might be described as grey and as a counterfeit rather than as a clandestine station ... The *Deutscher Kurzwellensender Atlantik* is not a clandestine station in the sense that *Gustav Siegfried Eins* pretends to be clandestine. It is a counterfeit of a German forces programme and gets its effect by interlarding German official news with subversive news and presenting the German public with a plausibly German point of view. It is black in so far as it repudiates any British origin and the British government accepts no responsibility for its statements.

But even if the German listener accepts the official German denunciation of this programme as an enemy programme, he will still listen to it and be influenced by it as it is: (*a*) full of entertainment and up-to-the-minute information (often in advance of competing news services); (*b*) speaks to him from a German point of view which he will accept as the plausible point of view of a large number of German citizens in present-day Germany.

The advantage of broadcasting black on a medium-wave band, additional to bringing black within range of a vast number of listeners without short-wave listening facilities, is the collection of many cautious listeners who are afraid to listen to enemy propaganda. They will have the answer: 'I thought it was a German broadcast!'

> This use of Aspidistra will not invite enemy reprisals against the BBC
> Home Service as is feared might follow counterfeit broadcasts on enemy
> wave-lengths. It is not intended to pick an enemy frequency for this
> purpose.[1]

Delmer's proposals gave rise to endless objections from the BBC and
its supporters, some of whom were powerful. And there was, too, a lot
of muddled thinking. One prize specimen of the latter was that our Allies
might be as easily deceived as the Germans. Delmer's reaction was that
he might just as well close down all his stations, on the grounds that if
we were to deceive the enemy we had to be prepared to deceive all
listeners, including friends.

In August 1943 Delmer's opponents relented to the extent that he
could have the use of Aspidistra daily for a very brief period. A month
later as a major concession he was to be allowed to employ it for three
hours after 8pm. At this time the *Atlantik* station was continuously on
the air between 6.30pm and 7am and was using ten different announcer
voices as well as six compères (to introduce the musical items). Most of
them were German PoWs so there was no shortage of fairly experienced
talent. By D-Day in June 1944 *Calais* and *Atlantik* were continuously
broadcasting from 8pm until 5am, and by the end of the war on a
round-the-clock basis. By this time a staff of fifty radio technicians was
required to operate the Aspidistra transmitter at Crowborough as well as
two further 100-kW short-wave transmitters for the benefit of U-boat
crews and other German seafarers.

It is important to make a distinction between Delmer's prisoners of war
who were actually captured and the relatively few who were deserters.
The first deserter to arrive was probably Zech-Nenntwich (locally Herr
Nansen), whom Delmer actually identified by name in *Black Boomerang*.
He claimed to have been a member of an SS resistance group and to
have collaborated with a Polish equivalent which smuggled him over the
border into Sweden. His story must have been extremely convincing to
satisfy the experts at the Combined Services Detailed Interrogation
Centre. Delmer, however, preferred to keep him away from MB and
installed him at Paris House in Woburn with Wolfgang von Putlitz for
company. The latter was the former German diplomat who had supplied
Lord Vansittart with information before the war and who had made a
speedy escape to England at the last possible moment. He then spent a
period in the USA. When he eventually returned to England 'C' (the
SIS chief) planted him on Delmer who could not use him effectively

because his knowledge of current conditions in Germany was minimal. It was considered safe to house him with 'Herr Nansen' on condition that he should not under any circumstances discuss MB personalities. Delmer was not particularly surprised when Zech-Nenntwich engineered a long interview with Dr Adenauer, the German Chancellor, in 1950 and told him all he knew. After the war von Putlitz was given a British passport in return for services rendered and then proceeded to defect to the German Democratic Republic.[2]

Zech-Nenntwich's arrival in England can be dated. All requests to start new RUs had to be approved by the Foreign Office and the application to employ him was dated 14 October 1943.[3]

> The station's fundamental idea would be that there is a small but powerful section in the *Waffen*-SS which has turned against Hitler, Himmler and the Party. These elements feel that the soldierly ideals which originally made them join and subscribe to the SS ideology had been largely betrayed by these men. They believe the war is lost. They are particularly hostile to the Gestapo and *Sicherheitsdienst* [Himmler's Security Service] of the SS and the Party. They are active witnesses of Party corruption and Party atrocities both against foreigners and against Germans.

Zech-Nenntwich's clandestine station (*Kampfgruppe Yorck*) broadcast at irregular intervals from 11 December 1943 until the end of the war and was supplied with sufficient plausible background material. He was also a useful local consultant on SS terminology and jargon.

Three other deserters were undoubtedly genuine and, furthermore, trustworthy. Two young *Luftwaffe* officers ('Steiner' and 'Wegely') and a sergeant ('Obermeyer') simply flew the latest German nightfighter to an aerodrome in Essex and gave themselves up. Sepp Obermeyer was soon asking if he could write his own scripts and delivered his talks in an unmistakeable Bavarian accent. His companions became useful specialists for *Luftwaffe* affairs and gossip.

Delmer also recalled with respect and affection Major 'von Virchow', one of Rommel's artillery regiments' intelligence officers until he was captured in North Africa. 'He was invaluable in helping us to avoid solecisms of language, procedure and other pitfalls of the counterfeiter.'

The disappearance of the *Luftwaffe* aircraft and crew – unfortunately their names were reported to the Red Cross – may have been responsible for the detailed instructions issued by the *Luftwaffe* High Command on 11 June 1944. They are too lengthy to be quoted in full but indicate that parked aircraft were to be drained of petrol and that, 'In the future the relatives of deserters are to be arrested and brought to trial.' This, and possibly similar escapades led to the formulation of the Allied 'Plan Huguenot' (18 January 1945), which outlined how similar cases were to be handled:[4]

> The fact that a pilot has deserted will be kept strictly secret by the Allies unless the pilot himself wishes it to be made public ... Covert and disavowable channels, and possibly deception channels, will be used to convey to the enemy authorities the impression that a number of pilots whom they believed dead or prisoners were in fact deserters, but no names of real or pseudo-deserters will be given in this operation. Covert radio will further help this suggestion by pointing out to German pilots that it is impossible for the German authorities to know whether a pilot is missing because he has been killed or because he has deserted.

As a further inducement it was suggested that German pilots who might be considering desertion should be informed that they would 'find employment on civilian airlines under Allied control after the war, or would be given jobs in the administration of Germany'. Needless to say, these 'promises' were completely cynical. Indeed, those who drafted 'Plan Huguenot' did not expect a succession of German pilots who were no longer prepared to fly for the *Führer*. What they hoped for, rather, was 'the sharpening-up of anti-desertion security measures generally and the issue of instructions to commanding officers and the *Feldgendarmerie* [Field Security Police] to keep a suspicious eye on everyone – a course of action which must have serious effects on morale'.

In the course of interrogation a pre-war Lufthansa pilot said in March 1945 that he would have flown to Croydon at night, perhaps because he knew the way there. However, the idea of desertion was at least discussed in some *Luftwaffe* circles because, 'he did hear second-hand that *Soldatensender West* [formerly *Calais*] had announced that there were French airfields lighted for desertion. He also believes, and says everyone else does, that Switzerland and Sweden return deserting airmen to Germany.'

The latter discouraging item of information may have been incorrect because, 'during the summer [of 1944], several hundred American pilots, their courage abraded by the horrific odds against their survival, had set down their aircraft in Switzerland or Sweden and had been interned'.[5]

However, it was not necessary to depart from Germany by air because a report on 'Morale of Germans in Belgium' dated 18 January 1944 stated that, 'During the last two weeks in August 1943 at least twenty deserters from Holland cycled to La Roche, where they received civilian clothing. All reached Vienna, thanks to a service which seems well organised and gives false papers to those interested.'

There is a small Belgian town called La Roche-en-Ardenne within easy cycling distance from the Dutch frontier at Maastricht so the story might conceivably be true.

When the high-powered medium-wave Aspidistra transmitter was installed near Crowborough no one was precisely sure of what it would be capable. For instance, it is unlikely that anyone expected that the *Soldatensender Calais*, which hoped to find an appreciative audience among the German armed forces in France, would discover yet another in Munich and Upper Bavaria, furthermore a circle of listeners which found its transmissions rather surprising. The text of the letter printed below would have been greeted with much appreciative laughter at MB if it had been available at the time.

Security Service of the *Reichsführer* SS     Munich 13
SD Directing Sector Munich     Franz Joseph Street 38
III C 4 – AZ 17/43 – Dr. Kn/Hi     16.3.1944

(*Stamped:* Bavarian State Ministry of the Interior: 20 March 1944)
Transmitted     Marked for
on 18.3.44     SS *Obergruppenführer* and General of Police
             Freiherr von Eberstein.

SS *Obergruppenführer*    Ref: Reception and effect of the transmissions
                      of the *Soldatensender Calais* among the
                      population.

Since October 1943 increasingly frequent references are being made by the population to the transmissions of the radio station which calls itself *Soldatensender Calais* and concerning whose nationality people were not clear.

The chief effect of the station's news transmissions, which have been described as psychologically excellent, emerges from its practice of giving absolutely unexceptionable information, which has also been carried verbatim in the German News Service and mixing in with it a number of isolated, more or less tendentious items. This has caused large portions of the population to believe that *Soldatensender Calais* was a German station, perhaps one of the many *Soldatensenders* started up in the Occupied Territories also without anything about them being officially communicated to the population. That the reports of the *Soldatensender Calais* often had a sharpness otherwise nowhere to be found in the German News Service was in some cases explained by the population on the following lines: 'After all they cannot present the soldier at the front with the same propaganda as they sell us at home. They have to be more honest with the soldiers at the front.'

As was shown in the course of the last two months of the year 1943,

*Soldatensender Calais*, which originally transmitted on a wave-length around 360 m., and only later started to broadcast on the frequency of Munich, owes a large part of its audience to one quite special circumstance. Since September 1943, it will be remembered, the *Reichssender* Munich carried in the evening hours transmissions for Fascist Republican Italy which, as they continued, caused the greatest indignation among listeners here and forced them to dial other stations in order not to lose their evening's entertainment. They twiddled and found the *Soldatensender Calais*, which was coming through with extraordinary power and held the population with its news service.

Since the New Year observers in Munich and in the provinces point out with all urgency that the transmitter has caused the greatest unrest and confusion among the population by news concerning the situation at the fronts and at home and that the population is showing ever-increasing trust in the station's news service as its reports have shown themselves more or less correct. There is general agreement that the majority of the opinions expressed among the population concerning the situation at the front are derived from the news of the *Sender Calais* which, in the words of a Munich radio expert of note, with Belgrade and the *Luftnot-Sender* Laibach, belongs to the three most listened-to radio stations.

Politically responsible observers demand with increasing urgency that action should be taken against this station with all means at our disposal, above all that the population must be enlightened as to its character as an enemy station. As this had not been done so far, the population feels it has the right to listen to the station, on the one hand because they cannot help listening to it on the Munich frequency, and on the other hand because its effectiveness is not being interfered with sufficiently.

As it was not possible to reduce listening to *Soldatensender Calais* by confidential hints as to its origin, it was considered justified that the station should be powerfully jammed.

But this jamming had unpleasant consequences, particularly of late. The noise of the jammer mobilised against *Calais* made reception of the *Reichssender* Munich quite impossible in many parts of the Gau Oberbayern and particularly in the Munich town area. *Calais* itself, on the other hand, could be received clearly. The *Reichssender Munich* is completely drowned (and it is noteworthy that many people have identified the jammer put on against *Calais* as an enemy jammer attacking the 'German station' *Calais*).

In view of the very grave effects of this enemy station from a morale and propaganda point of view, it seems very necessary to limit as far as possible the effectiveness of *Calais*, for the attempts to jam it that have been made hitherto must be considered insufficient in the light of the listener reports received here.

per pro (signature illegible)
SS *Sturmbannführer*.

*    *    *

241

Soon after the Normandy landings a large Anglo-American Psychological Warfare Division, in which American personnel dominated, was operating as a part of the Supreme Headquarters Allied Expeditionary Force in France. In this Crossman played a prominent role as Chief of Operations under the American General Robert McClure. However, the PWD team lacked Delmer and Co.'s flair and experience and Jay Lerner, who was a member of PWD, later wrote: 'Only about the very few "black" operations conducted mainly by the Americans has there been a regular "leak" of information (one might almost say a "flood"). But these were not the most skilful, successful and characteristic of "black" activities and it would be misleading to treat them as representative.'[6]

I have no reason to believe that collaboration between PWE and MB and PWD was ever particularly close, although Donald McLachan went to France with a watching brief for Delmer and to prevent, if possible, too many serious gaffes being perpetrated on the black side.

This preamble will explain the reference to 'the daily newspaper for the German troops in the West' (*Nachrichten für die Truppe*) which is mentioned in the 'Report on Special "Black" Operations during "Overlord" (3 August 1943)', which follows. Delmer mentioned in *Black Boomerang* that, 'Of all the enterprises I launched during the war this "News for the Troops" is the one of which I am proudest.' It was a joint Anglo-American production (four pages), was edited at MB and printed on a local newspaper rotary press at Luton. It was neither black nor grey but what Delmer described as 'a dirty off-white'. My own belief is that such success as it could claim was due more to the sheer inefficiency of the news service provided by the Germans for their troops than the actual merits of *Nachrichten*. Its contents contained Delmer's standard mixture of true and false news and the German soldiers who read it would soon have realised that it could not have been produced by Dr Goebbels or one of the *Wehrmacht*'s propaganda companies. A Magdeburg newspaper 'reviewed' the issue for 7 February 1945:

The *Nachrichtenblatt* [*sic*] prints facts on its front page which more or less tally with our own OKW reports. In this way it gains the confidence of the reader and appeals to his sense of impartiality. It even mentions decorations awarded to members of the Armed Forces and the special performances of German divisions. When it has thus lulled the reader's suspicions to sleep with its exemplary objectivity it serves up fat lies and filthy calumnies.

According to the enemy there are still wives of big-wigs in Germany who lazily travel from spa to spa and forget suitcases filled with diamonds which are now being feverishly hunted by the whole of the detective forces of central Europe. This attempt to destroy our confidence in our leaders is only surpassed by the story that certain prominent people had arrived at a neutral airport, inserting their own obituaries in the German press before their departure . . .

According to one issue an accurately described BDM [Nazi organisation for teenage girls] leader had arrived recently at one of the health resorts in our Gau [region] for prolonged treatment for a nervous breakdown. The fact that any ordinary citizen can get such treatment, in spite of the bomb terror, is of course omitted. Investigation revealed that the whole story is quite untrue.

All these 'revelations' had previously been broadcast by the *Wehrmacht-sender* and merely needed rewriting for press purposes.

A very large number of 'come-backs' indicate that the *Wehrmachtsender* had captured a large audience among the rank and file of the German troops in the west. In a memorandum written on 14 February 1944 Delmer expressed the view that,

. . . we ought, if possible, on the Black side of the preparation for Overlord build up some big leadership personality that could talk in an impressive way to German officers and raise in their consciences doubts as to whether they are doing the right thing in continuing to obey Hitler. I would like to suggest . . . that we should get General Thoma to put himself at the disposal of this Black campaign.[7]

General von Thoma, who was Rommel's successor as Commander-in-Chief of the *Afrika Korps*, had been captured soon after the decisive break through at El Alamein and was now in a prisoner of war camp in England. According to Delmer on 14 February 1944:

General von Thoma would be the anonymous chief speaker of a clandestine station whose main theme would be the need to break with Hitler and the politicians and rally Germany under the best elements in the army to the Western powers. We would spread in Germany by sibs [rumours] that Thoma was the speaker. We would thus have a disavowable station which was, at the same time, holding out an attractive phantom of Anglo-German co-operation for a Western peace . . . We could pick up some of the broadcasts of the Thoma RU and relay them on *Calais* so as to give it the widest possible circulation.

Robert Bruce Lockhart was sufficiently interested in this proposition to compose a long minute for the Foreign Secretary (Anthony Eden):

We have studied his utterances closely. He appears to have a colourful personality and would probably make a good speaker. Among his fellow prisoners of war he has always refused to hide his opinions and has consistently taken an anti-Nazi stand. He delights in lending his companions his anti-Nazi literature and has told a British officer that he enjoys sitting next to the Nazi generals at meals so that he can 'jolt their ideas a bit'.

Eden's minute records that he was attracted by the proposals, 'but the Prime Minister should be told first'. What probably killed the plan was Lockhart's statement (quoting von Thoma) that, 'He looks to us to protect Germany from Communism.' Sir Alexander Cadogan, the Permanent Under-Secretary, minuted (as if apprehensively): 'He wouldn't put this out, I suppose?' The Russians already had Field-Marshal von Paulus and their own Free German Committee in Moscow and it is likely that the last thing Sir Alexander wanted was suspicious enquiries from our Soviet allies.

The report of 3 August 1944 is of interest, however, because it provides information about the pre-invasion preparations for D-Day at MB and how their success was evaluated when the fighting in Normandy was at its height.[8] Paris was not liberated until 23–25 August.

### REPORT ON SPECIAL 'BLACK' OPERATIONS FOR 'OVERLORD'
#### (3 August 1944)

1   The media for covert propaganda during operation Overlord have been four:

(a) The radio programme *Soldatensender Calais angeschlossen der Deutsche Kurzwellensender Atlantik* (Soldiers' Station *Calais* with the German short-wave Station *Atlantik*), which carries a programme of news bulletins and entertainment for the German forces and adopts the convention of speaking as a German soldiers' station situated somewhere in France. The programme is radiated on three short-wave transmitters and on Aspidistra in the medium-wave band. The medium-wave broadcast is from 2000 until 0500, while the short-wave broadcast begins one and a half hours earlier and ends at 0800.

(b) The daily newspaper for the German troops in the West (*Nachrichten für die Truppe*), which is dropped by American aircraft in quantities varying from 250,000 to 750,000 a night over targets in the West selected by 21st Army Group.

(c) The medium-wave (and occasionally short-wave) programme of talks for the opposition movement within the SS which is broadcast irregularly at various hours of the day and night on wave-lengths used by official German programmes.

(d) Forged documents and subversive leaflets distributed in Germany and occupied countries by agents and by balloon. These purport to come either from German official sources or from the various brands of German opposition. They aim at promoting defeatist and subversive activity.

The first two media carry the same news material and comment and execute the same general propaganda policy. The newspaper, however, maintains a more neutral attitude, speaking neither from an Allied nor from an explicitly German standpoint.

## 2 *Operational Tasks*

Two months before D-Day the role of these media in Operation Overlord was discussed and agreed with G2 and G3 SHAEF. It was to direct subversive news and comment, both military and political, to the German armed forces in the West; to use SHAEF and other intelligence sources to present exclusive and expert versions of military events; to assist in maintaining deception plans with the advice of G3 SHAEF.

An audience for both our principal black media was built up in preparation for Overlord. It has since been learnt from prisoners and documents captured in Normandy that the broadcasts were widely heard in spite of warnings from the German military authorities that they were British and that those caught listening would be severely punished.

Aircraft distribution of the newspaper for the troops was begun a month before D-Day.

## 3 *Policy*

Both before and after D-Day the main task of 'black' propaganda has been to concentrate the attention of the German soldier on the enemy within (i.e. the Party authorities) rather than on the enemy without.

In the strictly military field it has endeavoured to keep before the mind of the soldier in the West the military disasters on the Eastern front; the growing weakness of German war production under stress of bombing, blockade and call-up; the impotence of the German air force at home and on the battlefields; and the breakdown of authority, in particular police authority, and the consequent increasing safety of defiance of the law.

After D-Day the course of operations in France was used to illustrate the hopelessness of Germany's continuation of the war, while every opportunity was taken to suggest to the German fighting men on the invasion front that they were being sacrificed uselessly and being let down by their leaders. We have striven to suggest the incompetence and selfishness of the German military leaders and their disunity, particularly with reference

245

to quarrels between Rommel and Rundstedt, between Rommel and Doll-mann, and between the various services.

## 4 *Technique*

The technique of the two main media, *Calais/Atlantik* and the news-sheet, has been to provide German soldier listeners with a news service comprising a mixture of harmless items of general interest to German soldiers (e.g., Sports News, Promotions, Decorations), of news taken from the German DNB wireless teleprinter services, and of radio, put out frequently ahead of the German official broadcasting services, often with a subversive twist. Propaganda by direct appeal has played no part.

Military situations and themes have been given special treatment in talks, these talks afterwards being rewritten into leading articles for the Troop Newspaper. Examples of such themes are:

i) The coastal divisions have been written off by the High Command as a loss and are there simply to serve as human land-mines in the way of the invasion.

ii) The Cherbourg peninsula has been abandoned by the High Command. No attempt is being made to reinforce it.

iii) Von Schlieben and 25,000 officers and men have set an example of military realism in refusing to obey the theatrical *Führer* order to fight to the last cartridge.

iv) Heavy losses incurred by U-boats in futile attempts to interfere in the Channel under suicidal conditions. The failure of the one-man torpedo in the Seine Bay owing to insufficient preparation.

v) Shortage of munitions, shortage of petrol, shortage of transport makes it impossible for the troops to carry out tactical tasks and justify their surrender. The breakdown of rear communications on the Normandy front owing to bombing and the efforts of the Maquis.

vi) The frittering away by the nervous, impulsive Rommel in the battle between the Orne and the Odon of his tanks and Panzer Grenadiers, rendering impossible the promised counter-offensive with masses of armour to which we had committed him.

vii) The realisation by Germany's best generals that the outlook is hopeless leads to an organised conspiracy to kill Hitler and set up a government which can make peace.

We have kept the home front well in the picture with particular reference to the approach of the Russian armies to Germany, the sufferings of the population under bombing. (We give lists of bombed streets so that soldiers may apply for compassionate leave.) Constant emphasis is laid on the inequality of sacrifice between the privileged Party officials and the ordinary Germans. Throughout we endeavour to give news with an appeal to the self-interest of the individual listener likely to cause him to act for himself against the collective interests of the German war effort.

## 5  Evidence of Reception of Wireless Propaganda

SHAEF interrogations of a number of prisoners during the week ending 1 July showed that over 50% had listened to the *Calais* station. They include men from infantry, armoured and artillery units, both regular and SS. General von Schlieben and other senior officers listened to *Calais* as a source of news during the siege of Cherbourg, and certain key phrases and themes of our propaganda have reappeared in statements made by Schlieben (as in those of other prisoners) suggesting that they may have been absorbed into his ordinary line of thinking. It is known that the station is listened to by U-boat officers and men at sea as well as at base. From prisoners' statements it is known that *Calais* has a large audience among officers and men of the German air force and is even turned on in the messes. Official documents, warning against the station, have been captured. Official statements have also been issued denying stories heard on *Calais* and subsequently circulated by officers and men.

## 6  Evidence of Leaflet Circulation

We have good evidence from Norway, France, Switzerland and inside Germany of the circulation of black leaflets which have been distributed by agents and balloons.

The enemy appear to regard as most dangerous a handbook on methods of malingering which has been printed under various disguises. An order from the High Command warning against this document and expressing concern at the spread of malingering among the troops is in our possession.

Our leaflets purporting to be issued by a German deserters' organisation, giving advice on ways of deserting to neutral countries, have been found circulating among German troops in Norway and France. Our forged ration cards, dropped by aircraft, are known to be circulating in Germany and seem to have caused considerable administrative difficulties to the German Food Ministry.

Our imitations of official publications for the troops similar to our own Army Bureau of Current Affairs booklets have been warned against by the German military authorities.

The Germans were often puzzled by the speed with which MB was able to report on news which appeared to emanate from the *Führer*'s headquarters and then broadcast the information on the *Soldatensender Calais*. Thus soon after Colonel von Stauffenberg's unsuccessful attempt to assassinate Hitler on 20 July 1944 the very large telephone installation at the *Führer*'s HQ was occupied at short notice by no fewer than 200 signals specialists who searched diligently for 'parallel lines' which would transmit conversations to unauthorised destinations but found nothing suspicious.[9]

In Great Britain MI6 was making discreet enquiries about the topography of the *Führer*'s headquarters two days *before* the *Putsch* attempt. According to a letter from Clifton Child to the present writer, 'a man from MI6, wearing the uniform and insignia of the rank of an army major, came down to MB on 18 July, saying that "we are going to bump off Hitler" and asking to see all the information we had about Hitler's HQ at Rastenburg.' It happened that some rough sketch maps were available. It is probable that MB was the one place in England where intelligence material of this kind was collected and filed.

According to an 'Evidence of Reception Report' dated 24 September 1944:

> There have in the past been numerous cases of individual listeners expressing astonishment at the accuracy of *Calais* intelligence. Now there are indications that the German authorities themselves are convinced that *Calais* has special information, not only of Allied intentions but of what is going on inside Germany. In private conversation at the end of July a senior German official in Sweden said it was officially believed that *Calais* had many correspondents in Germany itself, and a number of officials were engaged in checking its statements in the hope of checking these informants. He quoted as an example the *Calais* statement that the German naval attaché in Stockholm, von Wahlert, was implicated in the 20 July *Putsch*. In consequence some of the Legation officials decided to investigate the matter secretly and came to the conclusion that quite possibly the report was true.

It was Clifton Child, too, who explained the organisation of MB's intelligence department. He paid particular tribute to the contribution made by 'Joe' (later Professor Sir Cecil) Parrott, who was in charge of the Stockholm Press Reading Bureau, which was affectionately known as 'the Parrot House'. There were his daily telegrams containing useful snippets of information from the German and other Axis newspapers. The publications followed by the next available aircraft. Parrott had an uncanny instinct for the kind of material which Delmer could use. The polymathic C. E. Stevens, helped by former colleagues at the Ministry of Economic Warfare, specialised in economic intelligence. Max Braun, with the assistance of his brother Heinrich and Fritz Heine, assembled a card index (60,000 items!) relating to members of the Nazi Party and Frank Lynder gathered a vast store of information on the *Kriegsmarine* and the German army and air force. There were, too, the Ruth Hutchings files on general conditions in the Third Reich. According to Child, 'She kept all the useful bits and pieces of information derived from the Combined Services Detailed Interrogation Centre's "eaves-dropping" reports.' The story of Ley's butler and the diplomatic rations derived from this source (see p. 130).

As Child observed in a letter: 'One just had to read and read – Tom made everybody do this – and then put two and two together. We scored because what we said had the ring of truth (and often was no more than the truth) and was factually accurate down to the last minute detail.' Finally, hour after hour the radio-controlled *Hellschreiber* provided the official German News Agency's press releases and, most important, the Propaganda Ministry's directives to editorial staffs.

The 'Evidence of Reception' reports from the end of 1944 onwards follow the kind of pattern already well known: widespread listening and surprise at the accuracy of the *Soldatensender West*'s information. *Calais* became *West* shortly before the former was liberated. One new feature was the regularity with which the reactions of German *deserters* was reported. They had presumably flourished the distinctive leaflets – they were printed in German and English – which bore a facsimile of General Eisenhower's signature and stated that the bearer was to be 'well looked after, to receive food and medical attention as required, and be removed from the danger zone as soon as possible'. A selection extracted from these reports follows:

*November and December 1944:* A *Korvettenkapitän* attached to the Officer Commanding Cherbourg listened to nothing but *Calais* when in France because the sets they had were too small for anything else and *Calais* drowned every other broadcast. The officers liked it because it gave news which was suppressed in Germany. Another PoW listened in Copenhagen and was always surprised at the inside news of the German army. The former Managing Director of Tauchnitz also listened in Paris throughout the first half of 1944 with his fellow officers. He believes that *Calais* made a great impression on the rank and file, but intellectuals were often repelled.

A PoW from Berlin said that one great advantage of *Calais* was that it broadcast all night when other stations were off the air. It was so cleverly camouflaged that the first reaction of anybody was to say: 'That can't be an enemy station!' Two particular items confirmed its reliability. Soon after the Hitler attentat *Calais* announced that a picture of Gordeler would appear in the German newspapers and the very next day almost every German paper had in fact such a picture.

An Allied Intelligence Officer visited a PoW camp at Compiègne in October and found 70 per cent of those he questioned to have been regular listeners. For many of them *Calais* was a *Wehrmacht* or SS station operating inside Germany. An *Oberleutnant* captured at Liedly on 1 September said he knew Hitler, Goering and Goebbels intended to escape to Japan. He had heard it officially.

The later 'come-backs' all follow much the same pattern and are too numerous to require quotation here. However, my own favourite is the fan letter from a German deserter which actually reached the press department at our embassy in Stockholm.

In May 1943 I was on the Donetz front [he wrote]. We were sitting quietly in the woods. As batman to the company commander I was able to use the service receiving set – the only thing in the army I have ever been fond of – so every morning at 3am when on telephone duty, I twiddled the band for light music. Up bobbed *Herr Atlantik*. At first I thought it was in fact an official broadcast for the German army. The news was not exaggerated, and the other incidentals did not give anything away. Later I began to see through it; mainly English recordings and the manner of presenting the material showed the station was illegal, and since I listened pretty regularly to news broadcasts from foreign stations I also discovered a similarity between the BBC and *Atlantik*. Most of the Company thought it was a real German station. After three weeks the CO forbade listening, but of course I and a few friends continued all the same. The music was so good that it got talked about and after a short while the station had devotees throughout the whole division.

After the retreat I deserted from the army and travelled illegally to Hamburg. That was in August 1943 after the heavy RAF attacks. *Atlantik* was almost unknown when I first arrived; reception seemed to improve after a time and it soon became the habit amongst my anti-Nazi friends to listen both to the BBC and *Atlantik*.

Soon after, I escaped to Denmark and found *Atlantik* was a great source of entertainment for the Danes. We often danced to it. I remember two compatriots in Copenhagen commenting on how *Atlantik* had announced that their home street in Hanover had been bombed. In March 1944 I got to Sweden and noticed how widely known the station was in the [internment] camp. Most people thought it was in France or Switzerland; some said in Russia and others a mobile station inside Germany. But fancy a station using three short- and three medium-waves in a regular twelve-hour programme anywhere in occupied territory or in Germany!

Then one day to my great joy a voice came back on the air which had been a great favourite: *der Chef* of *Gustav Siegfried Eins*. When I first heard him in Denmark in 1941 talking about SS methods in Norway, we all listened to the talks three times over. Of course my circle of acquaintances at home is a little less vulgar perhaps than *der Chef*, but we forgave him everything. There was a lot of conjecture as to where GS1 might be, and then I hit on it. 'GS1 is of course an official designation for one of the

English short-wave stations!' I am so glad that *der Chef* is back on *Atlantik*, even though his tone and presentation have entirely changed. For me he is still *der Chef*. I wonder if he comes from Berlin. Anyway I hope to meet him one day.

What is the reason for *Atlantik*'s success? Of course the German soldier does not like it when he and the army are held responsible for defeats. He takes it as a *personal* affront. Very German! But if *Atlantik* attacks the Party or the SS he is full of childish delight. Moreover he believes what he is told and then he also believes what he hears in the news part of the broadcast, which does not happen when he listens to an official news service from abroad.

Yet another compliment dated 21 November 1944 was received from a Ministry of Information broadcasting official based at Stockholm:

I found that *Atlantik* is coming through and would not resist the temptation to listen to it for the rest of the evening. As a medium of mass propaganda the *Atlantik* technique is as far in advance of the technique of the BBC European Service as BBC today is in advance of BBC technique in 1939 ... I have often noticed that listeners who would not bother about listening to a badly jammed BBC transmission will put up with very bad reception of *Atlantik* and will glue their ears to the loudspeaker in order to catch what *Atlantik* is saying when jamming has reached an intensity that, if it affected a BBC transmission, would have discouraged them long ago.

The Swedish Home Service radio ran a broadcast on secret radio stations in wartime and gave a detailed description of the technique and contents of the almost legendary *Atlantik* which, 'as far as is known was the first with the news of the invasion of France, thus winning an undisputed reputation'.

With the swift liberation of France and Belgium during the summer and autumn of 1944 there were many who supposed that the end of the war was in sight, but there was to be much hard fighting until the instrument of final and unconditional surrender was at last signed at Rheims early on 7 May 1945. In the meantime work continued as usual at MB and the editorial staff of *Nachrichten für die Truppe* also played a supporting role. A batch of German PoWs was interrogated about their reaction to *Nachrichten*. They said that they were almost without news from home and one of them described it as 'like the morning mail' (Evidence of Reception Report, November–December 1944). However, the morning mail could contain completely misleading information because according to a warning issued by the German 353 Infantry division dated 16 September 1944, *Nachrichten* contained maps which gave the impression that in certain sectors the German troops were surrounded and cut off.

The same report contains a reference to an issue of *Skorpion-West*, described as a 'morale-building news propaganda sheet of the German army'. This, according to a December 1944 interrogation report, 'enlightened its readers a few days ago with the statement, "Troops are authorised to liquidate commanders who order them to retreat. *However, this privilege must not be abused* (author's italics)." ' It is conceivable that this last sentence was actually printed in No. 11 of a series of genuine German *Skorpion* leaflets even if it sounds suspiciously like one of the *Wehrmachtsender*'s jokes.

No. 11 was headed 'Who can surrender?', followed by the sub-headings 'Nobody can surrender! Not even the responsible commander!' Our version, which was produced by my unit and looked exactly like the genuine article, simply stated that whoever surrendered was a traitor who 'deserved to be shot down like a dog'.

The story of the rival *Skorpion* leaflets, i.e. those produced by the German 'Kurt Eggers' SS propaganda unit and our fakes, was not without its comic side. The German propaganda line was to encourage its battle-weary soldiers to stand fast because the Allied offensive would indubitably collapse like a pricked balloon. However, the German *Skorpions* were plausible up to a point. They admitted that the situation was desperate and did not read as if they were written by hacks at the Propaganda Ministry. They were delivered to German front-line troops by air.

Copies soon reached Donald McLachan, who was working for Delmer in France (supplying up-to-date information, captured documents, etc.). McLachan immediately suggested that we should print bogus *Skorpions* and I can recall producing the first of about half a dozen issues with considerable expedition. Ours were also disseminated by aircraft. It happened that in mid-November 1944 McLachan was with General Edwin Sibert, the US 12th Army Group's chief of intelligence, in the Belgian Ardennes region in an area which was thinly held by only three or four American divisions. Opposite them, but undetected, the Germans had assembled two tank divisions which were preparing for Hitler's last major offensive action in the west.

A German peasant crossed the lines bringing with him some useful fragments of information, some German newspapers and one of *our Skorpions* which was headed: 'Can the *Führer* be allowed to surrender?' The answer was *yes* and it was proposed, too, that Himmler was the right man to succeed him, thus following Delmer's usual 'Himmler for

# Willst Du die Wahrheit wissen, Kamerad, so frage den „Skorpion!"

## 13

**FRAGE:** Glaubt der „Skorpion" noch an das, was er vor vier Wochen gesagt hat?

**ANTWORT:** Ja!

Denn es handelt sich dabei nicht um eine Frage des Glaubens, sondern des Wissens. Die Kameraden, die den Skorpion fragen, wollen etwas wissen. Und der Skorpion antwortet ihnen, weil er es weiß. Er antwortet ihnen auch nur, wenn er etwas weiß. Das, was er gesagt hat, hat sich bisher alles bestätigt. Er hat gesagt, daß wir uns nichts vormachen wollen. Unsere Lage war kritisch. Wir haben gewisse Fehler gemacht und können das heute getrost zugeben.

Denn heute liegt nun das meiste hinter uns, was durch unsere Fehler entstanden ist. Außer ein paar unzuverlässigen fremdländischen Arbeitskräften und sonstigen staatsfeindlichen Elementen haben wir keine Partisanen mehr im Rücken, welche uns die Versorgung der Front zur Last und die Verwaltung des Hinterlandes zur Plage machen, und keine Bundesgenossen mehr an unserer Seite, die wir ununterbrochen mit Waffen und Hilfsmitteln versorgen müssen, ohne daß wir dabei an ihnen jemals eine nennenswerte Hilfe gehabt hätten. Und wir wissen heute auch, daß Fehler aus Leichtsinn, Trägheit und Gedankenlosigkeit natürlich Opfer kosten und mit Enttäuschungen, Tränen und Rückschlägen bezahlt werden müssen.

Aber wir können uns auch sagen, daß Erfolge, die der Feind nur unseren Fehlern zu verdanken hat, nicht so entscheidend sind, wie wenn wir alles richtig gemacht hätten und doch geschlagen worden wären. Dann wäre wohl nichts mehr zu hoffen gewesen. So aber haben wir aus unseren Fehlern lernen und die Konsequenzen ziehen können. Und wieder hat uns die Erfahrung gelehrt, was Glaube und Wille gegen noch so hohe materielle Feindüberlegenheit auszurichten vermögen ; noch in der Niederlage triumphieren sie.

Wir stehen sozusagen wieder in den alten Startlöchern von 1933, da wo wir standen, bevor wir in das Rheinland wiedereinrückten, und können getrost wieder von neuem anfangen.

**FRAGE:** Warum kämpfen wir weiter?

**ANTWORT:**

Diese Frage wird jetzt immer häufiger an den Skorpion gerichtet. Vor allem kommt sie von Kameraden, die sich von der Feindpropaganda haben beeinflussen lassen, oder von anderen kleinmütigen Geistern, deren Willenskraft den Rückschlägen der letzten Zeit nicht standgehalten hat. Es muß auch solche Leute geben. Auch ihnen ist der Skorpion bereit mit der gewohnten Offenheit zu anworten.

Wir kämpfen weiter, weil wir den Idealismus des Führers, der nationalsozialistischen Idee und ihrer Träger rechtfertigen müssen, auch wenn das vorübergehend die materielle Vernichtung unserer selbst, unseres Vaterlandes und der kommenden Generation bedeuten sollte.

Wir müssen uns des hohen Vertrauens würdig zeigen, das der Führer und die großen Nationalsozialisten an seiner Seite in uns kämpfende Soldaten gesetzt haben. Jeder von uns muß bereit sein, dem großen Beispiel der Selbst-

Bogus English version of a German propaganda leaflet. The former was designed to encourage *Wehrmacht* troops in France to spread misleading ideas.

President' line. This document created considerable interest at Sibert's HQ and it was proposed that General Bradley, the army commander, should be advised to launch an immediate attack in view of the apparently low morale of the German troops opposite. McLachan was present at the conference which discussed the implications of our bogus *Skorpion* but preferred to keep quiet until he could talk to Sibert privately when he informed the general that he had been deceived by a specimen of British black propaganda. Sibert was both amused and irritated because if the leaflet had reached Bradley and an attack had been launched the results could have been disastrous.

Sibert was not the only general to be deceived. A copy of one of our productions landed on the desk of the German Field-Marshal Walter Model who, when he read it, could scarcely contain his surprise. When he was given another specimen a week or two later he was so angry that he ordered the immediate suppression of this particular German propaganda activity because it was clear that the British could so easily deceive the German rank and file with their 'poison'. However, there was a compromise: in future the German *Skorpions* were only to be delivered by hand. 'The *Skorpion* which is on the ground is a fake. Don't touch it! It's poison!'[10]

We are approaching the last weeks of the war. On 7 March 1945 units of the US 1st Army crossed the Rhine over the railway bridge at Remagen which the Germans had failed to destroy. At the *Führer*'s conference held the following day the Chief of the Army Operations Staff reported that two naval demolition teams had been assigned to destroy the bridge but an enquiry directed to the Admiral commanding small combat units (naval frogmen, etc.) showed that nothing was known about such an operation. On 9 March the *Führer* was told that two detachments of frogmen were being sent to Remagen as fast as possible, also that they would use torpedo mines.

In the meantime on 11 March *Calais/Atlantik* committed the Germans to destroying the bridge by exactly the same methods decided upon in Berlin a couple of days earlier. This was a routine MB 'joke' for which Frank Lynder supplied the technical background information; it happened to be entirely correct. The next day Grand Admiral Dönitz informed the *Führer* that the *Atlantiksender* had already revealed the German plan, but he intended to proceed with it, 'because there is a possibility that the British made the announcement in order to mislead us'.[11] The frogmen set forth on their perilous journey but surfaced and surrendered to the Americans before they got anywhere near the bridge.

\*　　　\*　　　\*

Gambier-Parry's original concept for the employment of Aspidistra was that the transmitter should intrude on enemy wave-lengths. The first experiments were made between 18 September and 27 October 1943, soon after the Italian surrender. Mussolini had been liberated by a German commando unit on 12 September and broadcast on 18 September. No doubt it was the latter event which gave Delmer the excuse to produce a counterfeit of the National Fascist Government radio station on the same day. According to a report based on contemporary records:[12]

> The programme starting at 20.20 BST was continuous until midnight. It relayed the genuine National Fascist Radio programme, either direct, or from records, picked up from medium-wave German transmitters and inserted subversive news items and talks. Apart from these it was identical with the genuine programme.
>
> Most of the insertions were recorded in advance, but some of them were inserted 'live'. Operational items such as reports that an area of Central Italy had been declared a neutral zone, or that the German authorities had arranged for a free distribution of food for the population at Fascist HQ in certain towns were included in order to cause movement along roads on enemy lines of communication at certain times.
>
> Other features were an attack on the Vatican in the name of Fascism, talks announcing that Italian women were to assume the same war burdens as German women, and that a new Fascist *lire* would be issued at a new rate under German auspices.
>
> The success of the technique was such that all trained monitors were duped. It had an immediate crop of come-backs from monitors in Sweden, Switzerland, the USA and also the BBC.
>
> The difficulties attending the operation of W.6 were that if most of the material were relayed and counterfeit items inserted there would be a noticeable difference in quality between related and counterfeit material when reception was bad. There would also be a discrepancy between the programme announcement and the actual programme (unless the programme announcement was counterfeited – but this does not seem to have been tried).
>
> If the entire programme were counterfeit the transmission quality would be uniform. But there were actually insufficient skilled operators for this to be possible. In fact the programme, though successful, was abandoned owing to the lack of speakers and the requirements of another RU.[13]

No further 'Intruder' operations were attempted until late in March 1945 when the German armed forces in the west were close to defeat. It is true that Aspidistra could have been used earlier in conjunction with military operations but it was considered inadvisable to provide the Germans with the excuse that they had been defeated by a propaganda trick. According to a SHAEF report dated 31 March 1945 the first 'Intruder' operations were transmitted via Aspidistra on 24 March, their purpose being to create the maximum confusion in the German civil defence services and, of course, the civilian population. It must be emphasised that Field-Marshal Montgomery's 21st Army Group began to cross the Rhine at four places between Rees and a point south of Wesel during the night of 23–24 March, hence the 'Intruder' and military operations were closely linked. Furthermore, it was by then inevitable that the war could only last for a few more weeks.

Delmer knew from captured documents that the area on both sides of the Rhine was divided into zones under specially appointed Nazi functionaries and that the German code name for the possible evacuation of the civilian population was called 'Operation Siegfried'. Its counterpart was created at MB.

The surviving documents do not make it possible to provide a detailed account of the final 'Intruder' operations – Harold Robin told me that there were about ten of them – but we have a fair idea of what was contrived on 24 March when two separate 'Intruder' programmes were transmitted:

1   Operation ARP [Civil Defence] channel. 20.19 hrs. Aspidistra went on the air on 599 kilocycles with interval signal identical with that used by Germans to fill gaps in announcements about movements of Allied aircraft. Various announcements of this type broadcast. 20.30. Special announcement read twice. This was followed by interval signal and various ARP messages. 20.52 Aspidistra off the air.

The APR announcement was as follows:

Here is an announcement from the Reich Defence Commissioner of Gau Düsseldorf of R[*uckführung*, i.e., evacuation] Operation Siegfried in Gau Düsseldorf.

Zonal evacuation from Zones 4 and 5 on the established lines starts immediately. However, unless I give express instructions to the contrary only folk comrades liable for military service and of the age groups 29 to 31 are permitted to take part in the evacuation. All necessary measures to counteract panic among the remaining population are to be taken immediately. Individual evacuation independent of the march columns should be suppressed as far as possible.

All bridges and ferry crossings over the Lippe between Dorsten and Lünen are unusable for Operation Siegfried. New approach roads and crossing points only after agreement with the P1 [?] Leader of the Army Group.

*        *        *

This ARP instruction limited evacuation to a minute fragment of the population. Next there was an 'Intruder' operation on the Cologne frequency which was calculated to produce panic since it dismissed any hope of evacuation.

2 Operation on *Reichssender* Cologne. 658 ks. Cologne closed down owing to the approach of Allied aircraft. The period when it was off the air was used to relay the German programme, which Cologne should have broadcast on 658 ks, into which the special announcement was inserted.

21.40 Cologne closed down and Aspidistra went on the air with the Cologne programme [which it had 'captured' from another German transmitter]. 21.44 Special announcement (repeated at 21.55). 21.59 Aspidistra went off the air. 22.00 Cologne resumed transmission of the German Home Service.

The 'special announcement' was ostensibly from the Gauleiters and Reich Defence Commissioners of Essen, Düsseldorf, Westphalia North and Westphalia South. It began:

Folk Comrades! The enemy has reached the gates of our Gau. His intention to destroy the Reich and exterminate the German people will meet with fanatical resistance . . . On account of the enemy penetration on the eastern side of the Rhine, our population is open to all the effects of modern weapons and threatened with complete destruction. The utmost discipline must therefore be maintained in this hour. Since the evacuation measures originally planned have become impossible . . . only those compatriots who are suited to carry on the decisive struggle . . . will be evacuated. The evacuation of a great number of our compatriots will, for the time being, be impossible. Their duty, therefore, is to stick it out and, if need be, to face death bravely.

I must explain the 'capturing' process mentioned above. When a German station closed down with the approach of Allied aircraft there were always several others which continued to broadcast the programme that was no longer transmitted. Aspidistra was able to relay an active station without any perceptible break in continuity and then interrupt the programme with a 'special announcement'. The next stage was to continue the genuine article for a minute or two then fade out as 'enemy terror raiders' approached.

The *Reichssender* Frankfurt am Main was silent during the evening of 25 March because of the presence of enemy aircraft. Between the hours of 8.43pm and shortly after midnight Aspidistra relayed the German Home Service on the Frankfurt frequency but interrupted the relay with fifteen different announcements. Some of them gave the alleged positions of Allied tanks and armoured fighting vehicles while others were addressed to Red Cross workers, doctors and even butchers. Aspidistra returned to the Frankfurt frequency on the following evening (26 March) and put out messages and instructions in which evacuation columns were diverted in order to avoid imaginary penetrations. All motor vehicles with certain markings were to be commandeered and local Party leaders were informed of the arrival of relief trains at certain stations. Experts at the Ministry of Economic Warfare had worked out a convincing timetable.

The Germans did not react until the evening of 27 March when their Forces programme announced that the Allies were broadcasting on German wave-lengths. On 29 March the German authorities were obliged to confine instructions to the *Deutschlandsender* (long wave) on which Aspidistra could not intrude.

During the night of 30 March Aspidistra was busy on both the Hamburg and Berlin wave-lengths warning listeners that the Allies were trying to spread confusion among the civilian population by sending false telephone messages from occupied to unoccupied towns. 'To counter these enemy machinations once and for all, no action must from now on be taken on orders, instructions or reports received by telephone before they have been confirmed by ringing back. This applies to all State and Party authorities and to each individual German.' There was no immediate German reaction. If this instruction had been acted upon the work of the Reich telephone service would have been doubled and the system could have been brought to a standstill.

The date when the Reich Government confined itself to issuing its announcements and instructions over the *Drahtfunk*, a wired diffusion network on which we could not intrude, does not appear to be known.

On 8 April Aspidistra used the Hamburg and Leipzig frequencies to issue a police warning concerning the large number of forged RM 20 and RM 50 banknotes which were alleged to be in circulation. The serial numbers were stated. The objective was clearly to make the Germans suspicious of even their own currency. On the following evening (9 April) the Hamburg frequency was employed to announce the distribution of extra pork rations in three rural districts of Oldenburg in Lower Saxony. The supplies did not exist!

My own impression is that PWE never obtained any precise information about the effect of the 'Intruder' broadcasts or perhaps no information at all, if only because no research was attempted 'on the spot' immediately after the war. Germany had been defeated, the country was in a state of chaos, and no staff was available to investigate matters which would have been considered as being merely of academic interest or, more likely, of no interest at all.

In *Black Boomerang* Delmer stated that the *Wehrmachtsender* ceased to broadcast at 5.59am on 14 April 1945. When he was finishing his book he consulted Clifton Child who thought that the terminal date coincided with that of his own appointment to the staff of the Foreign Office Research Department. Unfortunately both of them had been too busy in 1945 to make diary entries and this conversation took place about fifteen years later.

Fortunately Harold Robin actually recorded the last hours of the *Soldatensender* on large glass-backed discs. The latter were then stored in his attic for the next thirty-six years. During the summer of 1981 these wartime 'souvenirs' were transferred (at my suggestion) to the Imperial War Museum's recorded sound archives. At the IWM everything was converted to magnetic tapes and the IWM kindly gave me a cassette containing an hour's 'speech' as I did not need the musical intermezzos. The official MB 'Record History Card', which accompanied the consignment was clearly marked 'G9. Last programme, 29–30 April 1945.' The 'last programme' contains two important evidential items: firstly there is a highly embroidered account of Heinrich Himmler's meeting with the Swedish Count Folke Berndotte at Lübeck on 27 April. This story, which happened to be true, was leaked from the USA to Reuters in London during the morning of 28 April. Secondly, the broadcast contained a brief reference to Mussolini's death at the hands of Italian partisans on 28 April.

What impressed me when I listened to the IWM's cassette was the *Soldatensender*'s aura of sheer professional skill. It must be remembered that the station was almost exclusively staffed by people who had no previous broadcasting experience. Its 'eye-witness' accounts of what was supposed to be happening in Berlin and elsewhere in Germany sounded completely authentic and I could at last begin to understand how and why the *Soldatensender* had captured a large audience in Germany and elsewhere in Europe. Apart from the fact that it appeared to be exceedingly well informed it provided excellent entertainment. And, furthermore, it provided an element of ironic, sometimes derisive humour that could certainly not be matched by Dr Goebbels's propagandists.

To sum up: Delmer's MB operation, in particular, was a side-show, brilliantly conceived and executed but nevertheless a modest affair by comparison with the total war effort. Frank Lynder (the Sergeant), who was devoted to Delmer, once asked me if this book could be considered as a tribute to his memory.

It is . . .

1  F & CO document

2  See Wolfgang von Putlitz, *Unterwegs nach Deutschland* (autobiography), published in the German Democratic Republic in 1956. This is an interesting but prejudiced source as far as Delmer and Zech-Nenntwich are concerned.

3  FO 898/51

4  FO 898/399

5  See David Irving, *The War Between the Generals*, 1981, p. 316.

6  See Daniel Lerner, *Psychological Warfare against Nazi Germany*, 1971, p. 264. Neither Delmer's nor McLachan's names are mentioned in the index. For Delmer's critical assessment of Lerner's book see *Black Boomerang*, p. 320.

7  For documents relating to the von Thoma 'plan' see FO 898/65.

8  FO 898/64

9  See Albert Praun, *Soldat in der Telegraphen und Nachrichtentruppe*, published privately by the author at Würzburg in *c*. 1965, p. 221 ff. Praun was in charge of the investigation at the *Führer*'s headquarters.

10  A fairly detailed account of the *Skorpion* operation (with illustrations) will be found in Ortwin Buchbender and Horst Schuh, *Heil Beil!*, 1974.

11  See *Lagervorträge des Oberbefehlshabers der Kriegsmarine vor Hitler 1939–45*, ed. G. Wagner, 1971.

12  F & CO document

13  F & CO document

# 23

# Black Prima Donna?

I did not read Richard Crossman's review of Delmer's *Black Boomerang* in the *New Statesman* of 9 November 1962 until almost twenty years after its publication. Perhaps I should not have been so surprised by its apparent animosity and, indeed, its inaccuracies. My conclusion was that Crossman was still jealous of Delmer's apparent successes and must have been at least vaguely aware that he (Crossman) had been a failure at PWE. I cannot say how the Americans reacted to him at Algiers after the spring of 1943 or during his period as Chief of Operations in the Psychological Warfare Division at Supreme Headquarters Allied Expeditionary Force (SHAEF) because I do not know. What is evident, however, is that Delmer's chiefs in PWE liked and trusted him, whereas there is plenty of evidence of the extent to which Crossman was mistrusted, at least by the British. It would be otiose to print the whole of Crossman's article or Delmer's dignified reply a week later, but extracts from both follow. Crossman's review, incidentally, was headed 'Black Prima Donna'!

The first part of *Black Boomerang* covers the whole story of this black propaganda from its first tentative beginning ... to the bogus German Forces programme which by the time of the Normandy landings was carried by a powerful medium-wave transmitter, competing with the official *Deutschlandsender* as well as the BBC, and issuing its own leaflet newspaper, with two [?] editions delivered daily to selected units of the German army by means of leaflet bombs dropped by two special squadrons of [American] Flying Fortresses. Judged in terms of the number of its listeners and readers, our black propaganda by the end of the war in Europe had become a serious rival to the Nazi radio and press, and may well have outstripped the German service of the BBC.

To man it up, Delmer recruited a motley army of internees, émigrés and, later, prisoners of war. Among his staff were Stalinists, Trotskyists, International Brigaders, SS men and, towards the end of the war, one junior member of the 20th July conspiracy who, after seeing his brother executed, escaped to Lisbon. It was as a result of proving his reliability on Delmer's staff that Otto John was later recommended by HMG – with disastrous consequences – to be the first head of counter-espionage in the German Federal Republic.

Neither the Stalinists nor the Trotskyists can be identified. The two former members of the International Brigade in Spain (Dr Ernst Adam and Alexander Maas) had both rejected Communism by the time they joined Delmer in 1941–2. There was only *one* SS man and Delmer never allowed him even to enter the MB compound. Otto John never saw his brother executed but escaped to Lisbon (via Madrid) on 24 July. He eventually reached England but there was a long delay before he finally arrived at Aspley Guise as Delmer's 'guest' in December 1944. However, at MB, where he was known as Oskar Jürgens, although his advice was asked on specific questions and problems he was never allowed to broadcast on the *Soldatensender*. His appointment as head of the *Bundesamt für Verfassungsschutz* (Federal Office for State Security) in December 1950 was not *recommended* by His Majesty's Government – the appointment itself was an internal affair – but nevertheless required the approval of the three Allied High Commissioners.

> Delmer enforced only two rules for his staff [Crossman continued]. First, they must observe the stringent security arrangements required by the fact that they officially did not exist. Secondly, as Germans they had to be prepared to carry out any form of subversion, however odious, on the orders of a chief who not only ate, drank and looked like Henry VIII but equalled that monarch in the genial absolutism with which he ran his kingdom.

'Any form of subversion, however odious ...'? Only a very small proportion of Delmer's output can be described as 'odious' (cf. the so-called 'Naples Letters' mentioned on page 217). As for gluttony I am convinced that no black market supplies ever reached RAG and Frank Lynder told me that the canteen food at MB was hardly attractive. If Delmer 'looked like Henry VIII' it was because razor blades were constantly in short supply so he allowed his beard to grow. Thanks to a friendly wine merchant whose customer he had been for many years he was able to maintain a modest stock of bottles at RAG and generously shared whatever he had with his weekend guests there, including the veteran members of his staff (the Corporal, the Sergeant, Max Braun and one or two others) who were permanent members of his household.

As for the 'stringent security arrangements', an increasingly large number of Delmer's people had relatives in Germany against whom the Nazis were quite capable of taking reprisals. 'Genial absolutism'? There is no doubt that Delmer maintained very high standards of discipline, if only because Aspley Guise and MB were certainly not holiday camps.

> In the realm of black propaganda [Crossman continued], indeed, only two men could talk to Delmer as an equal: his deputy editor Karl Robson of the *News Chronicle* and Donald McLachan ... It was McLachan's [Naval Intelligence Division] liaison office which ensured the necessary flow of naval, military and air force secrets on the basis of which the black broadcasts were able to tell bigger lies *and provide more accurate information about the course of the war and about life in Germany than any other radio station or newspaper in Europe* [author's italics].

It is hardly surprising that only two particularly close associates could talk to Delmer 'as an equal', because MB could not be run as a Socratic discussion circle. It was, in fact, an operational headquarters. Someone once said to me, 'Dick Crossman works best in meetings', presumably meaning that he preferred long discussions, although it does not necessarily mean that the decisions taken were 'democratic' ones. Delmer had a brief daily 'morning prayers' with a handful of senior colleagues, issued his instructions and left them to implement them. Someone had to take the responsibility for quick decisions and he assumed it. Nevertheless, during the last eighteen months of the war he was probably working at least an eighteen-hour day.

Crossman knew why it was that, 'the Service Chiefs, who remained to the end of the war suspicious of white propaganda, at once fell in love with black'. Still quoting Crossman: 'One motive was a penchant for secret dirt, a delight in looking at the "feelthy pictures" which Delmer assured them was helping to win the war.' This was absolute nonsense because only *one* pornographic item was ever printed (actually early in 1942); another, in fact a rather witty one, reached the proof stage in 1944 but was never used.[1]

Crossman's 'review' contains a number of further inaccuracies which are hardly worth discussing now that the protagonists are no longer alive. But perhaps the following (by Crossman) is worth recording:

> I happen to be able to vouch for the authenticity of Delmer's story because I spent nearly two years as overall director of political warfare against the enemy, trying to control and co-ordinate the black propaganda of PWE with the white propaganda of the BBC German service. Delmer and Hugh Carleton Greene, the BBC chief, detested each other and waged a departmental war in which no holds were barred ... Their feuding finally drove me to take refuge in Eisenhower's headquarters, first at Algiers and then

in SHAEF. There I could help to direct a relatively harmonious propaganda machine which issued the Supreme Commander's orders to both Delmer and Greene from a safe distance.

My own view is that Crossman spent nearly two years *hoping* to gain control of propaganda to Germany, i.e. as a maker of policy, and failed. Professor Michael Balfour, who was in a position to know what was happening, wrote to me on 17 February 1981:

The idea was that PWE should co-ordinate all propaganda to Germany and enemy-occupied territories so that Dick, on becoming German direc-tor, was entitled to expect that he would run all propaganda to Germany, at any rate as far as policy was concerned. This only happened in part, because the BBC never liked outside direction, accepted PWE orders with some reluctance and only acted on them if they were in fact joint conclu-sions agreed after discussion rather than orders. [Ivone] Kirkpatrick [PWE's senior Foreign Office representative in the BBC] defended this attitude and was too able and too well-connected to be over-ridden by Bruce Lockhart, Leeper or anyone. Hugh Greene was both a thoroughly competent broadcaster and knew Germany as well as Dick. I don't think they quarrelled badly but Dick wasn't in a position to run the show.

Next, it struck me as highly improbable that it was the alleged feuding between Delmer and Carleton Greene which finally drove Crossman to go to Algiers and then to SHAEF. Sir Hugh Carleton Greene wrote to me in July 1981 and said: 'I am sure that Delmer and I had nothing whatever to do with Crossman's departure for Algiers.' Thus the facts, as I deduce them, are that in April 1943 PWE needed a 'strong man' to join the basically inefficient American-British political warfare team at Algiers and was both relieved and delighted to be able to 'export' Crossman who, as I have already mentioned elsewhere, never effectively returned to PWE.

At the end of his review Crossman wrote:

Black propaganda is a secret weapon which can be tolerated – if at all – in total war. Like strategic bombing, it is nihilistic in purpose and solely de-structive in effect. Like Air-Marshall Harris, Delmer was permitted to wage war against Germany, the total war which Goering and Goebbels threatened but never waged against us. The job was brilliantly carried out. But would victory have been delayed for a day if 'black' had been forbidden and all our efforts had been concentrated on perfecting a white propa-ganda, designed first to win the confidence of the enemy in our truthfulness and then impose our will upon him? I suspect the answer is no. Reflecting once again on Delmer's extraordinary personal achievement I am more doubtful than ever whether this decision to plunge far below the Nazis' own level of lying, half-lying and news perversion was justified even by its undoubted results.

Delmer's urbane and tolerant reply was published in the following issue of the *New Statesman*. From this I need only quote one paragraph which seems to be important:

What the service chiefs valued about 'black' in distinction to 'white', was that all connected with its operations were government servants subject to the Official Secrets Act; that intelligence, planning and production were all under one hat in one unit; that its output could be fitted to service requirements at a moment's notice without any long committee palavers about directives, without the danger of security leaks or of the betrayal of the objectives of an operation by heavy-handed and all too straightforward implementation. And of course they also welcomed that they could not be held responsible for anything a 'black' station said. Yet a further point that attracted the service chiefs towards 'black' was that the sources of such intelligence as they let us have – and they became more and more generous with intelligence as their confidence in us increased – were not betrayed by 'black' because we did not *reproduce* intelligence but *used* it.

It is useless, in my opinion, to discuss the relative merits of the various kinds of propaganda: white, black, grey and what Delmer described as 'dirty off-white', because there was a place for all of them. In any case the Germans were ultimately defeated by the Allied and Russian armed forces and not by propaganda. Nor, unlike Crossman, do I have any particularly strong views about the ethics of black, at least as conducted by Delmer. We fought the last war, which was a strenuous and dangerous affair, with the weapons we had available and Delmer's brand of black was merely one of them.

When Sir Campbell Stuart founded the 'Propaganda to the Enemy Department' (EH) in 1938–9 he thought almost exclusively in terms of the precedents of 1918 and the important role that radio was to perform during the Second World War never occurred to him. It is possible that someone is already considering the possibilities of black TV relayed by satellite, but before the nuclear devices have begun to explode rather than later if only because there may be no one alive to watch it. And on that speculative note I end this book.

1   For Delmer's critical attitude to printed pornography see his article, 'The abuses of literacy - 2: HMG's secret pornographer' in *The Times Literary Supplement*, 21 January 1972. He wrote:

'My cloak-and-dagger friends in SOE (the Special Operations Executive) were constantly clamouring for printed pornography. But I still took the same view of printed pornography as I had in France in 1939. Looking back, I do not think my unit produced more than three items of printed pornography during the whole of the war, not because I was squeamish, but simply because I did not think the effort involved on our part would be justified by the subversive effect on the Germans.

'The first item was a two-page folding leaflet. Its theme was the Kaiser Germany's patriotic song "The Watch on the Rhine". A very gloomy picture of a snow-covered grave somewhere on the Russian front headed the first verse of the "Watch on the Rhine":

> *Lieb Vaterland magst ruhig sein -*
> (Dear Fatherland you may rest assured -)

By rights that inspiring thought would be followed by a second verse.

—*Fest steht und treu die Wacht am Rhein.* (—Firm stands and true the watch on the Rhine.)

'Instead, the picture of the soldier's grave and its reassuring caption was followed by a second page overleaf showing in colour a picture of a naked girl, painted in the photographic style favoured by Adolf Hitler in such beloved pictures as "Leda and the Swan", about to seat herself on the upright penis of some darkhaired and darkskinned non-German.

'The caption ran: "*Fest steckt's und treu der Fremdarbeiter 'rein.*" ("Firmly sticks it and true the foreign worker in"). Depending on the region selected for this document's distribution, we alternated the word *Fremdarbeiter* with *der Italiener* or even *der Makaroni*.

'My SOE friends ordered these leaflets by the thousands. But, ironically not because they found them to be subversive of German morale, but because they found them excellent for the morale of their men distributing them!'

Delmer's SOE friends did not order these leaflets by the thousand because only the *Fremdarbeiter* version was ever printed (probably a maximum of 5000 copies) in the summer of 1942. The *Nordisk Nyhedstjenste* (underground paper) reported on 11 August 1944 that copies were circulating among German soldiers in Denmark. According to this source, 'The framed notice on page four reads: "5,800,000 dead, severely wounded or missing" and an additional explanation says that the foreign workers in Germany exploit the prevailing distress and starvation in Germany and are admitted to soldiers' homes because of the food parcels they receive from their home country. They steal information from the factories and they will render soldiers unemployed if the war continues. The pamphlet concludes: We have lost the war. We must save what can still be saved for the peace. Out with the foreign workers. The war must finish, we have had sufficient losses.'

In retrospect it was just as well that only this one pornographic item was ever actually printed because there would have been an incredible fuss if even a single copy of anything similar had reached an unauthorised recipient, e.g. Sir Stafford Cripps.

Chronological list of Research Units (clandestine broadcasting stations) operated by PWE. All were short-wave with the exception of No. 36, G9 *Soldatensender Calais* (later *Soldatensender West*) which was the medium-wave development of the *Kurzwellensender Atlantik* and the short-lived No. 43, W6, 'Intruder into Italian Republican Fascist Radio'. With the exception of No. 36, G9, and No. 43, which were broadcast live from Milton Bryant (MB), all the short-wave broadcasts were recorded at 'Simpson's'. When the information is available the actual number of programmes recorded has been included. The necessarily brief annotations are based on documents at the PRO (FO 898 series) and the F & CO.

1 G1 **Das wahre Deutschland** (*German*), 26.5.40–15.3.41. 294 programmes.

2 G2 **Sender der Europäischen Revolution** (*German*), 7.10.40–22.6.42. 582 programmes.

3 R1 **Frats Romun** (*Romanian*), 10.11.40–20.7.43. 974 programmes.

4 F1 **Radio Inconnue** (*French*), 15.11.40–10.1.44. 1145 programmes.

5 W1 **Radio Italia** (*Italian*), 16.11.40–15.5.42. 545 programmes.

6 F2 **Radio Travail** (*French*), 17.11.40–21.5.42. 551 programmes.

7 N1 **Norwegian Freedom** (*Norwegian*), 5.2.41–16.12.42. 609 programmes. The RU's task was to stimulate opposition to the Germans in Norway. The need for an RU was strongly felt as the Norwegian government had complete control over BBC talks and the BBC bulletin was entirely given up to news. The most striking reaction to the RU was the '1918' campaign (September–October 1942) when many Norwegians commemorated Germany's defeat in that year by painting or chalking '1918' on any convenient wall. The RU was widely heard in Sweden and believed to be in Norway. It was closed when the Norwegian government refused to allow the Norwegian staff to continue working unless it assumed control over the station.

8 No code letter or number. **Italian Socialist** (*Italian*), 1.2.41–6.3.41. 8 programmes.

9 D1 **Radio Denmark** (*Danish*), 16.2.41–27.4.42. 432 programmes.

10 RD **Radio Nazdar** (*Czech*), 16.3.41–28.9.41. 65 programmes.

11 G3 **Gustav Siegfried Eins** (*German*), 23.5.41–18.11.43. 693 programmes.

12 Y1 **Radio Zrinski** (*Yugoslav Croat*), 31.5.41–1.12.43. 906 programmes. Was broadcasting 1¾ hours per week in October 43. The station's objective was to undermine the influence of the Quisling government in Croatia. Closed because military events and

267

the conflicting aims of Tito and Michailovitch were too powerful.

13 **Radio Libertà** (*Italian*), 8.6.41–27.11.41. 168 programmes.

14 F3 **La France Catholique** (*French*), 2.7.41–15.5. 44. Objective: to create resistance amongst the clergy and religious groups in France. Broadcast 3½ hours per week. Two transmissions daily (one was a repeat). In October 43 no evidence as to its effect.

15 B1 **Radio Vrijschutter** (*Belgian*), 4. 7.41–8.6. 44. Broadcast in Flemish 1½ hours per week in October 43. Transmitted six days per week at 22.30, 'late enough not to clash with BBC and not too late for Flemish peasants' bedtime'. Three voices used, one of them a woman's. This was an operational RU run for Flemish patriots, its aim being to organise resistance and support the main campaigns put out by 'white' radio. 'Our agents in the field who go to Flemish-speaking parts of Belgium are warned of the existence of this station and when they send their reports we are to implement their recommendations without delay.' In October 43 it was known that the station had an audience. 'Reactions from Flanders always take a much longer time to reach us than from the French-speaking parts of Belgium. The old B1 (also known as **Radio Heraus**) was in operation for a long time before any reactions were received, but evidence still reaches us of its popularity among Flemish peasants and industrial workers.'

16 H1 **Radio Flitspuit** (*Dutch*), 17.7.41–18.8.42. 286 programmes.

17 Y2 **Radio Shumadia** (*Yugoslav Serbian*), 7.8.41–19.11.43. 811 programmes. Broadcast 3½ hours per week in October 43. Objective: to destroy the authority and prestige of the Nedic government and hinder its attempt to obtain Serb collaboration with the Germans. 'This station appeals to the large remnant of Serbs who are neither Quislings nor Partisans (followers of

Tito) nor followers of Michailovitch.' It had a strictly nationalist line and addressed itself to middle-class Belgrade listeners. The RU was kept going by a single writer/voice owing to the difficulty 'in finding genuine Serbs in speech and outlook'. Campaigns included the encouragement of civil disobedience among provincial officials and to expose bad working conditions at the German controlled Bor mines and encouraging Serbs to avoid labour service there. 'American reactions have always indicated a belief that the transmitter was genuinely operated within Yugoslavia by Serb patriots.'

18 Y3 **Radio Triglav** (*Yugoslav, Slovene*), 23.8.41–9.4.42. 211 programmes.

19 F4 **Radio Gaulle** (*French*), 25.8.41–15.11.42. 426 programmes. The station was closed owing to difficulties arising from the divergence in policy with the De Gaulle organisation in London after the North African landings and the Anglo-American attitude to General Giraud and Admiral Darlan. The speakers on F4 were serving officers of the Free French Forces. 'Radio Gaulle was conceived as a medium through which to train certain types of resistance groups. But neither PWE nor the Fighting French evolved any concrete plan in this direction and little was done to direct activity into such channels as gathering information about enemy troops, supply dumps, aerodromes, etc. listing collaborators, forming contact with personnel holding key positions such as telephone operators, railway workers, police chiefs, etc.'

20 A1 **Radio Rotes Wien** (*Austria*), 3.10.41–27.12.41. 62 programmes.

21 X1 **Vasil Levski** (*Bulgarian*), 6.11.41–11.1.44. 762 programmes. The RU's objective, until his death, was to undermine the influence of King Boris (*d*. 28 August 43) and the Bulgarian government and expose their subservience to Germany. The station's political tone

was that of the left-wing Agrarian Party. Two voices were used (one male, one female) and the station normally transmitted for 15 minutes every evening. 'In a series of special transmissions the station reconstructed the circumstances of King Boris's death [allegedly] at the hands of the Germans; these revelations were transmitted day and night for six days in an attempt to exploit popular sentiment by canalising local rumours on the King's death in an anti-German direction.' Reception was reported from Bulgaria and from Istanbul, 'where·it was stated to be very clear'. A source who had heard X1 in Bulgaria reported that, 'Secret stations have a certain effect but are listened to by fewer people than London (BBC). Levski is believed to be British but there is no definite opinion as to its location.'

22  W3 **Andrea Viaghiello** (*Italian*), 1.1.42–14.3.43. 354 programmes. No information traced.

23  G6 **Astrologie und Okkultismus** (*German*), 28.3.42–19.4.42. 18 programmes recorded but not broadcast.

24  B2 **Sambre et Meuse** (*Belgium, French*), 9.5.42–4.6.44. Two transmissions six days weekly at 1 and 7pm. 'They are very good times for Walloon industrial workers as they occur at the lunch hour and just after they have returned home.' The station had a definite socialist complexion. 'The aim is to stimulate workers in industry to resist the Germans in their own country and to avoid deportation to Germany. It aims, too, at keeping their action in Belgium controlled and disciplined and to prevent them from following the more hot-headed councils of extreme communists to break into open revolt at the present moment. This programme also has a direct relation with the work of one or two of our own agents and followed their recommendations.' Nearly all the Belgians who

had escaped to England knew of B2 and most of them had heard it.

25  G5 **Wehrmachtsender Nord** (*German*) 9.5.42–7.2.43. 275 programmes.

26  D2 **Danish Freedom** (*Danish*), 1.7.42–24.9.43. 291 programmes. Was broadcasting 5¼ hours per week in September 43. Its objective was to acquaint listeners with techniques of news distribution based on clandestine broadcasts. The relatively few evidence of reception reports suggested that D2's transmissions were heard and discussed.

27  G8 **Workers' Station** (*German*), 17.7.42–23.3.43. 226 programmes.

28  M1 **Magyar Nemzet** (*Hungarian*), 6.9.42–7.1.45. Eight transmissions were given on Sundays only (two were repeats). One writer for all scripts and one speaker. The object was to increase opposition to Germany and to diminish the Hungarian aid to Germany. M1 was aimed at a middle-class audience and identified itself with the leading opposition newspaper *Magyar Nemzet* and claimed to be connected with it. A special feature was a transmission period devoted entirely to rumours. The latter were co-ordinated with Balkan and German RUs by denial, variation, reporting, etc. Reception was confirmed from Hungary, Istanbul, the Middle East and USA. There were indirect advertisements of the station in *Magyar Nemzet*. Other results were believed to be the sudden dropping of a pro-Nazi speaker from **Budapest Radio** immediately after an attack on him made by M1.

29  G7 **German Priest** ('Christus der König'), (*German*), 16.9.42–28.4.45.

30  P1 **Rozglosnia Polska Swit** (*Polish*), 2.11.42–25.11.44. The RU's chief function was to service the Polish underground movement with news and orders from London. It also transmitted code messages passed to it by the Polish government-in-exile for the

Directorate of Underground Warfare in Poland. PWE was not informed of the meaning of these messages. A Polish RU 'Kociuszko' was transmitting from Moscow and P1 was soon denounced by the Russians who claimed it was speaking for an aristocracy fighting for its own interests. Russian policy in Poland, as everywhere else, was to bring about immediate armed risings at whatever cost to later resistance. Swit issued warnings against this. After the failure of the Warsaw Rising (September 44) it became difficult to keep the station running and it was temporarily closed on several occasions.

31 F5 **Honneur et Patrie** (*French*), 11.10.42–2.4.44. This was a purely operational RU whose purpose was to transmit all the orders and directives of the *Conseil de Résistance* in London. Its aim was the gradual instruction of the French people in methods of underground warfare in accordance with official directives. 'The general line therefore is necessarily dependent on the agreed policy between HMG (as interpreted by SOE and PWE), the French National Committee of Liberation and the heads of the resistance movements in France.' Two transmissions daily of which one was a repeat. The clandestine press in France was closely linked with F5.

32 Y4 **Ya Staro Pravdo** ('For Ancient Justice'), (*Yugoslavia, Slovene*), 23.1.43–19.12.43. This RU transmitted for one period every evening with an additional early period on Saturdays and Sundays. Two writer-speakers were used. The main objective originally was to undermine Italian morale by stories and rumours spread by Slovenes in their contacts with the Italian population. After the surrender of Italy the station switched to trying to obtain maximum collaboration between Slovenes and Italians against the Germans. During the Tunisian campaign the RU made great efforts to compromise the Slovenes in the Italian army in the eyes of the Italian military authorities in order to make them withdraw 20,000 Slovenes from line regiments and draft them to Slovene labour battalions in Italy. In June 1943 the Italian authorities did in fact begin to send new Slovene recruits exclusively to the labour units.

33 D3 **Radio Skagerak** (*Danish*), 6.2.43 –5.5.43. 26 programmes recorded.

34 H2 **Fluistergids** (*Dutch*), 6.2.43– 28.3.43. 30 programmes recorded.

35 W4 **Italia Risorgi** (*Italian*), 6.2.43– 15.9.43. 152 programmes recorded.

36 **Kurzwellensender Atlantik** (*German*), 22.3.43–30.4.45. Linked with medium-wave **Soldatensender Calais** (later **Soldatensender West**) from 14.11.43. All G9 broadcasts were transmitted 'live' from MB.

37 H3 **Blauwvoet** (*Belgian, Flemish*), 24.3.43–4.5.44. Transmitted three or four times a week at 7.15pm. Two speakers (one male, one female). The programme professed to emanate from a group of dissident collaborators who felt that they had been let down by the Germans. It aimed at stirring up suspicions between Germans and collaborators on the one hand and rival groups of collaborators on the other. It bitterly opposed the extremist elements in Flanders who were in favour of the complete annexation of their country by Germany. Another aim was to complicate the German administration by encouraging desertions in the lower ranks of the collaborationist parties in Belgium and Holland.

38 **Nova Europa** (*Czech*), 23.6.43– 30.6.44. The station purported to be broadcasting from the Protectorate. It functioned as a pseudo-collaborationist station and in such a way as to turn the Czechs against it.

39 X2 **The Voice of New Europe** (*Bul-*

*garian*), 2.7.43–15.7.44. The RU transmitted a daily 15-minute news bulletin. 'It presents this in the form of a German black station to Bulgaria, playing in with the opening bars of the German and Bulgarian national anthems. The bulletins open regularly with the German High Command communiqué, followed by six to eight news items, some false, some falsified, some straight for cover purposes and chosen for their effect on the Bulgarian as distinct from the German listener. Apart from straight creation of news, the RU uses the technique of over-emphasis, falsification, denials, tactlessness or juxtaposition of genuine but contradictory German items. In its presentation of war news it maintains an undertone of desperation and depression, which protrudes through all the bombast and exaggerated strategic claims. It is particularly outspoken in its treatment of air-raids on Germany.'

40 W5 **Giustizia e Libertà** (*Italian*), 27.7.43–26.6.44. The RU purported to be the mouthpiece of a group of anti-fascists belonging to the *Giustizia e Libertà* group, in contact with all active anti-fascist organisations in Italy but having no connection with the Allies or anti-fascists outside Italy. This was actually the case and the only deception practised was that the station claimed to be in Italy when it was actually at Woburn. The personnel originally consisted of five prominent members of the G.e.L. group, of whom three were speakers. Their great political and psychological understanding of the position in Italy was invaluable for PWE.

41 R2 **Porunca Maresululi** ('The Marshal's Order', *Romanian*), 21.7.43–26.6.44. The RU's objective was to reduce Romanian aid to Germany and lower Romanian morale. The station was taken over from the old R1 (No.3) by 'ghost-voicing' with an overlap of one month and then closing R1. 'The

audience aimed at was the Romanian middle and upper class. Whereas R1 was anti-German, making a direct approach, R2 was impossibly pro-German and pro-Antonescu. Rumours, stories and operational propaganda were put out by slips, exaggeration, denials, misconstructions and patently weak German or Antonescu propaganda.' The station ran a number of successful rumour campaigns, e.g. there was a protest from Budapest about the anti-Hungarian material put out in the name of Marshal Antonescu. There was one speaker who was part-author of the scripts.

42 S1 **Bradlo** (*Czech, Slovak*), 4.9.43–19.7.44. The RU's objective was to increase the unpopularity of those who collaborated with the Germans and add to German difficulties by encouraging Slovak hatred of the Hungarians, not to mention undermining the loyalty of Slovak troops serving in the German army.

43 W6 **'Intruder into Italian Republican Fascist Radio'**, 18.9.43–27.10.43. This was a short-lived medium-wave Aspidistra operation managed by Delmer at MB. The programme started at 20.20 pm and was continuous until midnight. It relayed the genuine NFR programme either direct (or from records), picked up from German transmitters and inserted subversive news items and talks. Apart from the latter it was identical with the genuine programme. Most of the insertions were recorded in advance. Operational items such as that the German authorities had arranged for a free distribution of food for the population at Fascist HQ in certain towns were included in order to cause movement along roads on enemy lines of communication at certain times. Other features were an attack on the Vatican in the name of fascism, also that Italian women were to assume the same war burdens as German women

and that a new fascist *lire* would be issued at a new rate under German auspices. The success of the operation was such that many trained monitors were duped and there was an immediate crop of come-backs from Sweden, Switzerland, the USA and the BBC. There were insufficient trained operators for a complete counterfeit programme and the experiment was soon abandoned.

44 R3 **Prahova** (*Romania*), 18.10.43–30.4.44. The RU's objective was to reduce supplies of Romanian oil to Germany by encouraging go-slow methods in order to conserve Romanian oil supplies. Sabotage was not suggested as this would have destroyed the RU's cover. It implied that it had the support of the Romanian government. The RU was run on the above lines until January 1944 when a new policy of greater violence was introduced, also suggestions of sabotage not only with regard to oil, but also oil-seeds, transport, cereals, etc. The Ministry of Economic Warfare and the Ministry of Fuel and Power collaborated with advice and information.

45 P2 **Glos Polskiej Kobiety** ('Voice of a Polish Woman', *Polish*), 26.10.43–30.5.44. This RU was run by a small group of Polish women and was chiefly devoted to servicing the clandestine press.

46 D4 **Hjemmefronte Radio** (*Danish*), 6.12.42–18.4.45. No information available.

47 G10 **Kampfgruppe Yorck, Waffen SS** (*German*), 11.12.43–18.4.45. This must have been the SS man's station.

48 U1 **Hagedorn** (*German*), 26.1.45–27.4.45. Probably a pseudo-German 'resistance' station. No information available.

Austrian 20
Belgian 15, 24
Bulgarian 21, 39
Czech 10, 38
Danish 9, 26, 33, 46
Dutch 16, 34
French 4, 6, 14, 19, 31
German 1, 2, 11, 23, 25, 27, 29, 36, 47, 48
Hungarian 28
Italian 5, 8, 13, 22, 35, 40, 43
Norwegian 7
Polish 30, 45
Romanian 3, 41, 44
Slovak 42
Yugoslav 12, 17, 18, 32

# INDEX